# OPERATING SYSTEM
# PRINCIPLES

Prentice-Hall
Series in Automatic Computation

MARTIN AND NORMAN,  *The Computerized Society*
MATHISON AND WALKER,  *Computers and Telecommunications: Issues in Public Policy*
MCKEEMAN, et al.,  *A Compiler Generator*
MEYERS,  *Time-Sharing Computation in the Social Sciences*
MINSKY,  *Computation: Finite and Infinite Machines*
NIEVERGELT et al.,  *Computer Approaches to Mathematical Problems*
PLANE AND MCMILLAN,  *Discrete Optimization: Integer Programming and Network Analysis for Management Decisions*
PRITSKER AND KIVIAT,  *Simulation with GASP II: a FORTRAN-Based Simulation Language*
PYLYSHYN, editor,  *Perspectives on the Computer Revolution*
RICH,  *Internal Sorting Methods: Illustrated with PL/1 Program*
RUSTIN, editor,  *Algorithm Specification*
RUSTIN, editor,  *Computer Networks*
RUSTIN, editor,  *Data Base Systems*
BUSTIN, editor,  *Debugging Techniques in Large Systems*
RUSTIN, editor,  *Design and Optimization of Compilers*
RUSTIN, editor,  *Formal Semantics of Programming Languages*
SACKMAN AND CITRENBAUM, editors,  *On-line Planning: Towards Creative Problem-Solving*
SALTON, editor,  *The SMART Retrieval System: Experiments in Automatic Document Processing*
SAMMET,  *Programming Languages: History and Fundamentals*
SCHAEFER,  *A Mathematical Theory of Global Program Optimization*
SCHULTZ,  *Spline Analysis*
SCHWARZ, et al.,  *Numerical Analysis of Symmetric Matrices*
SHERMAN,  *Techniques in Computer Programming*
SIMON AND SIKLOSSY,  *Representation and Meaning: Experiments with Information Processing Systems*
STERBENZ,  *Floating-Point Computation*
STERLING AND POLLACK,  *Introduction to Statistical Data Processing*
STOUTEMYER,  *PL/1 Programming for Engineering and Science*
STRANG AND FIX,  *An Analysis of the Finite Element Method*
STROUD,  *Approximate Calculation of Multiple Integrals*
TAVISS, editor,  *The Computer Impact*
TRAUB,  *Iterative Methods for the Solution of Polynomial Equations*
UHR,  *Pattern Recognition, Learning, and Thought*
VAN TASSEL,  *Computer Security Management*
VARGA,  *Matrix Iterative Analysis*
WAITE,  *Implementing Software for Non-Numeric Application*
WILKINSON,  *Rounding Errors in Algebraic Processes*
WIRTH,  *Systematic Programming: An Introduction*

*To Milena, Mette, and Thomas*
*for making it all worthwhile*

# OPERATING SYSTEM PRINCIPLES

PER BRINCH HANSEN

*California Institute of Technology*

PRENTICE-HALL, INC., Englewood Cliffs, New Jersey

*Library of Congress Cataloging in Publication Data*

Brinch Hansen, Per,
    Operating system principles.

    Bibliography: p.
    1. Time sharing computer systems. 2. Computer
programming management. I. Title.
QA76.5.B76    001.6'44'04    73-491
ISBN 0-13-637843-9

10  9  8  7  6  5  4  3

Printed in the United States of America

PRENTICE-HALL INTERNATIONAL, INC., *London*
PRENTICE-HALL OF AUSTRALIA, PTY. LTD., *Sydney*
PRENTICE-HALL OF CANADA, LTD., *Toronto*
PRENTICE-HALL OF INDIA PRIVATE LIMITED, *New Delhi*
PRENTICE-HALL OF JAPAN, INC., *Tokyo*

# PREFACE

## THE MAIN GOAL

This book tries to give students of computer science and professional programmers a general understanding of *operating systems*—the programs that enable people to share computers efficiently.

To make the sharing of a computer tolerable, an operating system must enforce certain rules of behavior on all its users. One would therefore expect the designers of operating systems to do their utmost to make them as simple, efficient, and reliable as possible.

A number of operating systems made in the early 1960's had these characteristics; but in the late 1960's designers were often overambitious and built enormous systems with poor performance.

I see no inherent reason why operating systems should not reach the quality of program construction found in present compilers; this will require an understanding of the principles common to all operating systems and a consistent use of safe methods of designing large programs. It is my hope that this book will give you a start in this direction.

I assume that you are familiar with the basic structure of computers and programming languages and have some experience in writing and testing non-trivial programs. In a few cases a knowledge of elementary calculus and probability theory is also needed.

## THEMES

The main theme of the book is that operating systems are not radically different from other programs. The difficulties encountered in the design of efficient, reliable operating systems are the same as those one encounters in the design of other large programs, such as compilers or payroll programs.

The historical importance of operating systems is that they led to the discovery of new principles of *resource sharing, multiprogramming*, and *program construction*. These principles have a general validity beyond operating systems, and I think that they should be taught as part of a core of computer science courses, following courses on *programming languages, data structures*, and *computer structures*.

The purpose of an operating system is to share computational resources among competing users. To do this efficiently *a designer must respect the technological limitations of these resources.*

Present computers consist of a small number of components (processors, store modules, and peripherals) which operate strictly sequentially. It is possible to multiplex a single processor and a small internal store (supported by a large backing store) among several computations to create the illusion that they are executed concurrently and have access to a large, homogeneous store. But these abstractions are not supported by the underlying technology, and if they are carried too far, the result is a total collapse of computational service known as thrashing.

*One of the difficulties of operating systems is the highly unpredictable nature of the demands made upon them.* Independent users submit jobs with varying resource requirements at irregular intervals. An operating system is expected to schedule this unpredictable mixture of jobs in such a manner that the resources are utilized efficiently and the users can expect response within reasonably predictable times!

The only way to satisfy these expectations is probably to put restrictions on the characteristics of jobs so *the designer can take advantage of the expected usage of resources.* This is certainly the main reason for the success of small, specialized operating systems. It also gives a plausible explanation of the failure of recent "general-purpose" operating systems which try to handle a much greater variety of jobs (in some cases for a variety of machine configurations as well).

Although most components of present computers are sequential in nature, they can work simultaneously to some extent. This influences the design of operating systems so much that the subject can best be described as *the management of shared multiprogramming systems.*

The main difficulty of multiprogramming is that concurrent activities can interact in a time-dependent manner which makes it practically impossible to locate programming errors by systematic testing. Perhaps, more than anything else, this explains the difficulty of making operating systems reliable.

*If we wish to succeed in designing large, reliable multiprogramming systems, we must use programming tools which are so well-structured that most time-dependent errors can be caught at compile time.* It seems hopeless to try to solve this problem at the machine level of programming, nor can we expect to improve the situation by means of so-called "implementation languages," which retain the traditional "right" of systems programmers to manipulate addresses freely.

I use the programming language *Pascal* throughout the text to define operating system concepts concisely by algorithms. Pascal combines the clarity needed for teaching with the efficiency required for design. It is easily understood by programmers familiar with Algol 60 or Fortran, but

Pascal is a far more natural programming tool than these languages, particularly with respect to data structuring. As we go along, I extend Pascal with a well-structured notation for multiprogramming.

## STRUCTURE

The book contains eight chapters:

Chapter 1 is *an overview of operating systems*. It defines the purpose of operating systems and outlines their historical development from early batch processing to recent interactive systems. It also points out the influence of technological constraints on the services offered by operating systems.

Chapter 2 on *sequential processes* discusses the role of abstraction and structure in problem solving and the nature of computations. It summarizes structuring principles of data and sequential programs and gives an example of hierarchal program construction.

Chapter 3 on *concurrent processes* emphasizes the role of reproducible behavior in program testing and compares various methods of process synchronization: simple and conditional critical regions, semaphores, message buffers, and event queues. It concludes with an analysis of the prevention of deadlocks by a hierarchal ordering of process interactions.

Chapters 2 and 3 present an abstract view of computational processes and their representation in programming languages. The following Chapters, 4 to 6, discuss techniques of implementing processes on computers with limited resources. This problem is mainly technological, and it seems unrealistic to look for a unifying view of how different kinds of components are used efficiently. I try to describe various techniques and point out under which circumstances they are successful.

Chapter 4 on *processor management* discusses the short-term problems of scheduling concurrent processes on a limited number of processors at the lowest level of programming. It also explains the implementation of synchronizing primitives and evaluates the influence of these abstractions on the real-time characteristics of a system.

Chapter 5 on *store management* considers the short-term problems of sharing an internal store of limited capacity among concurrent processes. It summarizes current store technology and explains the influence of recursive procedures, concurrent processes, and dynamic relocation on store addressing. It ends with an analysis of placement algorithms and store multiplexing.

Chapter 6 analyzes the performance of various medium-term *scheduling algorithms*. It uses elementary queuing theory to derive analytical results for the average response time to user requests in a single processor system with these priority rules: first-come first-served, shortest job next, highest response ratio next, and round robin. Foregound-background scheduling is discussed informally.

Chapter 7 is concerned with *resource protection*—the problem of ensuring that physical resources and data are accessed by well-defined operations within computations authorized to use them. This is a fundamental problem of program design which should have been presented earlier in the book, if only I understood it better. It is handled inadequately in all present operating systems. As fragments of a solution I mention two of the more systematic techniques used: the class concept in Simula 67 and the capability concept.

It is important that a designer of operating systems understand the underlying common principles. But the danger of this division of the subject into separate chapters is that you may find it difficult to see how they fit together into a working system and be unaware of the more subtle interactions between, say, process communication, store management, input/output, and preemptive scheduling.

I have therefore tried to describe a complete operating system in some detail in Chapter 8. It is *a case study* of the *RC 4000 multiprogramming system*. It is by no means an ideal system, but it is the only one I know in detail, and is regarded as a consistent, simple, and reliable design which illustrates the concepts and implementation of concurrent processes.

It should perhaps be explained why there are no chapters on input/output and filing systems. For a particular operating system, considerations about how these tasks are handled are highly relevant. But in this book I have concentrated on the more elementary aspects of these complicated tasks, namely process synchronization, store management, scheduling, and resource protection.

## VOCABULARY

In each chapter many words are first used intuitively to give you a feeling for the subject. Later I return to these words and try to give reasonably precise verbal definitions of their meaning. My use of a common word may not always agree completely with the various shades of meaning it has acquired elsewhere, but I hope to justify the usefulness of the concept behind the word and show that it is possible to describe operating systems in an informal but consistent terminology.

The most important terms are collected in a Vocabulary section at the end of the book.

## LITERATURE

This book is only one designer's view of operating systems. I urge you to examine my viewpoints critically and compare them with other literature on the subject. As a guide to such a study I have included an *annotated selective bibliography* at the end of each chapter.

For the sake of completeness I have listed all *references* mentioned in the text at the end of the book.

## ACKNOWLEDGEMENTS

Niels Ivar Bech and Poul Dahlgaard enabled me to gain valuable experience in the design of the RC 4000 multiprogramming system at Regnecentralen, Denmark. Alan Perlis and Joseph Traub made the writing of this book possible by inviting me to visit Carnegie-Mellon University from November 1970 to June 1972. The writing was supported in part by the Advanced Research Projects Agency of the Office of the Secretary of Defense (F44620-70-C-0107).

Parts of the manuscript have been published earlier under the titles:

RC 4000 software: multiprogramming system.
Regnecentralen, Copenhagen, Denmark, April 1969.

A comparison of two synchronizing concepts.
*Acta Informatica* 1, 3, 1972.

Structured multiprogramming.
*Communications of the ACM* 15, 7, July 1972.

Permissions to reprint excerpts from these papers have kindly been granted by Regnecentralen, Springer-Verlag, and the Association for Computing Machinery.

The idea of looking upon the management of shared computers as a general data-processing problem was inspired by a similar attitude of Peter Naur (1966) towards program translation. This viewpoint determined the structure of the book since it was conceived in March 1970. It is also a pleasure to acknowledge the influence of Tony Hoare on my attitude towards multiprogramming.

Jim Horning and Alan Shaw gave helpful comments on the overall structure of the manuscript. And many useful suggestions were made by Giorgio Ingargiola and Howard Morgan. Finally, I wish to thank my wife, Milena, for her patience and encouragement during the past two years. I also thank her for an extremely careful reading of the manuscript which led to numerous improvements in style.

PER BRINCH HANSEN

*California Institute of Technology*

# CONTENTS

# 1

# AN OVERVIEW OF OPERATING SYSTEMS

This chapter describes the purpose and technological background of operating systems. It stresses the similarities of all operating systems and points out the advantages of special-purpose over general-purpose systems.

## 1.1. THE PURPOSE OF AN OPERATING SYSTEM

### 1.1.1. Resource Sharing

An *operating system* is a set of manual and automatic procedures that enable a group of people to share a computer installation efficiently.

The key word in this definition is *sharing*: it means that people will *compete* for the use of physical resources such as processor time, storage space, and peripheral devices; but it also means that people can *cooperate* by exchanging programs and data on the same installation. The sharing of a computer installation is an economic necessity, and the purpose of an operating system is to make the sharing tolerable.

An operating system must have a *policy* for choosing the order in which competing users are served and for resolving conflicts of simultaneous requests for the same resources; it must also have means of *enforcing* this policy in spite of the presence of erroneous or malicious user programs.

Present computer installations can execute several user programs simultaneously and allow users to *retain data* on backing storage for weeks or months. The simultaneous presence of data and programs belonging to different users requires that an operating system *protect* users against each other.

Since users must pay for the cost of computing, an operating system must also perform *accounting* of the usage of resources.

In early computer installations, operators carried out most of these functions. The purpose of present operating systems is to carry out these tasks automatically by means of the computer itself. But when all these aspects of sharing are automated, it becomes quite difficult for the installation management to find out what the computer is actually doing and to modify the rules of sharing to improve performance. A good operating system will assist management in this evaluation by collecting *measurements* on the utilization of the equipment.

Most components of present computer installations are sequential in nature: they can only execute operations or transfer data items one at a time. But it is possible to have activities going on simultaneously in several of these components. This influences the design of operating systems so much that our subject can best be described as the *management of shared multiprogramming systems*.

### 1.1.2.  Virtual Machines

An operating system defines several languages in which the rules of resource sharing and the requests for service can be described. One of these languages is the *job control language*, which enables users to identify themselves and describe the requirements of computational jobs: the types and amounts of resources needed, and the names of programs and data files used.

Another language is the *virtual machine language*: the set of machine operations available to a user during program execution. To maintain control of a computer installation and isolate users from each other, an operating system must prevent user programs from executing certain operations; otherwise, these programs could destroy procedures or data inside the operating system or start input/output on peripheral devices assigned to other users. So the set of machine operations available to users is normally a subset of the original machine language.

But users must have some means of doing input/output. The operating system enables them to do so by calling certain standard procedures that handle the peripherals in a well-defined manner. To the user programs, these standard procedures appear to be extensions of the machine language available to them. The user has the illusion of working on a machine that can execute programs written in this language. Because this machine is partly simulated by program, it is called a *virtual machine*. So an operating system makes a virtual machine available to each user and prevents these machines from interfering destructively with each other. The simultaneous presence of several users makes the virtual machines much slower than the physical machine.

An operating system can make the programming language of the virtual machine more attractive than that of the original machine. This can be done by relieving the user of the burden of technological details such as the physical identity of peripheral devices and minor differences in their operation. This enables the user to concentrate on logical concepts such as the names of data files and the transfer of data records to and from these files. The virtual machine can also be made more attractive by error correction techniques; these make the virtual machine appear more reliable than the real one (for example, by automatic repetition of unsuccessful input/output operations). In this way an operating system may succeed in making a virtue out of a necessity.

Yet another language is the one used inside the operating system itself to define the policy of sharing, the rules of protection, and so on. A certain amount of bitter experience with present operating systems has clearly shown that an operating system may turn out to be inefficient, unreliable, or built on wrong assumptions just like any other large program. Operating systems should be designed so that they are simple to understand, and easy to use and modify. Even if an operating system works correctly, there is still a need for experimenting with its policy towards users and for adapting it to the requirements of a particular environment, so it is important not only to give users an attractive programming language, but also to design good programming tools to be used inside the operating system itself. But since the operating system is imposed on everyone, it is extremely important that the language used to implement it reflect the underlying machine features in an efficient manner.

### 1.1.3.  Operating Systems and User Programs

Operating systems are *large programs* developed and used by a changing group of people. They are often modified considerably during their lifetimes. Operating systems must necessarily impose certain restrictions on all users. But this should not lead us to regard them as being radically different from other programs—they are just complicated *applications* of general programming techniques.

During the construction of operating systems over the past decade, new methods of multiprogramming and resource sharing were discovered. We now realize that these methods are equally useful in other programming applications. Any large programming effort will be heavily influenced by the characteristics and amounts of physical resources available, by the possibility of executing smaller tasks simultaneously, and by the need for sharing a set of data among such tasks.

It may be useful to distinguish between operating systems and user computations because the former can *enforce* certain rules of behavior on the latter. But it is important to understand that each level of programming solves some aspect of resource allocation.

Let me give a few examples of the influence of resource sharing on the design of standard programs and user programs.

*Store allocation.* One of the main reasons for dividing a compiler into smaller parts (called *passes*) is to allocate storage efficiently. During a compilation, the passes can be loaded one at a time from drum or disk into a small internal store where they are executed.

*Job scheduling.* A data processing application for an industrial plant can involve quite complicated rules for the sequence in which smaller tasks are scheduled for execution. There may be a daily job which records details of production; weekly and monthly jobs which compute wages; a yearly job associated with the fiscal year; and several other jobs. Such long-term scheduling of related jobs which share large data files is quite difficult to control automatically. In contrast, most operating systems only worry about the scheduling of independent jobs over time spans of a few minutes or hours.

*Multiprogramming.* To control an industrial process, engineers must be able to write programs that can carry out many tasks simultaneously, for example, measure process variables continuously, report alarms to operators, accumulate measurements of production, and print reports to management.

*Program protection.* The ability to protect smaller components of a large program against each other is essential in real-time applications (such as banking and ticket reservation) where the service of reliable program components must be continued while new components are being tested.

So the problems of resource sharing solved by operating systems repeat themselves in user programs; or, to put it differently, every large application of a computer includes a local operating system that coordinates resource sharing among smaller tasks of that application. What is normally called "the operating system" is just the one that coordinates the sharing of an entire installation among users.

When you realize that resource sharing is not a unique characteristic of operating systems, you may wonder whether the simulation of virtual machines makes operating systems different from other programs. But alas, a closer inspection shows that all programs simulate virtual machines.

Computer programs are designed to solve a *class of problems* such as the editing of all possible texts, the compilation of all possible Algol programs, the sorting of arbitrary sets of data, the computation of payrolls for a varying number of employees, and so on. The user specifies a particular case of the class of problems by means of a set of data, called the *input*, and the program delivers as its result another set of data, called the *output*.

One way of looking at this flexibility is to say that the input is a sequence of instructions written in a certain language, and the function of the program is to follow these instructions.

From this point of view, an editing program can execute other programs written in an editing language consisting of instructions such as *search*, *delete*, and *insert* textstring. And an Algol compiler can execute programs written in the Algol 60 language. The computer itself can be viewed as a physical implementation of a program called the *instruction execution cycle*. This program can carry out other programs written in a so-called machine language.

If we adopt the view that a computer is a device able to follow and carry out descriptions of processes written in a formal language, then we realize that each of these descriptions (or programs) in turn makes the original computer appear to be another computer which interprets a different language. In other words, an editing program makes the computer behave like an editing machine, and an Algol compiler turns it into an Algol 60 machine. Using slightly different words, we can say that a program executed on a physical machine makes that machine behave like a virtual machine which can interpret a different programming language. And this language is certainly more attractive *for its purpose* than the original machine language; otherwise, there would be no reason to write the program in the first place!

From these considerations it is hard to avoid the conclusion that operating systems must be regarded merely as large application programs. Their purpose is to manage resource sharing, and they are based on general programming methods. The proper aim of education is to identify these methods. But before we do that, I will briefly describe the technological development of operating systems. This will give you a more concrete idea of what typical operating systems do and what they have in common.

## 1.2. TECHNOLOGICAL BACKGROUND

### 1.2.1. Computer and Job Profiles

We now go back to the middle of the 1950's to trace the influence of the technological development of computers on the structure of operating systems.

When many users share a computer installation, queues of computations submitted for execution are normally formed, and a decision has to be made about the order in which they should be executed to obtain acceptable overall service. This decision rule is called a *scheduling algorithm.*

A computation requested by a user is called a *job*; it can involve the execution of several programs in succession, such as editing followed by compilation and execution of a program written in a high-level language. A job can also require simultaneous execution of several programs cooperating on the same task. One program may, for example, control the printing of data, while another program computes more output.

In the following, I justify the need for automatic scheduling of jobs by quite elementary considerations about a *computer installation* with the following characteristics:

| | |
|---|---|
| instruction execution time | 2 $\mu$sec |
| internal store | 32 K words |
| card reader | 1,000 cards/min |
| line printer | 1,000 lines/min |
| magnetic tape stations | 80,000 char/sec |

($1\ \mu = 10^{-6}$, and 1 K = 1024).

We will consider an environment in which the main problem is to schedule a *large number of small jobs* whose response times are as short as possible. (The *response time* of a job is the interval between the request for its execution and the return of its results.) This assumption is justified for universities and engineering laboratories where program development is the main activity.

A number of people have described the typical *job profile* for this type of environment (Rosin, 1965; Walter, 1967). We will assume that the average job consists of a compilation and execution of a program written in a high-level language. The source text read from cards and listed on a printer, is the major part of the input/output. More precisely, the average job will be characterized by the following figures:

| | |
|---|---|
| input time (300 cards) | 0.3 min |
| output time (500 lines) | 0.5 min |
| execution time | 1  min |

### 1.2.2. Batch-processing Systems

For the moment we will assume that *magnetic tape* is the only form of backing store available. This has a profound influence on the possible forms of scheduling. We also impose the technological restriction on the computer that its mode of operation be *strictly sequential.* This means that: (1) it can only execute one program at a time; and (2) after the start of an input/output operation, program execution stops until the transfer of data has been completed.

The simplest scheduling rule is the *open shop* where users each sign up for a period of, say, 15 min and operate the machine themselves. For the individual user this is an ideal form of service: it enables him to correct minor programming errors on the spot and experiment with programs during their execution. Unfortunately, such a system leads to prohibitive costs of idle machinery: for an average job, the central processor will only be working for one out of every 15 min; the rest of the time will be spent waiting for the operator. The situation can be characterized by two simple measures of average performance:

processor utilization = execution time/total time

throughput = number of jobs executed per time unit

For the open shop, processor utilization is only about 7 per cent with a throughput of no more than 4 jobs per hour, each requiring only one minute of execution time(!).

Idle processor time caused by manual intervention can be greatly reduced by even the most *primitive* form of *automatic scheduling*. Figure 1.1 illustrates an installation in which users no longer can interact with programs during execution. They submit their jobs to an operator who stacks them in the card reader in their order of arrival. From the card reader, jobs are input directly to the computer, listed on the printer, and executed one by one. This scheduling is done by an operating system which resides permanently in the internal store.

Under this form of scheduling an average job occupies the computer for 1.8 min (the sum of input/output and execution times). This means that processor utilization has been improved to 55 percent with a corresponding throughput of 33 jobs per hour.

But even this simple form of automatic scheduling creates new problems: How do we *protect the operating system* against erroneous user programs? How can we force user programs to *return control* to the operating system when they are finished, or if they fail to terminate after a

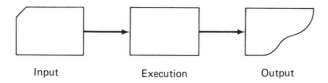

Input        Execution        Output

Fig. 1.1 Automatic scheduling of a job queue input directly
from a card reader, executed, and output directly
on a line printer by a single processor.

period of time defined by the operating system? Early operating systems offered no satisfactory solutions to these problems and were frequently brought down by their jobs. We will ignore this problem at the moment and return to it in the chapters on processor management and resource protection.

This argument in favor of automatic scheduling has ignored the processor time that is lost while the operator handles the peripheral devices: inserting paper in the printer, mounting tapes for larger jobs, and so forth. The argument has also ignored processor time that is wasted when the operator makes a mistake. But these factors are ignored throughout the chain of arguments and do not affect the *trend* towards better utilization of the processor.

The main weakness is that the argument did not include an evaluation of the amount of processor time used by the new component—the operating system. The reason for this omission is that an operating system carries out certain indispensable functions (input/output, scheduling, and accounting) which previously had to be done elsewhere in the installation by operators and users. The relevant factor here—the amount of processor time lost by an inefficient implementation of the operating system—unfortunately cannot be measured. But in any case, the figures given in the following are not my estimates, but measurements of the actual performance of some recent operating systems.

The bottleneck in the previous simple system is the slow input/output devices; they keep the central processor waiting 45 per cent of the time during an average job execution. So the next step is to use the fast tape stations to implement a *batch processing system* as shown in Fig. 1.2. First, a number of jobs are collected from users by an operator and copied from

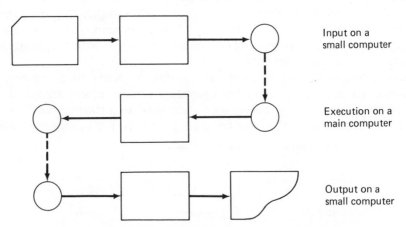

Fig. 1.2   Batch processing of jobs in three phases: input of cards to tape on a small computer; execution with tape input/output on a main computer; and output of tape to printer on a small computer.

cards to magnetic tape on a small, cheap computer. This tape is carried by the operator to the main computer, which executes the batch of jobs one by one, delivering their output to another tape. Finally, this output tape is carried to the small computer and listed on the printer. Notice that although jobs are executed in their order of arrival inside a batch, the printed output of the first job is not available until the entire batch has been executed.

During the execution of a batch on the main computer, the operator uses the small computer to print the output of an earlier batch and input a new batch on tape. In this way the main computer, as well as the card reader and printer, is kept busy all the time. Input/output delays on the main computer are negligible in this system, but another source of idle time has appeared: the mounting and dismounting of tapes. This can only be reduced by batching many jobs together on a single tape. But in doing so we also increase the waiting time of users for the results of their jobs. This dilemma between idle processor time and user response time can be expressed by the following relation:

$$\text{processor utilization} = \frac{\text{batch execution time}}{\text{batch response time}}$$

where

batch response time = batch mounting time + batch execution time

This can also be rewritten as follows:

$$\text{batch response time} = \frac{\text{batch mounting time}}{1 - \text{processor utilization}}$$

Since there is a limit to the amount of idle processor time management is prepared to accept, the net result is that response time for users is still determined by the manual speed of operators! In the installation considered a *batch cycle* typically proceeds as follows:

| | |
|---|---|
| Delivery time of 50 jobs | 30 min |
| Conversion of cards to tape | 15 min |
| Mounting of tapes | 5 min |
| Batch execution | 50 min |
| Conversion of tape to printer | 25 min |
| Manual separation of output | 15 min |
| Total batch cycle | 140 min |

With a tape mounting time of 5 min per batch, utilization of the main processor is now as high as 50/55 = 90 per cent, and throughput has reached 55 jobs per hour. But at the same time, the shortest response time for any job is 140 min. And this is obtained only if the job joins a batch immediately after submission.

We have also ignored the problem of the large jobs: When jobs requiring hours for execution are included in a batch, the jobs following will experience much longer response times. Most users are only interested in fast response during working hours. So an obvious remedy is to let the operators *sort jobs manually* and schedule the shorter ones during the daytime and the longer ones at night.

If the operator divides the jobs into three groups, the users might typically expect response times of the following order:

$$
\begin{array}{ll}
\text{1-min jobs:} & \text{2- 3 \ hours} \\
\text{5-min jobs:} & \text{8- 10 hours} \\
\text{other jobs:} & \text{1- 7 \ days}
\end{array}
$$

We have followed the rationale behind the classical batch-processing system of the late 1950's (Bratman, 1959). The main concern has been to reduce idle processor time, unfortunately with a resultant increase in user response time.

In this type of system the most complicated aspects of sharing are still handled by operators, for example, the scheduling of simultaneous input/output and program execution on two computers, and the assignment of priorities to user jobs. For this reason I have defined an operating system as a set of *manual and automatic procedures* that enable a group of people to *share* a computer installation *efficiently* (Section 1.1.1).

### 1.2.3. Spooling Systems

It is illuminating to review the technological restrictions that dictated the previous development towards batch processing. The first one was the strict sequential nature of the computer which made it necessary to prevent conversational interaction with running programs; the second limitation was the sequential nature of the backing store (magnetic tapes) which forced us to schedule large batches of jobs strictly in the order in which they were input to the system.

The sequential restrictions on scheduling were made much less severe (but were by no means removed) by technological developments in the early 1960's. The most important improvement was the design of *autonomous peripheral devices* which can carry out input/output operations independently while the central processor continues to execute programs.

The problem of synchronizing the central processor and the peripheral devices after the completion of input/output operations was solved by the interrupt concept. An *interrupt* is a timing signal set by a peripheral device in a register connected to a central processor. It is examined by the central processor after the execution of each instruction. When an interrupt occurs, the central processor suspends the execution of its current program and starts another program—the operating system. When the operating system has responded properly to the device signal, it can either resume the execution of the interrupted program or start a more urgent program (for example, the one that was waiting for the input/output).

This technique made *concurrent operation* of a central processor and its peripheral devices possible. The programming technique used to control concurrent operation is called *multiprogramming*.

It was soon realized that the same technique could be used to simulate concurrent execution of several user programs on a single processor. Each program is allowed to execute for a certain period of time, say of the order of 0.1–1 sec. At the end of this interval a *timing device* interrupts the program and starts the operating system. This in turn selects another program, which now runs until a timing interrupt makes the system switch to a third program, and so forth.

This form of scheduling, in which a single resource (the central processor) is shared by several users, one at a time in rapid succession, is called *multiplexing*. Further improvements are made possible by enabling a program to ask the operating system to switch to other programs while it waits for input/output.

The possibility of more than one program being in a state of execution at one time has considerable influence on the organization of storage. It is no longer possible to predict in which part of the internal store a program will be placed for execution. So there is no fixed correspondence at compile time between the names used in a program to refer to data and the addresses of their store locations during execution. This problem of *program relocation* was first solved by means of a *loading program*, which examined user programs before execution and modified addresses used in them to correspond to the store locations actually used.

Later, program relocation was included in the logic of the central processor: a *base register* was used to modify instruction addresses automatically during execution by the start address of the storage area assigned to a user. Part of the *protection problem* was solved by extending this scheme with a *limit register* defining the size of the address space available to a user; any attempt to refer to data or programs outside this space would be *trapped* by the central processor and cause the operating system to be activated.

The protection offered by base and limit registers was, of course, illusory as long as user programs could modify these registers. The recognition of this flaw led to the design of central processors with two states of execution: a *privileged state*, in which there are no restrictions on the operations executed; and a *user state*, in which the execution of operations controlling interruption, input/output, and store allocation is forbidden and will be trapped if attempted. A transition to the privileged state is caused by interrupts from peripherals and by protection violations inside user programs. A transition to the user state is caused by execution of a privileged operation.

It is now recognized that it is desirable to be able to distinguish in a more flexible manner between many levels of protection (and not just two). This early protection system is safe, but it assigns more responsibility to the operating system than necessary. The operating system must, for example, contain code which can start input/output on every type of device because no other program is allowed to do that. But actually, all that is needed in this case is a mechanism which ensures that a job only operate devices assigned to it; whether a job handles *its own devices* correctly or not is irrelevant to the operating system. So a centralized protection scheme tends to increase the complexity of an operating system and make it a bottleneck at run time. Nevertheless, this early protection scheme must be recognized as an invaluable improvement: clearly, the more responsibility management delegates to an operating system, the less they can tolerate that it breaks down.

Another major innovation of this period was the construction of *large backing stores*, disks and drums, which permit fast, *direct access* to data and programs. This, in combination with multiprogramming, makes it possible to build operating systems which handle a continuous stream of input, computation, and output on a single computer. Figure 1.3 shows the organization of such a *spooling system*. The central processor is multiplexed between four programs: one controls input of cards to a queue on the backing store; another selects user jobs from this input queue and

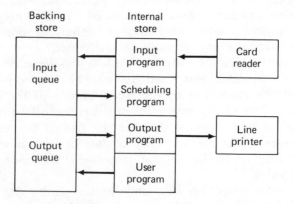

Fig. 1.3   A spooling system controlling continuous buffering
of input/output on backing storage and sequential
scheduling of user jobs.

starts their execution one at a time; and a third one controls printing of output from the backing store. These three programs form the operating system. The fourth program held in the internal store is the current user program which reads its data from the input queue and writes its results in an output queue on the backing store.

The point of using the backing store as a *buffer* is that the input of a job can be fed into the machine in advance of its execution; and its output can be printed during the execution of later jobs. This eliminates the manual overhead of tape mounting. At the same time, direct access to the backing store makes it possible to schedule jobs in order of *priority* rather than in order of arrival. The spooling technique was pioneered on the *Atlas* computer at Manchester University (Kilburn, 1961).

A very successful operating system with input/output spooling, called *Exec II*, was designed by Computer Sciences Corporation (Lynch, 1967 and 1971). It controlled a *Univac 1107* computer with an instruction execution time of 4 $\mu$sec. The backing store consisted of two or more fast drums, each capable of transferring 10,000 characters during a single revolution of 33 msec. The system typically processed 800 jobs per day, each job requiring an average of 1.2 min. It was operated by the users themselves: To run a job, a user simply placed his cards in a reader and pushed a button. As a rule, the system could serve the users faster than they could load cards. So a user could immediately remove his cards from the reader and proceed to a printer where his output would appear shortly.

Less than 5 per cent of the jobs required magnetic tapes. The users who needed tapes had to mount them in advance of program execution.

Fast response to student jobs was achieved by using the scheduling algorithm *shortest job next*. Priorities were based on estimates of execution time supplied by users, but jobs that exceeded their estimated time limits were terminated by force.

Response times were so short that the user could observe an error, repunch a few cards, and resubmit his job immediately. System performance was measured in terms of the *circulation time* of jobs. This was defined as the sum of the response time of a job after its submission and the time required by the user to interpret the results, correct the cards, and resubmit the job; or, to put it more directly, the circulation time was the interval between two successive arrivals of the same job for execution.

About a third of all jobs had a circulation time of less than 5 min, and 90 per cent of all jobs were recirculated ones that had already been run one or more times the same day. This is a remarkable achievement compared to the earlier batch-processing system in which small jobs took a few hours to complete! At the same time, the processor utilization in the *Exec II* system was as high as 90 per cent.

The *Exec II* system has demonstrated that many users do not need a direct, conversational interaction with programs during execution. Users will often be quite satisfied with a non-interactive system which offers them informal access, fast response, and minimal cost.

*Non-interactive scheduling* of small jobs with fast response is particularly valuable for *program testing*. Program tests are usually short in duration: After a few seconds the output becomes meaningless due to a programming error. The main thing for the programmer is to get the initial output as soon as possible and to be able to run another test after correcting the errors shown by the previous test.

There are, however, also cases in which the possibility of interacting with running programs is highly desirable. In the following section, I describe operating systems which permit this.

### 1.2.4. Interactive Systems

To make direct conversation with running programs tolerable to human beings, the computer must respond to requests within a few seconds. As an experiment, try to ask a friend a series of simple questions and tell him to wait ten seconds before answering each of them; I am sure you will agree that this form of communication is not well-suited to the human temperament.

A computer can only respond to many users in a few seconds when the processing time of each request is very small. So the use of multiprogramming for conversation is basically a means of giving fast response to *trivial requests*; for example, in the editing of programs, in ticket reservation systems, in teaching programs, and so forth. These are all situations in which the pace is limited by human thinking. They involve very moderate amounts of input/output data which can be handled by low-speed terminals such as typewriters or displays.

In interactive systems in which the processor time per request is only a few hundred milliseconds, scheduling cannot be based on reliable user estimates of service time. This uncertainty forces the scheduler to allocate processor time in small slices. The simplest rule is *round-robin* scheduling: each job in turn is given a fixed amount of processor time called a *time slice*; if a job is not completed at the end of its time slice, it is interrupted and returned to the end of a queue to wait for another time slice. New jobs are placed at the end of the queue. This policy guarantees fast response to user requests that can be processed within a single time slice.

Conversational access in this sense was first proposed by Strachey (1959). The creative advantages of a closer interaction between man and machine were pointed out a few years later by Licklider and Clark (1962). The earliest operational systems were the *CTSS* system developed at Massachusetts Institute of Technology and the *SDC Q-32* system built by the System Development Corporation. They are described in excellent papers by Corbato (1962) and Schwartz (1964 and 1967).

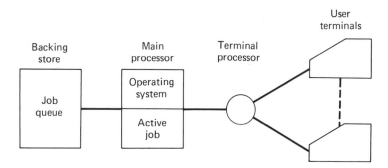

**Fig. 1.4** An interactive system with low-speed user terminals and swapping of jobs between internal and backing storage.

Figure 1.4 illustrates the *SDC Q-32* system in a simplified form, ignoring certain details. An internal store of 65 K words is divided between a resident operating system and a single active user job; the rest of the jobs are kept on a drum with a capacity of 400 K words.

The average time slice is about 40 msec. At the end of this interval, the active job is transferred to the drum and another job is loaded into the internal store. This exchange of jobs between two levels of storage is called *swapping*. It takes roughly another 40 msec. During the swapping, the central processor is idle so it is never utilized more than 50 per cent of the time.

During the daytime the system is normally accessed simultaneously by about 25 user terminals. So a user can expect response to a simple request (requiring a single time slice only) in 25*80 msec = 2 sec.

A small computer controls terminal input/output and ensures that users can continue typing requests and receiving replies while their jobs are waiting for more time. A disk of 4000 K words with an average access time of 225 msec is used for semi-permanent storage of data files and programs.

The users communicate with the operating system in a simple job control language with the following instructions:

LOGIN:    The user identifies himself and begins using the system.

LOAD:     The user requests the transfer of a program from disk to drum.

START:    The user starts the execution of a loaded program or resumes the execution of a stopped program.

STOP:     The user stops the execution of a program temporarily.

DIAL:     The user communicates with other users or with system operators.

LOGOUT:   The user terminates his use of the system.

The system has been improved over the years: Processor utilization has been increased from 50 to 80 per cent by the use of a more complicated scheduling algorithm. Nevertheless, it is still true that this system and similar ones are forced to spend processor time on unproductive transfers of jobs between two levels of storage: Interactive systems achieve *guaranteed response* to short requests at the price of decreased processor utilization.

In the *SDC Q-32* system with an average of 25 active users, each user is slowed down by a factor of 50. Consequently, a one-minute job takes about 50 min to complete compared to the few minutes required in the *Exec II* system. So interactive scheduling only makes sense for trivial requests; it is not a realistic method for computational jobs that run for minutes and hours.

Later and more ambitious projects are the *MULTICS* system (Corbato, 1965) also developed at MIT, and the IBM system *TSS-360* (Alexander, 1968). In these systems, the problem of *store multiplexing* among several users is solved by a more refined method: Programs and data are transferred between two levels of storage in smaller units, called *pages*, when they are actually needed during the execution of jobs. The argument is that this is less wasteful in terms of processor time than the crude method of swapping entire programs. But experience has shown that this argument is not always valid because the overhead of starting and completing transfers increases when it is done in smaller portions. We will look at this problem in more detail in the chapter on store management. The paging concept was originally invented for the *Atlas* computer (Kilburn, 1962).

Another significant contribution of these systems is the use of large disks for semi-permanent storage of data and programs. A major problem in such a *filing system* is to ensure the *integrity* of data in spite of occasional hardware failures and *protect* them against unauthorized usage. The integrity problem can be solved by *periodic copying* of data from disk to magnetic tape. These tapes enable an installation to restore data on the disk after a hardware failure. This is a more complicated example of the design goal mentioned in Section 1.1.2: An operating system should try to make the virtual machine appear more reliable than the real one.

The protection problem can be solved by a *password* scheme which enables users to identify themselves and by maintaining as part of the filing system a *directory* describing the authority of users (Fraser, 1971).

Interactive systems can also be designed for *real-time control* of industrial processes. The central problem in a real-time environment is that the computer must be able to receive data as fast as they arrive; otherwise, they will be lost. (In that sense, a conversational system also works under real-time constraints: It must receive input as fast as users type it.)

Usually, a process control system consists of several programs which are executed simultaneously. There may, for example, be a program which is started every minute to measure various temperatures, pressures, and flows and compare these against preset alarm limits. Each time an alarm condition is detected, another program is started to report it to an operator, and while this is being done, the scan for further alarms continues. Still other programs may at the same time accumulate measurements on the production and consumption of materials and energy. And every few hours these data are probably printed by yet another program as a report to plant management.

This concludes the overview of the technological background of shared computer installations. I have tried through a series of simple arguments to illustrate the influence of *technological constraints* on the service offered by operating systems. Perhaps the most valid conclusion is this: In spite of the ability of present computer installations to perform some operations simultaneously, they remain basically *sequential* in nature; a central processor can only execute one operation at a time, and a drum or disk can only transfer one block of data at a time. There are computers and backing stores which can carry out more than one operation at a time, but never to the extent where the realistic designer of operating systems can afford to forget completely about sequential resource constraints.

## 1.3.  THE SIMILARITIES OF OPERATING SYSTEMS

The previous discussion may have left the impression that there are basic differences between batch processing, spooling, and interactive systems. This is certainly true as long as we are interested mainly in the relation between the user service and the underlying technology. But to gain a deeper insight into the nature of operating systems, we must look for their similarities before we stress their differences.

To mention one example: All shared computer installations must handle concurrent activities at some level. Even if a system only schedules one job at a time, users can still make their requests simultaneously. This is a real-time situation in which data (requests) must be received when they arrive. The problem can, of course, be solved by the users themselves (by forming a waiting line) and by the operators (by writing down requests on paper); but the observation is important since our goal is to handle the problems of sharing automatically.

It is also instructive to compare the batch-processing and spooling systems. Both achieve high efficiency by means of a small number of concurrent activities: In the batch processing system, independent processors work together; in the spooling system, a single processor switches among independent programs. Furthermore, both systems use backing storage (tape and drum) as a buffer to compensate for speed variations of the producers and consumers of data.

As another example, consider real-time systems for process control and conversational programming. In these systems, concurrently executed programs must be able to exchange data to cooperate on common tasks. But again, this problem exists in all shared computer installations: In a spooling system, user computations exchange data with concurrent input/output processes; and in a batch processing system, another set of concurrent processes exchanges data by means of tapes mounted by operators.

As you see, all operating systems face a common set of problems. To recognize these, we must reject the established classification of operating systems (into batch processing, spooling, and interactive systems) which stresses the dissimilarities of various forms of technology and user service. This does not mean that the problems of adjusting an operating system to the constraints of a particular environment should be ignored. But the designer will solve them much more easily when he fully understands the principles common to all operating systems.

## 1.4. DESIGN OBJECTIVES

The key to success in programming is to have a realistic, clearly-defined goal and use the simplest possible methods to achieve it. Several operating systems have failed because their designers started with very vague or overambitious goals. In the following discussion, I will describe two quite opposite views on the overall objectives of operating systems.

### 1.4.1. Special-purpose Systems

The operating systems described so far have one thing in common: Each of them tries to use the available resources in the most simple and efficient manner to give a restricted, but useful form of computational service.

The *Exec II* spooling system, for example, strikes a very careful balance between the requirements of fast response and efficient utilization. The overhead of processor and store multiplexing is kept low by executing jobs one at a time. But with only one job running, processor time is lost when a job waits for input/output. So to reduce input/output delays, data are buffered on a fast drum. But since a drum has a small capacity, it becomes essential to keep the volume of buffered data small. This again depends on the achievement of short response time for the following reason: the faster the jobs are completed, the less time they occupy space within the system.

The keys to the success of the *Exec II* are that the designers: (1) were aware of the *sequential nature* of the processor and the drum, and deliberately kept the degree of multiprogramming low; and (2) took advantage of their knowledge of the *expected workload*—a large number of small programs executed without conversational interaction. In short, the *Exec II* is a simple, very efficient system that serves a special purpose.

The *SDC Q-32* serves a different special purpose: conversational programming. It sacrifices 20 per cent of its processor time to give response within a few seconds to 25 simultaneous users; its operating system occupies only 16 K words of the internal store. This too is a simple, successful system.

The two systems do not compete with each other. Each gives the users a special service in a very efficient manner. But the spooling system is useless for conversation, and so is the interactive system for serious computation.

On the other hand, neither system would be practical in an environment where many large programs run for hours each and where operators mount a thousand tapes daily. This may be the situation in a large atomic research center where physicists collect and process large volumes of experimental data. An efficient solution to this problem requires yet another operating system.

The design approach described here has been called design according to *performance specifications.* Its success strongly suggests that efficient sharing of a large installation requires a *range of operating systems*, each of which provides a special service in the most efficient and simple manner. Such an installation might, for example, use three different operating systems to offer:

(1) conversational editing and preparation of jobs;

(2) non-interactive scheduling of small jobs with fast response; and

(3) non-interactive scheduling of large jobs.

These services can be offered on different computers or at different times on the same computer. For the users, the main thing is that programs written in high-level languages can be processed directly by all three systems.

### 1.4.2. General-purpose Systems

An alternative method is to make a single operating system which offers a variety of services on a whole range of computers. This approach has often been taken by computer manufacturers.

The *OS/360* for the *IBM 360* computer family was based on this philosophy. Mealy (1966) described it as follows:

"Because the basic structure of *OS/360* is equally applicable to batched-job and real-time applications, it may be viewed as one of the first instances of a second-generation operating system. The new objective of such a system is to accommodate an environment of diverse applications and operating modes. Although not to be discounted in importance, various other objectives are not new—they have been recognized to some degree in prior systems. Foremost among these secondary objectives are:

☐ Increased throughput

☐ Lowered response time

☐ Increased programmer productivity

☐ Adaptability (of programs to changing resources)

☐ Expandability

"A second-generation operating system must be geared to change and diversity. *System/360* itself can exist in an almost unlimited variety of machine configurations."

Notice that performance (throughput and response) is considered to be of secondary importance to functional scope.

An operating system that tries to be all things to all men naturally becomes very large. *OS/360* is more than an operating system—it is a library of compilers, utility programs, and resource management programs. It contains several million instructions. Nash gave the following figures for the resource management components of *OS/360* in 1966:

| | |
|---|---|
| Data management | 58.6 K statements |
| Scheduler | 45.0 |
| Supervisor | 26.0 |
| Utilities | 53.0 |
| Linkage editor | 12.3 |
| Testran | 20.4 |
| System generator | 4.4 |
| | 219.7 K |

(Nato report, 1968, page 67).

Because of its size, the *OS/360* is also quite unreliable. To cite Hopkins: "We face a fantastic problem in big systems. For instance, in *OS/360* we have about 1000 errors each release and this number seems to be reasonably constant" (Nato report, 1969, page 20).

This is actually a very low percentage of errors considering the size of the system.

This method has been called design according to *functional specifications*. The results have been generally disappointing, and the reason is simply this: Resource sharing is the main purpose of an operating system, and resources are shared most efficiently when the designer takes full advantage of his knowledge of the *special characteristics* of the resources and the jobs using them. This advantage is immediately denied him by requiring that an operating system must work in a much more general case.

This concludes the overview of operating systems. In the following chapters, operating systems are studied at a detailed level in an attempt to build a sound theoretical understanding of the general principles of multiprogramming and resource sharing.

## 1.5. LITERATURE

This chapter owes much to a survey by Rosin (1969) of the technological development of operating systems.

With the background presented, you will easily follow the arguments in the excellent papers on the early operating systems mentioned: *Atlas* (Kilburn, 1961; Morris, 1967), *Exec II* (Lynch, 1967 and 1971), *CTSS* (Corbato, 1962), and *SDC Q-32* (Schwartz, 1964 and 1967). I recommend that you study these papers to become more familiar with the purpose of operating systems before you proceed with the analysis of their fundamentals. The *Atlas*, *Exec II*, and *SDC* systems are of special interest because they were critically reevaluated after several years of actual use.

The paper by Fraser (1971) explains in some detail the practical problems of maintaining the integrity of data in a disk filing system in spite of occasional hardware malfunction and of protecting these data against unauthorized usage.

CORBATO, F. J., MERWIN-DAGGETT, M., and DALEY, R. C., "An experimental time-sharing system," *Proc. AFIPS Fall Joint Computer Conf.*, pp. 335-44, May *1962*.

FRASER, A. G., "The integrity of a disc based file system," *International Seminar on Operating System Techniques*, Belfast, Northern Ireland, Aug.-Sept. *1971*.

KILBURN, T., HOWARTH, D. J., PAYNE, R. B., and SUMNER, F. H., "The Manchester University Atlas operating system. Part I: Internal organization," *Computer Journal 4*, 3, 222-25, Oct. *1961*.

LYNCH, W. C. "Description of a high capacity fast turnaround university computing center," *Proc. ACM National Meeting*, pp. 273-88, Aug. *1967*.

LYNCH, W. C., "An operating system design for the computer utility environment," *International Seminar on Operating System Techniques*, Belfast, Northern Ireland, Aug.-Sept. *1971*.

MORRIS, D., SUMNER, F. H., and WYLD, M. T., "An appraisal of the Atlas supervisor," *Proc. ACM National Meeting*, pp. 67-75, Aug. *1967*.

ROSIN, R. F., "Supervisory and monitor systems," *Computing Surveys 1*, 1, pp. 15-32, March *1969*.

SCHWARTZ, J. I., COFFMAN, E. G., and WEISSMAN, C., "A general purpose time-sharing system," *Proc. AFIPS Spring Joint Computer Conf.*, pp. 397-411, April *1964*.

SCHWARTZ, J. I. and WEISSMAN, C., "The SDC time-sharing system revisited," *Proc. ACM National Meeting*, pp. 263-71, Aug. *1967*.

*2*

# SEQUENTIAL PROCESSES

This chapter describes the role of abstraction and structure in problem solving, and the nature of computations. It also summarizes the structuring principles of data and sequential programs and gives an example of hierarchal program construction.

## 2.1. INTRODUCTION

The starting point of a theory of operating systems must be a *sequential process*—a succession of events that occur one at a time. This is the way our machines work; this is the way we think. Present computers are built from a small number of large sequential components: store modules which can access one word at a time, arithmetic units which can perform one addition at a time, and peripherals which can transfer one data block at a time. Programs for these computers are written by human beings who master complexity by dividing their tasks into smaller parts which can be analyzed and solved one at a time.

This chapter is a summary of the basic concepts of sequential programming. I assume you already have an intuitive understanding of many of the problems from your own programming experience. We shall begin by discussing the role of abstraction and structure in problem solving.

## 2.2. ABSTRACTION AND STRUCTURE

Human beings can think precisely only of simple problems. In our efforts to understand complicated problems, we must concentrate at any moment on a small number of properties that we believe are essential for our present purpose and ignore all other aspects. Our partial descriptions of the world are called *abstractions* or *models*.

One form of abstraction is the use of *names* as abbreviations for more detailed explanations. This is the whole purpose of terminology. It enables us to say "operating system" instead of "a set of manual and automatic procedures that enable a group of people to share a computer installation efficiently."

In programming, we use names to refer to *variables*. This abstraction permits us to ignore their actual values. Names are also used to refer to *programs* and *procedures*. We can, for example, speak of "the editing program." And if we understand *what* editing is, then we can ignore, for the moment, *how* it is done in detail.

Once a problem is understood in terms of a limited number of aspects, we proceed to analyze each aspect separately in more detail. It is often necessary to repeat this process so that the original problem is viewed as a hierarchy of abstractions which are related as components within components at several levels of detail.

In the previous example, when we have defined what an editing program must do, we can proceed to construct it. In doing so, we will discover the need for more elementary editing procedures which can "search," "delete," and "insert" a textstring. And within these procedures, we will probably write other procedures operating on single characters. So we end up with several levels of procedures, one within the other.

As long as our main interest is the properties of a component as a whole, it is considered a *primitive component*, but, when we proceed to observe smaller, related components inside a larger one, the latter is regarded as a *structured component* or *system*. When we wish to make a distinction between a given component and the rest of the world, we refer to the latter as the *environment* of that component.

The environment makes certain assumptions about the properties of a component and vice versa: The editing program assumes that its input consists of a text and some editing commands, and the user expects the program to perform editing as defined in the manual. These assumptions are called the *connections* between the component and its environment.

The set of connections between components at a given level of detail defines the *structure* of the system at that level. The connections between the editing program and its users are defined in the program manual. Inside the editing program, the connections between the components "search," "delete," and "insert" are defined by what these procedures assume about the properties and location of a textstring and by what operations they perform on it.

Abstraction and recognition of structure are used in all intellectual disciplines to present knowledge in forms that are easily understood and remembered. Our concern is the systematic use of abstraction in the design of operating systems. We will try to identify problems which occur in all shared computer installations and define a set of useful components and rules for connecting them into systems.

In the design of large computer programs, the following difficulties must be taken for granted: (1) improved understanding of the problems will change our *goals* in time; (2) technological innovations will eventually change our *tools*; and (3) our intellectual limitations will often cause us to make *errors* in the construction of large systems. These difficulties imply that large systems will be modified during their entire existence by designers and users, and it is essential that we build such systems with this in mind. If it is difficult to understand a large system, it is also difficult to predict the consequences of modifying it. So *reliability* is intimately related to the *simplicity* of structure at all levels.

Figure 2.1(a) shows a complicated system $S$, consisting of $n$ components $S1, S2, \ldots, Sn$. In this system, each component depends directly on the behavior of all other components. Suppose an average of $p$ simple steps of reasoning or testing are required to understand the relationship between one component and another and to verify that they are properly connected. Then the connection of a single component to its environment can be verified in $(n-1)p$ steps, and the complete system requires $n(n-1)p$ steps.

This can be compared with the system shown in Fig. 2.1(b): There, the connections between the $n$ components are defined by a common set of constraints chosen so that the number of steps $q$ required to verify whether

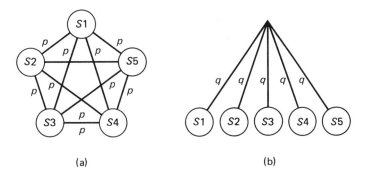

(a)　　　　　　　　　　(b)

Fig. 2.1　Two examples of system structures.

a component satisfies them is independent of the number of components $n$. The proof or test effort is now $q$ steps per component and $nq$ steps for the whole system.

The argument is, of course, extreme, but it does drive home the following point: If the intellectual effort required to understand and test a system increases more than linearly with the size of the system, we shall never be able to build reliable systems beyond a certain complexity. Our only hope is to restrict ourselves to simple structures for which the effort of verification is proportional to the number of components.

The importance of *precise documentation* of system structure can hardly be overemphasized. Quite often, a group of designers intend to adopt a simple structure, but they fail to state precisely what the assumptions are at each level of programming, and instead rely on informal, spoken agreements. Inevitably, the result is that each member of the group adds complexity to the structure by making unnecessary or erroneous assumptions about the behavior of components designed by his colleagues. The importance of making assumptions explicit is especially felt when an initial version of a system must be modified; perhaps by a different group of people.

## 2.3.  COMPUTATIONS

In Chapter 1 the word computation was used intuitively to refer to program execution. In the following, this concept and its components data and operations are defined explicitly.

### 2.3.1.  Data and Operations

The exchange of facts or ideas among human beings by speech is based on mutual agreement on the meaning of certain sounds and combinations of sounds. Other conventions enable us to express the same ideas by means of text and pictures, holes in punched cards, polarity of magnetized media, and modulated electromagnetic waves. In short, we communicate by means of physical phenomena chosen by us to represent certain aspects of our world. These physical representations of our abstractions are called *data*, and the meanings we assign to them are called their *information*.

Data are used to transmit information between human beings, to store information for future use, and to derive new information by manipulating the data according to certain rules. Our most important tool for the manipulation of data is the digital computer.

A datum stored inside a computer can only assume a finite set of values called its *type*. Primitive types are defined by *enumeration* of their values, for example:

$$\textbf{type } \textit{boolean} = (\textit{false, true})$$

or by definition of their *range*:

$$\textbf{type } \textit{integer} = -8388608. \; .8388607$$

Structured types are defined in terms of primitive types, as is explained later in this chapter.

The rules of data manipulation are called operations. An *operation* maps a finite set of data, called its *input*, into a finite set of data, called its *output*. Once initiated, an operation is executed to completion within a finite time. These assumptions imply that the output of an operation is a *time-independent function* of its input, or, to put it differently: An operation always delivers the same output values when it is applied to a given set of input values.

An operation can be defined by *enumeration* of its output values for all possible combinations of its input values. This set of values must be finite since an operation only involves a finite set of data with finite ranges. But in practice, enumeration is only useful for extremely simple operations such as the addition of two decimal digits. As soon as we extend this method of definition to the addition of two decimal numbers of, say, 10 digits each, it requires enumeration of $10^{20}$ triples $(x, y, x + y)$!

A more realistic method is to define an operation by a *computational rule* involving a finite sequence of simpler operations. This is precisely the way we define the addition of numbers. But like other abstractions, computational rules are useful intellectual tools only as long as they remain simple.

The most powerful method of defining an operation is by *assertions* about the type of its variables and the relationships between their values before and after the execution of the operation. These relationships are expressed by statements of the following kind: If the assertion $P$ is true before initiation of the operation $Q$, then the assertion $R$ will be true on its completion. I will use the notation

$$\text{``}P\text{''} \; Q \; \text{``}R\text{''}$$

to define such relationships.

As an example, the effect of an operation *sort* which orders the $n$ elements of an integer array $A$ in a non-decreasing sequence can be defined as follows:

> "$A$: **array** $1. \; .n$ **of** *integer*"
> $sort(A)$;
> "**for all** $i, j$: $1. \; .n$ ($i \leqslant j$ **implies** $A(i) \leqslant A(j)$)"

Formal assertions also have limitations: They tend to be as large as the programs they refer to. This is evident from the simple examples that have been published (Hoare, 1971a).

The whole purpose of abstraction is *abbreviation*. You can often help the reader of your programs much more by a short, informal statement that appeals to a common background of more rigorous definition. If your reader knows what a Fibonacci number is, then why write

"*F*: **array** 0. .*n* **of** *integer* & *j*: 0. .*n* &
**for all** *i*: 0. *j* (*F*(*i*) = **if** *i* < 2 **then** *i* **else** *F*(*i* − 2) + *F*(*i* − 1))"

when the following will do

"*F*(0) to *F*(*j*) are the first *j* + 1 Fibonacci numbers"

Definition by formal or informal assertion is an abstraction which enables us to concentrate on what an operation does and ignore the details of how it is carried out. The *type* concept is an abstraction which permits us to ignore the actual values of variables and state that an operation has the effect defined for all values of the given types.

### 2.3.2. Processes

Data and operations are the primitive components of computations. More precisely, a *computation* is a finite set of operations applied to a finite set of data in an attempt to solve a problem. If a computation solves

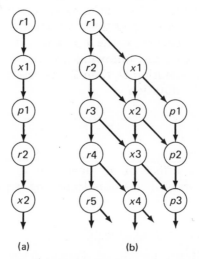

(a)                    (b)

**Fig. 2.2** A precedence graph of (a) a sequential and (b) a concurrent computation.

the given problem, it is also called an *algorithm*. But it is possible that a computation is meaningless in the sense that it does not solve the problem it was intended to solve.

The operations of a computation must be carried out in a certain order of precedence to ensure that the results of some operations can be used by others. The simplest possible precedence rule is the execution of operations in strict sequential order, one at a time. This type of computation is called a *sequential process*. It consists of a set of operations which are *totally ordered* in time.

Figure 2.2(a) shows a *precedence graph* of the process performed by an operating system that schedules user computations one at a time. Each node represents an instance of one of the following operations: $r$ (read user request), $x$ (execute user computation), and $p$ (print user results). The directed branches represent precedence of operations. In this case:

$r1$ precedes $x1$,
$x1$ precedes $p1$,
$p1$ precedes $r2$,
$r2$ precedes $x2$,
. . . . .

Most of our computational problems require only a *partial ordering* of operations in time: Some operations must be carried out before others, but some of them can also be carried out concurrently. This is illustrated in Fig. 2.2(b) by a precedence graph of a spooling system (see Chapter 1, Fig. 1.3). Here the precedence rules are:

$r1$ precedes $x1$ and $r2$,
$x1$ precedes $p1$ and $x2$,
$p1$ precedes $p2$,
$r2$ precedes $x2$ and $r3$,
. . . .

Partial ordering makes *concurrent execution* of some operations possible. In Fig. 2.2(b), the executions of the following operations may overlap each other in time:

$r2$ and $x1$,
$r3$ and $x2$ and $p1$,
. . . . .

In order to understand concurrent computations, it is often helpful to try to partition them into a number of sequential processes which can be analyzed separately. This decomposition can usually be made in several ways, depending on what your purpose is.

If you wish to design a spooling system, then you will probably partition the computation in Fig. 2.2(b) into three sequential processes of a cyclical nature each in control of a physical resource:

$$reader\ process: \qquad r1; r2; r3; \ldots$$
$$scheduler\ process: \qquad x1; x2; x3; \ldots$$
$$printer\ process: \qquad p1; p2; p3; \ldots$$

These processes can proceed simultaneously with independent speeds, except during short intervals when they must exchange data: The scheduler process must receive user requests from the reader process, and the printer process must be informed by the scheduler process of where user results are stored. Processes which cooperate in this manner are called *loosely connected processes*.

On the other hand, if you are a user, it makes more sense to recognize the following processes in Fig. 2.2(b):

$$job\ 1: r1; x1; p1;$$
$$job\ 2: r2; x2; p2;$$
$$job\ 3: r3; x3; p3;$$
$$\ldots \ldots$$

Both decompositions are useful for a particular purpose, but each of them also obscures certain facts about the original computation. From the first decomposition it is not evident that the reader, scheduler, and printer processes execute a stream of jobs; the second decomposition hides the fact that the jobs share the same reader, processor, and printer. A decomposition of a computation into a set of processes is a partial description or an abstraction of that computation. And how we choose our abstractions depends on our present purpose.

The abstractions chosen above illustrate a general principle: In a successful decomposition, the connections between components are much weaker than the connections inside components. It is the loose connections or infrequent interactions between the processes above which make it possible for us to study them separately and consider their interactions only at a few, well-defined points.

One of the recurrent themes of this book is *process interaction*. It is a direct consequence of the sharing of a computer. Processes can interact for various reasons: (1) because they *exchange data*, such as the reader, scheduler, and printer processes; (2) because they *share physical resources*, such as job1, job2, job3, and so on; or (3) because interaction *simplifies our understanding* and verification of the correctness of a computation—this is a strong point in favor of sequential computations.

Concurrent computations permit better utilization of a computer installation because timing constraints among physical components are reduced to a minimum. But since the order of operations in time is not completely specified, the output of a concurrent computation may be a time-dependent function of its input unless special precautions are taken. This makes it impossible to reproduce erroneous computations in order to locate and correct observed errors. In contrast, the output of a sequential process can always be reproduced when its input is known. This property of sequential processes along with their extreme simplicity makes them important components for the construction of concurrent computations.

The main obstacles to the utilization of concurrency in computer installations are economy and human imagination. Sequential processes can be carried out cheaply by repeated use of simple equipment; concurrent computations require duplicated equipment.

Human beings find it very difficult to comprehend the combined effect of activities which evolve simultaneously with independent speeds. Those who have studied the history of nations in school, one by one—American history, French history, and so on—recall how difficult it was to remember, in connection with a crucial time of transition in one country, what happened in other countries at the same time. The insight into our historical background can be greatly improved by presenting history as a sequence of stages and by discussing the situation in several countries at each stage—but then the student finds it equally difficult to remember the continuous history of a single nation!

It is hard to avoid the conclusion that we understand concurrent events by looking at sequential subsets of them. This would mean that, even though technological improvements may eventually make a high degree of concurrency possible in our computations, we shall still attempt to partition our problems conceptually into a moderate number of sequential activities which can be programmed separately and then connected loosely for concurrent execution.

In contrast, our understanding of a sequential process is independent of its actual speed of execution. All that matters is that operations are carried out one at a time with finite speed and that certain relations hold between the data before and after each operation.

### 2.3.3. Computers and Programs

The idea of defining complicated computations rigorously implies the use of a formal language to describe primitive data types and operations as well as combinations of them. A formal description of a computation is called a *program*, and the language in which it is expressed is called a *programming language*.

Programs can be used to communicate algorithms among human beings,

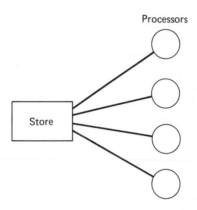

Fig. 2.3   A model of a computer installation.

but, in general, we write programs to solve problems on computers. We will indeed define a *computer installation* as a physical system capable of carrying out computations by interpreting programs.

Figure 2.3 shows a model of a computer installation. It consists of a store and one or more processors. The *store* is a physical component in which data and programs can be retained for future use. It is divided into a finite set of primitive components called *locations*. Each location can store any one of a finite set of data values.

A *processor* is a physical component which can carry out a sequential process defined by a program. During its execution, a program is stored as a sequence of data called *instructions*. An instruction consists of four components defining an operation, its input and output, and a successor instruction. Data used to identify store locations are called *addresses*.

The processors can work concurrently and share the common store. Some of the processors are called *terminals* or *peripheral devices*; they are dedicated to the transfer of data between the environment and the store. Other processors are called *central processors*; they operate mainly on stored data. For our purposes, the distinction between peripheral devices and central processors is not fundamental; it merely reflects various degrees of specialization.

The rest of this chapter is a discussion of the fundamental abstraction, sequential processes. It summarizes methods of structuring data and sequential programs, and serves as a presentation of the programming language used throughout the text, a *subset* of the language *Pascal*, created by Wirth. The algorithmic statements of Pascal are based on the principles and notation of *Algol 60*. But the data structures of Pascal are much more general than those of Algol 60.

Pascal permits *hierarchal structuring* of data and program, extensive *error checking* at compile time, and production of *efficient machine code* on present computers. It combines the clarity needed for teaching the subject with the efficiency required for designing operating systems. If you are familiar with Algol 60, you will find it quite natural to adopt Pascal as your programming tool.

The following is a brief and very informal description of a subset of Pascal with the emphasis on the language features that make it different from Algol 60. Although my summary of Pascal is sufficient for understanding the rest of the book, I recommend that you study the official Pascal report, which is written in clear, informal prose (Wirth, 1971a).

I have taken a few minor liberties with the Pascal notation. They are not mentioned explicitly because my subject is not rigorous language definition, but operating system principles.

## 2.4. DATA STRUCTURES

### 2.4.1. Primitive Data Types

*Constants* are denoted by numbers or identifiers. A definition of the form:

$$\textbf{const } a1 = c1, a2 = c2, \ldots , ak = ck;$$

introduces the identifiers $a1, a2, \ldots , ak$ as synonyms of the constants $c1, c2, \ldots , ck$, for example:

$$\textbf{const } e = 2.718281828;$$

*Variables* are introduced by declarations of the form:

$$\textbf{var } v1, v2, \ldots , vk: <\text{type}>;$$

which associates the identifiers $v1, v2, \ldots , vk$ with a data type.

A *data type* is the set of values which can be assumed by a variable. A type can be defined either directly in the declaration of a variable or separately in a type definition which associates an identifier $T$ with the type:

$$\textbf{type } T = <\text{type}> ;$$
$$\textbf{var } v1, v2, \ldots , vk: T;$$

A *primitive type* is a finite, ordered set of values. The primitive types:

> *boolean*
> *integer*
> *real*

are predefined for a given computer.

Other primitive types can be defined by *enumeration* of a set of successive values:

$$(a1, a2, \ldots , ak)$$

denoted by identifiers $a1, a2, \ldots , ak$, for example:

> **type** *name of month* =
> (*January, February, March, April, May, June, July,*
> *August, September, October, November, December*);

A primitive type can also be defined as a *range* within another primitive type:

$$cmin. .cmax$$

where *cmin* and *cmax* are constants denoting the minimum and maximum values in the range, for example:

> **type** *number of day* = 1. .31;
> **var** *payday*: *number of day*;

> **var** *summer month*: *June. .August*;

The first example is a variable *payday*, which can assume the values 1 to 31 (a subrange of the standard type *integer*). The second example is a variable *summer month*, which can assume the values *June* to *August* (a subrange of the type *name of month* defined previously).

The set of values which can be assumed by a variable $v$ of a primitive type $T$ can be *generated* by means of the standard functions:

$$min(T) \qquad max(T) \qquad succ(v) \qquad pred(v)$$

in ascending order:

> $v:= min(T);$
> **while** $v \neq max(T)$ **do** $v:= succ(v);$

or in descending order:

$$v := max(T);$$
$$\textbf{while } v \neq min(T) \textbf{ do } v := pred(v);$$

### 2.4.2. Structured Data Types

*Structured types* are defined in terms of primitive types or in terms of other structured types using the connection rules of arrays and records.

The type definition:

**array** $D$ **of** $R$

defines a data structure consisting of a fixed number of components of type $R$. Each component of an array variable $v$ is selected by an index expression $E$ of type $D$:

$$v(E)$$

Examples:

**type** *table* = **array** 1. .20 **of** *integer;*
**var** $A$: *table*; $i$: 1. .20;
. . . $A(i)$ . . .

**var** *length of month*:
    **array** *name of month* **of** *number of day*;
. . . *length of month (February)* . . .

The type definition:

**record** $f1$: $T1$; $f2$: $T2$; . . . ; $fk$: $Tk$ **end**

defines a data structure consisting of a fixed number of components of types $T1$, $T2$, . . . , $Tk$. The components are selected by identifiers $f1$, $f2$, . . . , $fk$. A component $fj$ within a record variable $v$ is denoted:

$$v . fj$$

Example:

**type** *date* = **record**
        *day*: *number of day;*
        *month*: *number of month;*
        *year*: 0. .2000;
    **end**
**var** *birthday*: *date;*
. . . *birthday . month* . . .

Good programmers do not confine themselves exclusively to the structures defined by an available programming language. They invent notations for abstractions that are ideally suited to their present purpose. But they will choose abstractions which later can be represented efficiently in terms of the standard features of their language.

I will occasionally do the same and postulate extensions to Pascal which help me to stress essential concepts and, for the moment, ignore trivial details.

As one example, I will assume that one can declare a variable $s$ consisting of a *sequence* of components of type $T$:

**var $s$: sequence of $T$**

Initially, the sequence is empty. The value of a variable $t$ of type $T$ can be appended to or removed from the sequence $s$ by means of the standard procedures

$$put(t, s) \qquad get(t, s)$$

The components are removed in the order in which they are appended to the sequence. In other words, a sequence is a first-in, first-out store.

The boolean function

$$empty(s)$$

defines whether or not the sequence $s$ is empty.

The implementation of sequences by means of arrays will be explained in Chapter 3. For a more detailed discussion of the representation of various data structures see Knuth (1969).

## 2.5. PROGRAM STRUCTURES

### 2.5.1. Primitive Statements

Operations and combinations of them are described by statements. The *primitive statements* are exit statements, assignment statements, and procedure statements.

The *exit statement*

**exit $L$**

is a restricted form of a *go to* statement. It causes a jump to the end of a compound statement *labeled $L$*:

label $L$ **begin** . . . **exit** $L$; . . . **end**

This use of jumps is an efficient way of leaving a compound statement in the exceptional cases when a solution to a problem is found earlier than expected, or when no solution exists. But in contrast to the unstructured *go to* statement, the exit statement simplifies the verification of program correctness.

Suppose an assertion $P$ holds before a compound statement $Q$ is executed. There are now two cases to consider: Either $Q$ is executed to completion, in which case an assertion $R$ is known to hold; or an exit is made from $Q$ when an exceptional case $S$ holds. So the effect of statement $Q$ is the following:

$$\text{``}P\text{''} \ Q \ \text{``}R \ \textbf{or} \ S\text{''}$$

The *assignment statement*

$$v := E$$

assigns the value of an *expression E* to a variable $v$. The expression must be of the same type as $v$. Expressions consist of operators and functions applied to constants, variables, and other expressions. The *operators* are:

| | | | | | |
|---|---|---|---|---|---|
| arithmetic: | $+$ | $-$ | $*$ | $/$ | **mod** |
| relational: | $=$ | $\neq$ | $<$ | $>$ $\leqslant$ | $\geqslant$ |
| boolean: | $\&$ | **or** | **not** | | |

The *function designator*

$$F(a1, a2, \ \ldots \ , ak)$$

causes the evaluation of a function $F$ with the actual parameters $a1$, $a2$, . . . , $ak$.

The *procedure statement*

$$P(a1, a2, \ \ldots \ , ak)$$

causes the execution of a procedure $P$ with the actual parameters $a1$, $a2$, . . . , $ak$.

The *actual parameters* of functions and procedures can be variables and expressions. Expressions used as parameters are evaluated before a function or procedure is executed.

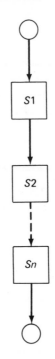

Fig. 2.4   A compound statement.

### 2.5.2.  Structured Statements

*Structured statements* are formed by connecting primitive statements or other structured statements according to the following rules:

(1) *Concatenation* of statements $S1$, $S2$, ... , $Sn$ into a compound statement:

**label** $L$ **begin** $S1; S2;$ ... ; $Sn$ **end**

**begin** $S1; S2;$ ... ; $Sn$ **end**

(See Fig. 2.4).

(2) *Selection* of one of a set of statements by means of a boolean expression $B$:

**if** $B$ **then** $S1$ **else** $S2$

**if** $B$ **then** $S$

or by means of an expression $E$ of a primitive type $T$:

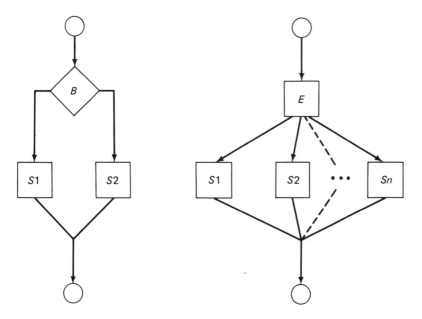

**Fig. 2.5** The **if** and **case** statements.

**type** $T = (c1, c2, \ldots, cn)$;

. . .

**case** $E$ **of**
$c1: S1; c2: S2; \ldots cn: Sn$;
**end**

If $E = cj$ then statement $Sj$ is executed (See Fig. 2.5).

(3) *Repetition* of a statement $S$ while a boolean expression $B$ remains true:

**while** $B$ **do** $S$

or repetition of a sequence of statements $S1, S2, \ldots, Sn$ until a boolean expression $B$ becomes true:

**repeat** $S1; S2; \ldots ; Sn$ **until** $B$

(See Fig. 2.6).

Another possibility is to repeat a statement $S$ with a succession of primitive values assigned to a control variable $v$:

**for** $v:= Emin$ **to** $Emax$ **do** $S$

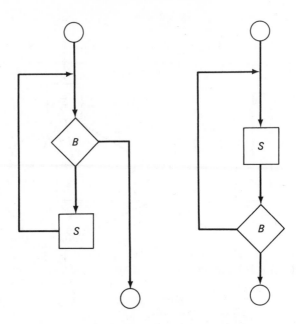

Fig. 2.6   The while and repeat statements.

(4) *Recursion* of a procedure *P* which calls itself:

**procedure** *P*( . . . );
**begin** . . . *P*; . . . **end**

(See Fig. 2.7.)

Notice that the analytical effort required to understand the effect of these structures is proportional to the number of component statements. For example, in the analysis of an *if* statement, we must first prove that a certain assertion *R* will be true after execution of statement *S*1, provided assertions *B* and *P* hold before *S*1 is initiated, and similarly for *S*2:

$$\text{``}B \ \& \ P\text{''} \ S1 \ \text{``}R\text{''} \qquad \text{``not } B \ \& \ P\text{''} \ S2 \ \text{``}R\text{''}$$

From this we infer that

$$\text{``}P\text{''} \text{ if } B \text{ then } S1 \text{ else } S2 \ \text{``}R\text{''}$$

The repetition statements are understood by mathematical induction. From

$$\text{``}B \ \& \ P\text{''} \ S \ \text{``}P\text{''}$$

we infer that

$$\text{``}P\text{''} \text{ while } B \text{ do } S \ \text{``not } B \ \& \ P\text{''}$$

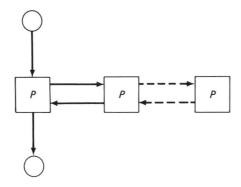

Fig. 2.7  A recursive procedure statement.

The aim is to find an *invariant P*—an assertion which is true before the iteration is started and remains true after each execution of the statment *S*. For records, the following structured statement can be used:

**with** *v* **do** *S*

It enables the statement *S* to refer to the components of a record variable *v* by their identifiers *f*1, *f*2, ... , *fk* without qualifying them with the record identifier *v*, for example:

**with** *birthday* **do**
**begin** *day*:= 19; *month*:= *April*; *year*:= 1938 **end**

Finally, we have the important abstraction of assigning a name to a sequence of statements *S*1, *S*2, ... , *Sn* by means of *procedure* and *function declarations* of the form:

**procedure** *P*(*p*1; *p*2; ... ; *pk*);
< local declarations >
**begin** *S*1; *S*2; ... ; *Sn* **end**

**function** *F*(*p*1; *p*2; ... ; *pk*): < result type > ;
< local declarations >
**begin** *S*1; *S*2; ... ; *Sn* **end**

where *p*1, *p*2, ... , *pk* are declarations of *formal parameters*. The declaration *pj* of a constant or variable parameter *vj* of type *Tj* has the form:

**const** *vj*: *Tj*          **var** *vj*: *Tj*

The preceding specifier can be omitted for constant parameters.
A function *F* computes a value that must be of a primitive type. At

least one of its statements $S1, S2, \ldots, Sn$ must assign a result value to the function identifier $F$

$$F := E$$

where $E$ is an expression of the result type.

The function statements must not assign values to actual parameters and non-local variables. This rule simplifies program verification as will be explained in Chapter 3.

The *declarations* of identifiers which are *local* to a procedure or function are written *before* the *begin* symbol of the statement part. They are written in the following order:

> **const** <constant definitions>
> **type** <type definitions>
> **var** <variable declarations>
> <local procedure and function declarations>

A *program* consists of a declaration part and a compound statement. Finally, I should mention that *comments* are enclosed in quotes:

> *"This is a comment"*

This concludes the presentation of the Pascal subset.

## 2.6. PROGRAM CONSTRUCTION

We design programs the same way we solve other complex problems: by step-wise analysis and refinement. In this section, I give an example of hierarchal program construction.

### 2.6.1. The Banker's Algorithm

The example chosen is a *resource sharing* problem first described and solved by Dijkstra (1965). Although the problem involves concurrent processes, it is used here as an example of sequential programming.

An operating system shares a set of resources among a number of concurrent processes. The resources are *equivalent* in the sense that when a process makes a request for one of them, it is irrelevant which one is chosen. Examples of equivalent resources are peripheral devices of the same type and store pages of equal size.

When a resource has been allocated to a process, it is occupied until the process releases it again. When concurrent processes share resources in this manner, there is a danger that they may end up in a *deadlock*, a state in which two or more processes are waiting indefinitely for an event that will never happen.

Suppose we have 5 units of a certain resource, and we are in a state where 2 units are allocated to a process $P$ and 1 unit to another process $Q$. But both processes need two more units to run to completion. If we are lucky, one of them, say $Q$, will acquire the last two units, run to completion, and release all three of its units in time to satisfy further requests from $P$. But it is also possible that $P$ and $Q$ both will acquire one of the last two units and then (since there are no more) will decide to wait until another unit becomes available. Now they are deadlocked: $P$ cannot continue until $Q$ releases a unit; $Q$ cannot continue until $P$ releases a unit; and each of them expects the other to resolve the conflict.

The deadlock could have been prevented by allocating all units needed by $P$ (or $Q$) at the same time rather than one by one. This policy would have forced $P$ and $Q$ to run at different times, and as we have seen in Chapter 1, this is often the most efficient way of using the resources. But for the moment, we will try to solve the problem without this restriction.

Let me define the problem more precisely in Dijkstra's terminology: A *banker* wishes to share a fixed *capital* of *florins* among a fixed number of *customers*. Each customer specifies in advance his maximum *need* for florins. The banker will accept a customer if his need does not exceed the capital.

During a customer's *transactions*, he can only borrow or return florins one by one. It may sometimes be necessary for a customer to wait before he can borrow another florin, but the banker guarantees that the waiting time will always be finite. The current loan of a customer can never exceed his maximum need.

If the banker is able to satisfy the maximum need of a customer, then the customer guarantees that he will complete his transactions and repay his loan within a finite time.

The current situation is *safe* if it is possible for the banker to enable all his present customers to complete their transactions within a finite time; otherwise, it is *unsafe*.

We wish to find an algorithm which can determine whether the banker's current situation is safe or unsafe. If the banker has such an algorithm, he can use it in a safe situation to decide whether a customer who wants to borrow another florin should be given one immediately or told to wait. The banker makes this decision by pretending to grant the florin and then observing whether this leads to a safe situation or not.

The situation of a customer is characterized by his current *loan* and his further *claim* where

$$claim = need - loan$$

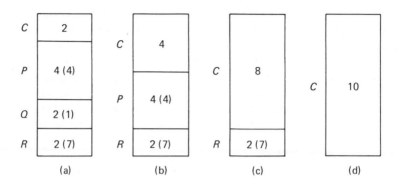

**Fig. 2.8**　The banker's algorithm: a safe situation.

The situation of the banker is characterized by his original *capital* and his current amount of *cash* where

*cash = capital - sum of loans*

The algorithm that determines whether the overall situation is safe or not is quite simple. Let me illustrate it by an example: Fig. 2.8 shows a situation in which three customers, $P$, $Q$, and $R$, share a capital of 10 florins. Their combined need is 20 florins. In the current situation, Fig. 2.8(a), customer $Q$ has a loan of 2 florins and a claim of 1 florin; this is denoted 2 (1). For $P$ and $R$ the loans and claims are 4 (4) and 2 (7) respectively. So the available cash $C$ at the moment is $10 - 4 - 2 - 2 = 2$.

The algorithm examines the customers one by one, looking for one who has a claim not exceeding the cash. In Fig. 2.8(a), customer $Q$ has a claim of 1. Since the cash is 2, customer $Q$ will be able in this situation to complete his transactions and return his current loan of 2 florins to the banker.

After the departure of customer $Q$, the situation will be the one shown in Fig. 2.8(b). The algorithm now scans the remaining customers and compares their claims with the increased cash of 4 florins. It is now possible to satisfy customer $P$ completely.

This leads to the situation in Fig. 2.8(c) in which customer $R$ can complete his transactions. So finally, in Fig. 2.8(d) the banker has regained his capital of 10 florins. Consequently, the original state Fig. 2.8(a) was safe.

It is possible to go from the safe state in Fig. 2.8(a) to an unsafe situation, such as the one in Fig. 2.9(a). Here, the banker has granted a request from customer $R$ for another florin. In this new situation, customer $Q$ can be satisfied. But this leads us to the situation in Fig. 2.9(b) in which we are stuck: neither $P$ nor $R$ can complete their transactions.

If the banker's algorithm finds that a situation is unsafe, this does not necessarily mean that a deadlock will occur—only that it might occur. But if the situation is safe, it is always possible to prevent a deadlock. Notice

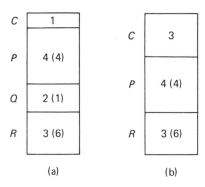

Fig. 2.9   The banker's algorithm: an unsafe situation.

that the banker prevents deadlocks in the same way as we originally proposed: by serving the customers one at a time; but the banker only does so in situations where it is strictly necessary.

We will now program the banker's algorithm for the general case considered by Habermann (1969), in which the banker's capital consists of several *currencies*: florins, dollars, pounds, and so on.

### 2.6.2.  A Hierarchal Solution

The first version of the banker's algorithm is trivial:

> **type** $S$ = ?

> **function** *safe(current state: S): boolean*;

It consists of a boolean function *safe* with a parameter defining the *current state*. The details of the function and the type of its parameter are as yet unknown.

The first refinement (Algorithm 2.1) expresses in some detail what the

*ALGORITHM 2.1   The Banker's Algorithm*

```
type S = ?

function safe(current state: S): boolean;
var state: S;
begin
  state:= current state;
  complete transactions(state);
  safe:= all transactions completed(state);
end
```

function *safe* does: It simulates the completion of customer transactions as far as possible. If all transactions can be completed, the current state is safe.

In the second refinement (Algorithm 2.2), the state is decomposed into: (1) an array defining the *claim* and *loan* of each customer and whether or not that customer's transactions have been *completed*; and (2) two components defining the *capital* and *cash* of the banker. The exact representation of currencies (type *C*) is still undefined.

The procedure *complete transactions* is now defined in some detail. It examines the transactions of one customer at a time: If they have not already been completed and completion is possible, the procedure simulates the return of the customer's loan to the banker. This continues until no more transactions can be completed.

*ALGORITHM 2.2   The Banker's Algorithm (cont.)*

```
type S = record
            transactions: array B of
                             record
                                claim, loan: C;
                                completed: boolean;
                             end
            capital, cash: C;
         end
   B = 1. .number of customers;
   C = ?

procedure complete transactions(var state: S);
var customer: B; progress: boolean;
begin
  with state do
  repeat
    progress:= false;
    for every customer do
    with transactions(customer) do
    if not completed then
    if completion possible(claim, cash) then
    begin
      return loan(loan, cash);
      completed:= true;
      progress:= true;
    end
  until not progress;
end
```

The statement

**for every** *customer* **do** . . .

is equivalent to

**for** *customer*:= *min*(B) **to** *max*(B) **do** . . .

Algorithm 2.3 shows that the current state is safe if the banker eventually can get his original capital back.

*ALGORITHM 2.3   The Banker's Algorithm (cont.)*

> **function** *all transactions completed*(*state*: S): *boolean*;
> **begin**
>   **with** *state* **do**
>   *all transactions completed*:= *capital* = *cash*;
> **end**

In the third refinement (Algorithm 2.4), we define the representation of a set of currencies as an array of integers and write the details of the function *completion possible,* which shows that the transactions of a single customer can be completed if his claim of each currency does not exceed the available cash.

*ALGORITHM 2.4    The Banker's Algorithm (cont.)*

> **type** C = **array** D **of** *integer*;
>   D = 1. .*number of currencies*;
>
> **function** *completion possible*(*claim, cash*: C): *boolean*;
> **var** *currency*: D;
> **label** *no*
> **begin**
>   **for every** *currency* **do**
>   **if** *claim*(*currency*) > *cash*(*currency*) **then**
>   **begin**
>     *completion possible*:= *false*;
>     **exit** *no*;
>   **end**
>   *completion possible*:= *true*;
> **end**

Algorithm 2.5 shows the final details of the banker's algorithm.

*ALGORITHM 2.5  The Banker's Algorithm (cont.)*

```
procedure return loan(var loan, cash: C);
var currency: D;
begin
  for every currency do
  cash(currency):= cash(currency) + loan(currency);
end
```

To be honest, I do not construct my first version of any program in the orderly manner described here. Nor do mathematicians construct proofs in the way in which they present them in textbooks. We must all experiment with a problem by trial and error until we understand it intuitively and have rejected one or more incorrect solutions. But it is important that the final result be so well-structured that it can be described in a step-wise hierarchal manner. This greatly simplifies the effort required for other people to understand the solution.

### 2.6.3.  Conclusion

I have constructed a non-trivial program (Algorithm 2.6) step by step in a hierarchal manner. At each level of programming, the problem is described in terms of a small number of variables and operations on these variables.

*ALGORITHM 2.6  The Complete Banker's Algorithm*

```
type S = record
           transactions:  array B of
                            record
                              claim, loan: C;
                              completed: boolean;
                            end
           capital, cash: C;
         end
B = 1. .number of customers;
C = array D of integer;
D = 1. .number of currencies;

function safe(current state: S): boolean;
var state: S;

  procedure complete transactions(var state: S);
  var customer: B; progress: boolean;
```

```
function completion possible(claim, cash: C): boolean;
var currency: D;
label no
begin
  for every currency do
  if claim(currency) > cash(currency) then
  begin
    completion possible:= false;
    exit no;
  end
  completion possible:= true;
end

procedure return loan(var loan, cash: C);
var currency: D;
begin
  for every currency do
  cash(currency):= cash(currency) + loan(currency);
end

begin
  with state do
  repeat
    progress:= false;
    for every customer do
    with transactions(customer) do
    if not completed then
    if completion possible(claim, cash) then
    begin
      return loan(loan, cash);
      completed:= true;
      progress:= true;
    end
  until not progress;
end

function all transactions completed(state: S): boolean;
begin
  with state do
  all transactions completed:= capital = cash;
end

begin
  state:= current state;
  complete transactions(state);
  safe:= all transactions completed(state);
end
```

At the most abstract level, the program consists of a single variable, *current state*, and a single operation, *safe*. If this operation had been available as a machine instruction, our problem would have been solved. Since this was not the case, we wrote another program (Algorithm 2.1), which can solve the problem on a simpler machine using the operations *complete transactions* and *all transactions completed*.

This program in turn was rewritten for a still simpler machine (Algorithms 2.2 and 2.3). The refinement of previous solutions was repeated until the level of detail required by the available machine was reached.

So the design of a program involves the construction of a series of *programming layers*, which gradually transform the data structures and operations of an ideal, non-existing machine into those of an existing machine. The non-existing machines, which are simulated by program, are called *virtual machines* to distinguish them from the physical machine.

It was mentioned in Section 1.1.3 that every program simulates a virtual machine that is more ideal than an existing machine for a particular purpose: A machine that can execute the banker's algorithm is, of course, ideally suited to the banker's purpose. We now see that the construction of a *large program* involves the simulation of a *hierarchy of virtual machines*. Figure 2.10 illustrates the virtual and physical machines on which the banker's algorithm is executed.

At each level of programming, some operations are accepted as *primitives* in the sense that it is known *what* they do as a whole, but the details of *how* it is done are unknown and irrelevant at that level. Consequently, it is only meaningful at each level to describe the effect of

| Machine | Operations | Data types |
|---|---|---|
| 1 | *safe* | *S* |
| 2 | *complete transactions* <br> *all transactions completed* | *S* |
| 3 | *completion possible* <br> *return loan* | *C* |
| 4 | Pascal statements | *D* |
| 5 | Machine language | Machine types |
| 6 | Instruction execution cycle | Registers |

**Fig. 2.10  The banker's algorithm viewed as a hierarchy of virtual and physical machines.**

the program at discrete points in time before and after the execution of each primitive. At these points, the *state* of the sequential process is defined by *assertions* about the relationships between its variables, for example:

"*all transactions completed* ≡ *capital = cash*"

Since each primitive operation causes a *transition* from one state to another, a *sequential process* can also be defined as a *succession of states* in time.

As we proceed from detailed to more abstract levels of programming, some concepts become irrelevant and can be ignored. In Algorithm 2.2, we must consider assertions about the local variable, *progress*, as representing distinct states during the execution of the partial algorithm. But at the level of programming where Algorithm 2.2 is accepted as a primitive, *complete transactions*, the intermediate states necessary to implement it are completely irrelevant.

So a state is a partial description of a computation just like the concepts sequential process and operation. A precise definition of these *abstractions* depends on the level of detail desired by the observer. A user may recognize many intermediate states in his computation, but for the operating system in control of its execution, the computation has only a few relevant states, such as "waiting" or "running."

In order to *test* the correctness of a program, we must run it through all its relevant states at least once by supplying it with appropriate input and observing its output. I remarked in Section 2.3.1 that the definition of operations by enumeration of all possible data values is impractical except in extremely simple cases. The same argument leads to the conclusion that exhaustive testing of operations for all possible input values is out of the question.

If we were to test the addition of two decimal numbers of 10 digits each exhaustively, it would require $10^{20}$ executions of a program loop of, say 10 $\mu$sec, or, all in all, $3 * 10^7$ years. The only way to reduce this time is to use our knowledge of the internal *structure* of the adder. If we know that it consists of 10 identical components, each capable of adding two digits and a carry, we also know that it is sufficient to test each component separately with $10 * 10 * 2$ combinations of input digits. This insight immediately reduces the number of test cases to 2000 and brings the total test time down to only 20 msec.

Returning to the problem of testing the correctness of a program such as the banker's algorithm, we must accept that such a test is impossible at a level where it is only understood as a primitive: *safe*. We would have to exhaust all combinations of various currencies and customers in every possible state! But if we take advantage of the layered structure of our programs (see Fig. 2.10), we can start at the machine level and demonstrate once and for all that the machine instructions work correctly. This proof can then be appealed to at higher programming levels independent of the actual data values involved. At the next level of programming, it is proved once and for all that the compiler transforms Pascal statements correctly into machine instructions. And when we reach the levels at which the banker's algorithm is programmed, it is again possible to test each level separately, starting with Algorithm 2.5 and working towards Algorithm 2.1.

In this chapter, I have stressed the need for simplicity in programming. I cannot accept the viewpoint that the construction of programs with a pleasant structure is an academic exercise that is irrelevant or impractical to use in real life. Simplicity of structure is not just an aesthetic pursuit—It is the key to survival in programming! Large systems can only be fully understood and tested if they can be studied in small, simple parts at many levels of detail.

## 2.7. LITERATURE

This chapter has briefly summarized concepts which are recognized and understood, at least intuitively, by most programmers.

The role of hierarchal structure in biological, physical, social, and conceptual systems is discussed with deep insight by Simon (1962).

In the book by Minsky (1967) you will find an excellent and simple presentation of the essential aspects of sequential machines and algorithms. Horning and Randell (1972) have analyzed the concept "sequential process" from a more formal point of view.

Hopefully, this book will make you appreciate the Pascal language. It is defined concisely in the report by Wirth (1971a).

A subject which has only been very superficially mentioned here is correctness proofs of algorithms. It was suggested independently by Naur and Floyd and further developed by Hoare (1969).

The practice of designing programs as a sequence of clearly separated layers is due to Dijkstra (1971a). He has successfully used it for the construction of an entire operating system (1968). Eventually, this constructive approach to programming may change the field from a hazardous application of clever tricks into a mature engineering discipline.

DIJKSTRA, E. W., "The structure of THE multiprogramming system," *Comm. ACM 11*, 5, pp. 341-46, May *1968*.

DIJKSTRA, E. W., *A short introduction to the art of programming*, Technological University, Eindhoven, The Netherlands, Aug. *1971a*.

HOARE, C. A. R., "An axiomatic basis for computer programming," *Comm. ACM 12*, 10, pp. 576-83, Oct. *1969*.

HORNING, J. J. and RANDELL, B., "Process structuring," University of Newcastle upon Tyne, England, *1972*.

MINSKY, M. L., *Computation: finite and infinite machines*, Prentice-Hall Inc., Englewood Cliffs, New Jersey, *1967*.

SIMON, H. A., "The architecture of complexity," *Proc. American Philosophical Society 106*, 6, pp. 468-82, *1962*.

WIRTH, N., "The programming language Pascal," *Acta Informatica 1*, 1, pp. 35-63, *1971a*.

# 3

# *CONCURRENT PROCESSES*

This chapter is a study of concurrent processes. It emphasizes the role of reproducible behavior in program verification and compares various methods of process synchronization: critical regions, semaphores, message buffers, and event queues. It concludes with an analysis of the prevention of deadlocks by hierarchal ordering of process interactions.

## 3.1. CONCURRENCY

The process concept was introduced in the previous chapter (see Section 2.3.2). In the following, I will summarize the basic properties of sequential and concurrent processes, and introduce a language notation for the latter.

### 3.1.1. Definition

A *process* is a sequence of operations carried out one at a time. The precise definition of an *operation* depends on the level of detail at which the process is described. For some purposes, you may regard a process as a single operation $A$, as shown on top of Fig. 3.1. For other purposes, it may be

Level of detail

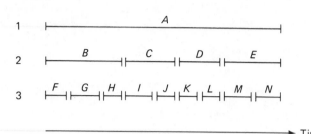

Fig. 3.1 The same process viewed at different levels
of detail as a succession of operations $A$ or $B, C, \ldots$
or $F, G, \ldots$ in time.

more convenient to look upon the same process as a sequence of simpler
operations $B$, $C$, $D$, and $E$. And when you examine it in still more detail,
previously recognized operations can be partitioned into still simpler ones:
$F, G, H, and \, so \, on.$

If you compare this picture with the hierarchy of machines on which
the banker's algorithm is executed (see Fig. 2.10), you will see that *as we
proceed to more detailed levels of programming, a process is described in
terms of increasingly simpler operations which are carried out in increasingly smaller grains of time.*

At all levels of programming, we assume that when an operation is
initiated, it terminates within a finite time and delivers output which is a
time-independent function of its input (see Section 2.3.1).

If the variables of a process are inaccessible to other processes, it is easy
to show by induction that the final output of a sequence of operations will
be a time-independent function of the initial input. In this case, a process
can be regarded as a single operation, provided that it terminates.

But if one process can change the variables of another process, the
output of the latter may depend on the relative speed of the processes. In
this case, a process cannot be regarded as a single operation. I will describe
the problem of multiprogramming systems with time-dependent behavior
later and proceed here to describe the basic properties of concurrent
processes.

Processes are *concurrent* if their executions overlap in time. Figure 3.2
shows three concurrent processes, $P$, $Q$, and $R$.

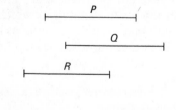

Fig. 3.2 Three concurrent processes $P$,
Time                    $Q$, and $R$.

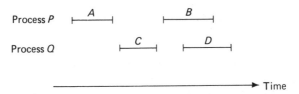

**Fig. 3.3** Two concurrent processes $P$ and $Q$ consisting of operations $A, B$ and $C, D$ which are partly interleaved, partly overlapped in time.

Whether the individual operations of concurrent processes are overlapped or interleaved in time, or both (as shown in Fig. 3.3), is irrelevant. Whenever the *first* operation of one process is started before the *last* operation of another process is completed, the two processes are concurrent.

In an installation where several processors work simultaneously, the machine instructions of concurrent processes can overlap in time. But if one processor is multiplexed among concurrent processes, the machine instructions of these processes can only be interleaved in time. The logical problems turn out to be the same in both cases; they are caused by our ignorance of the relative speeds of concurrent processes.

### 3.1.2. Concurrent Statements

The language notation

$$\textbf{cobegin } S1; S2; \ldots ; Sn \textbf{ coend}$$

indicates that the statements $S1$, $S2$, ..., $Sn$ can be executed concurrently. It was first proposed by Dijkstra (1965).

To define the effect of a *concurrent statement*, we must take into account the statements $S0$ and $Sn+1$, which precede and follow it in a given program:

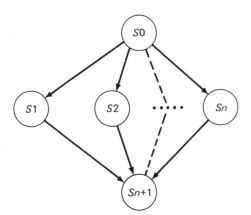

**Fig. 3.4 Precedence graph of a concurrent statement.**

$$S0 \ \textbf{cobegin} \ S1; S2; \ldots ; Sn \ \textbf{coend} \ Sn+1$$

This piece of program can be represented by the precedence graph shown in Fig. 3.4. The desired effect is to execute $S0$ first, and then execute $S1$, $S2$, ... , $Sn$ concurrently; when all the statements $S1$, $S2$, ... , $Sn$ have been terminated, the following statement $Sn+1$ is executed.

Concurrent statements can be arbitrarily *nested*, for example:

> **cobegin**
>   $S1$;
>   **begin**
>     $S2$;
>     **cobegin** $S3$; $S4$ **coend**
>     $S5$;
>   **end**
>   $S6$;
> **coend**

This corresponds to the precedence graph shown in Fig. 3.5.

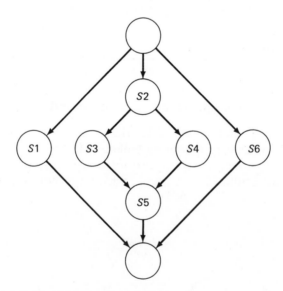

Fig. 3.5 Precedence graph of nested concurrent statements.

### 3.1.3.  An Example: Copying

The use of the concurrent statement is illustrated by Algorithm 3.1, which *copies* records from one sequence to another.

*ALGORITHM 3.1   Copying of a Sequence of Records*

```
procedure copy(var f, g: sequence of T);
var s, t: T; completed: boolean;
begin
  if not empty(f) then
  begin
    completed:= false;
    get(s, f);
    repeat
      t:= s;
      cobegin
        put(t, g);
        if empty(f) then completed:= true
                    else get(s, f);
      coend
    until completed;
  end
end
```

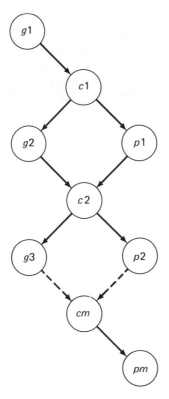

Fig. 3.6 Precedence graph of the copying of a sequence of records.

The variables used are two sequences, $f$ and $g$, of records of type $T$; two buffers, $s$ and $t$, each holding one record; and a boolean, indicating whether or not the copying has been *completed*.

The algorithm gets a record from the input sequence, copies it from one buffer to another, puts it on the output sequence, and, at the same time, gets the next record from the input sequence. The copying, output, and input are repeated until the input sequence is empty.

Figure 3.6 shows a precedence graph of this computation using the operations: $g$ (get record), $c$ (copy record), and $p$ (put record).

## 3.2. FUNCTIONAL SYSTEMS

In the following, we consider more precisely what time-independent or functional behavior means, and under what circumstances multiprogramming systems have this property. As an introduction to this topic, we will first examine our ability to verify the correctness of programs.

### 3.2.1. Program Verification

The ideal program is one which is known with *absolute certainty* to be correct. It has been argued that this can be achieved by rigorous *proofs* (Hoare, 1969 and 1971a). I believe that the use of proof techniques contributes to the correctness of programs by forcing programmers to express solutions to problems in two different ways: by an algorithm and by a proof. But it must be remembered that a proof is merely another formal statement of the same size as the program it refers to, and as such it is also subject to human errors. This means that some other form of program verification is still needed, at least for large programs.

The next best thing to absolute correctness is immediate *detection of errors when they occur*. This can be done either at compile time or at run time. In either case, we rely on a certain amount of *redundancy* in our programs, which makes it possible to check automatically whether operations are consistent with the types of their variables and whether they preserve certain relations among those variables.

Error detection at *compile time* is possible only by restricting the language constructions; error detection at *run time* is possible only by executing redundant statements that check the effect of other statements. In practice, both methods are used, but there are limits to how far one can go in each direction: At some point, severe language restrictions and excessive run-time checking will make the system useless for practical purposes.

This leaves a class of errors that is caught neither at compile time nor at run time. It seems fair to say that these errors can only be located and corrected if programs have functional behavior which enables the designer to reproduce errors under controlled circumstances.

One can subject a sequential program to a fairly systematic *initial testing* by examining its internal structure and defining a sequence of input data which will cause it to execute all statements at least once.

Dijkstra once remarked that "program testing can be used to show the presence of errors, but never their absence" (Nato report, 1969). Even a systematically tested program may contain some undetected errors after it has been released for normal use. If it has been subject to intensive initial testing, the remaining errors are usually quite subtle. Often, the designer must repeat the erroneous computation many times and print successive values of various internal variables to find out in which part of the program the error was made.

So program testing is fundamentally based on the ability to *reproduce computations*. The difficulty is that we must reproduce them *under varying external circumstances*. In a multiprogramming system, several user computations may be in progress simultaneously. These computations are started at unpredictable times at the request of users. So, strictly speaking, the environment of a program is unique during each execution. Even when computations are scheduled one at a time, a programming error is frequently observed by a user on one installation and corrected by a designer on another installation with a different configuration.

This has the following consequences: (1) an operating system must protect the data and physical resources of each computation against unintended interference by other computations; and (2) the results of each computation must be independent of the speed at which the computation is carried out.

The protection problem is discussed in a later chapter. Here we are concerned with the assumption of *speed-independence*. This assumption is necessary because a computation has no influence on the rate at which it proceeds. That rate depends on the presence of other computations and the possibly dynamic policy of scheduling. It is also a highly desirable assumption to make, considering our difficulty in understanding concurrent processes in terms of their absolute speeds.

The next section illustrates the consequences of time-dependent behavior of erroneous programs.

## 3.2.2. Time-dependent Errors

Consider again Algorithm 3.1, which copies records from a sequence $f$ to another sequence $g$. Initially, $f$ contains a sequence of records 1, 2, ... , $m$, while $g$ is empty. We will denote this as follows:

$$f = (1, 2, \ldots , m) \qquad g = (\square)$$

When the copying has been completed, $g$ contains all the records in their original order while $f$ is empty:

$$f = (\Box) \qquad g = (1, 2, \ldots, m)$$

The repetition statement in Algorithm 3.1 contains three component statements, which will be called *COPY*, *PUT*, and *GET*:

$$COPY \equiv\ t := s$$
$$PUT\ \ \equiv\ put(t, g)$$
$$GET\ \ \equiv\ \textbf{if}\ empty(f)\ \textbf{then}\ completed := true$$
$$\textbf{else}\ get\ (s, f)$$

They are used as follows:

> **repeat**
>     *COPY* **cobegin** *PUT*; *GET* **coend**
> **until** *completed*;

Now suppose the programmer expresses the repetition by mistake as follows:

> **repeat**
>     **cobegin** *COPY*; *PUT*; *GET* **coend**
> **until** *completed*;

The copying, output, and input of a single record can now be executed concurrently.

To simplify the argument, we will only consider cases in which the statements *COPY*, *PUT*, and *GET* can be arbitrarily *interleaved* in time, but we will ignore the possibility that they can *overlap* in time.

Suppose the first record is copied correctly from sequence $f$ to $g$. The computation will then be in the following state after the first execution of the repetition statement:

$$s = 2\ \&\ f = (3, \ldots, m)\ \&\ t = 1\ \&\ g = (1)$$

The following table shows the possible execution sequences of *COPY*, *PUT*, and *GET* during the second execution of the repetition statement. It also shows the resulting output sequence $g$ after each execution sequence.

| | | | | |
|---|---|---|---|---|
| *COPY*; | *PUT*; | *GET* | leads to | $g = (1, 2)$ |
| *COPY*; | *GET*; | *PUT* | leads to | $g = (1, 2)$ |
| *PUT*; | *COPY*; | *GET* | leads to | $g = (1, 1)$ |

$$PUT; \quad GET; \quad COPY \text{ leads to} \quad g = (1, 1)$$
$$GET; \quad COPY; \quad PUT \quad \text{leads to} \quad g = (1, 3)$$
$$GET; \quad PUT; \quad COPY \text{ leads to} \quad g = (1, 1)$$

One of these sequences is shown below in detail:

$$\text{"} s = 2 \ \& \ f = (3, \ \ldots \ , m) \ \& \ t = 1 \ \& \ g = (1) \text{"}$$
$$GET;$$
$$\text{"} s = 3 \ \& \ f = (4, \ \ldots \ , m) \ \& \ t = 1 \ \& \ g = (1) \text{"}$$
$$COPY;$$
$$\text{"} s = 3 \ \& \ f = (4, \ \ldots \ , m) \ \& \ t = 3 \ \& \ g = (1) \text{"}$$
$$PUT;$$
$$\text{"} s = 3 \ \& \ f = (4, \ \ldots \ , m) \ \& \ t = 3 \ \& \ g = (1, 3) \text{"}$$

The erroneous concurrent statement can be executed in six different ways with three possible results: (1) if copying is completed before input and output are initiated, the *correct* record will be output; (2) if output is completed before copying is initiated, the *previous* record will again be output; and (3) if input is completed before copying is initiated and this in turn completed before output is initiated, the *next* record will instead be output.

This is just for a single record of the output sequence. If we copy a sequence of 10000 records, the program can give of the order of $3^{10000}$ different results! It is therefore extremely unlikely that the programmer will ever observe the same result twice.

If we consider the general case in which concurrent operations overlap in time, we are unable even to enumerate the possible results of a programming error without knowing in detail how the machine reacts to attempts to perform more than one operation simultaneously on the same variable.

The actual sequence of operations in time will depend on the presence of other (unrelated) computations and the scheduling policy used by the operating system to share the available processors among them. The programmer is, of course, unaware of the precise combination of external events that caused his program to fail and is unable to repeat it under controlled circumstances. When he repeats the program execution with the same input, it will sometimes produce correct results, sometimes different erroneous results.

The programmer's only hope of locating the error is to study the program text. This can be very frustrating (if not impossible) if the text consists of thousands of lines and one has no clues about where to look for the error.

It can be argued that such errors are perfectly reproducible in the sense that if we had observed and recorded the behavior of all computations and physical resources continuously during the execution of a given computation, it would also have been possible to reproduce the complete behavior of the computer installation. But this is a purely hypothetical possibility. Human beings are unable to design programs which take into account all simultaneous events occurring in a large computer installation. We must limit ourselves to programs which can be verified independently of other programs. So, in practice, events causing time-dependent results are not observed and recorded, and must therefore be considered irreproducible.

Concurrent programming is far more hazardous than sequential programming unless we ensure that the results of our computations are *reproducible in spite of errors*. In the example studied here, this can easily be checked at compile time, as I will describe in the next section.

### 3.2.3.  Disjoint Processes

The two concurrent processes in Algorithm 3.1

> **cobegin**
> $put(t, g)$;
> **if** *empty*($f$) **then** *completed*:= *true*
>                **else** *get*($s$, $f$);
> **coend**

are completely independent processes which operate on disjoint sets of variables ($t, g$) and ($s, f, completed$).

Concurrent processes which operate on disjoint sets of variables are called *disjoint* or *non-interacting processes*.

In the erroneous version of Algorithm 3.1

> **cobegin**
> $t:= s$;
> $put(t, g)$;
> **if** *empty*($f$) **then** *completed*:= *true*
>                **else** *get*($s,f$);
> **coend**

the processes are not disjoint: The output process refers to a variable $t$ changed by the copying process, and the copying process refers to a variable $s$ changed by the input process.

When a process refers to a variable changed by another process, it is inevitable that the result of the former process will depend on the *time* at which the latter process makes an assignment to this variable.

These time-dependent errors can be caught at compile time if the following *restriction* on concurrent statements is made: The notation

$$\textbf{cobegin } S1; S2; \ldots ; Sn \textbf{ coend}$$

indicates that statements $S1$, $S2$, ... , $Sn$ define disjoint processes which can be executed concurrently. This means that a variable $vi$ changed by a statement $Si$ cannot be referenced by another statement $Sj$ (where $j \neq i$).

In other words, we insist that a variable subject to change by a process must be strictly *private* to that process; but disjoint processes can refer to *common* variables not changed by any of them.

To enable the compiler to *check* the *disjointness* of processes, the language must have the following property: It must be possible to determine the identity of a statement's constant and variable parameters by inspecting the statement.

In Pascal this is certainly possible for assignment statements and expressions involving variables of *primitive types* and *record types* only.

Components of *arrays* are selected by indices determined at run time only. So, at compile time it is necessary to require that an entire array be private to a single process within a concurrent statement.

*Functions* present no problems in Pascal since they cannot perform assignment to non-local variables. But with *procedures*, it is necessary to observe a certain discipline in the use of parameters.

The language notation must distinguish between *constant* and *variable parameters*. Pascal already does this: A comparison of a procedure statement

$$P(a, b)$$

with the corresponding procedure declaration

$$\textbf{procedure } P(\textbf{const } c: C; \textbf{var } v: V)$$

immediately shows that the procedure statement will leave variable $a$ unchanged, but may change variable $b$.

To make a clear distinction between constant and variable parameters, we will not permit a variable to occur both as a constant and as a variable parameter in the same procedure statement.

Without this rule one cannot make simple assertions about the effect of procedures. Consider, for example, the following procedure:

$$\textbf{procedure } P(\textbf{const } c: integer; \textbf{var } v: integer);$$
$$\textbf{begin } v:= c + 1 \textbf{ end}$$

If we call this procedure as follows:

$$P(a, b)$$

where $a$ and $b$ are integer variables, we can make the assertion that upon return from the procedure, $b = a + 1$. But this assertion leads to a contradiction in the following case:

$$P(a, a)$$

namely $a = a + 1$.

Another contradiction occurs if the same variable is used twice as a variable parameter in a procedure statement. For example, if a program contains the following procedure:

**procedure** $P(\textbf{var } v, w: \textit{integer})$;
**begin** $v := 1; w := 2$ **end**

then the call

$$P(a, b)$$

leads to the result $a = 1$ & $b = 2$. But when the same assertion is used for the call

$$P(a, a)$$

it leads to the contradiction $a = 1$ & $a = 2$.

These contradictions can be avoided by obeying the following rule: All variables used as *variable parameters* in a procedure statement must be *distinct* and *cannot occur* as *constant parameters* in the same statement.

A Pascal procedure can also have side effects: It can change non-local variables directly, as is shown in the following example:

**var** $v: T$;

**procedure** $P$;
**begin** ... $v := E$ ... **end**

or call other procedures which have side effects. So, it is not possible to identify the variables involved by simple inspection of a procedure statement and the corresponding procedure declaration.

One possibility is to specify all global variables referred to within a procedure $P$ (and within other procedures called by $P$) explicitly in the procedure declaration:

**var** $v: T$;

**procedure** $P$;
**global** $v$;
**begin** ... $v := E$ ... **end**

A more radical solution is to forbid side effects and check that *a procedure only refers to non-local variables used as parameters.*

A final difficulty is the exit statement. Consider the following program:

```
label L
begin ... label M
            begin ...
                cobegin
                    ... exit L;
                    ... exit M;
                coend
                ...
            end
        ...
    end
```

Here we have two processes trying to exit different compound statements labeled $L$ and $M$ at the same time. But this is meaningless: First, we have defined that a concurrent statement is terminated only when all its processes are terminated; so a single process cannot terminate it by an exit statement; second, it is possible for the program to continue as a purely sequential process after the concurrent statement (this is indeed the case in the above example), so the desire to continue the process simultaneously at two different points is a contradiction.

We will therefore also *forbid jumps out of concurrent statements.*

The rules presented here are due to Hoare (1971b). They enable a compiler to identify the constant and variable parameters of every statement by simple inspection and check the disjointness of concurrent processes. This property also simplifies the analysis of programs by people and should therefore be regarded as a helpful guideline for program structuring—not as a severe language restriction.

When these rules are obeyed, the *axiomatic properties of concurrent statements* become very simple. Suppose statements $S1$, $S2$, ..., $Sn$ define disjoint processes, and each $Si$ is an operation that makes a result $Ri$ true if a predicate $Pi$ holds before its execution. In other words, it is known that the individual statements have the following effects:

$$\text{“}P1\text{” } S1 \text{ “}R1\text{”}$$
$$\text{“}P2\text{” } S2 \text{ “}R2\text{”}$$
$$\ldots\ldots$$
$$\text{“}Pn\text{” } Sn \text{ “}Rn\text{”}$$

(I assume that statements and assertions made about them only refer to *variables* which are *accessible* to the statements according to the rule of disjointness).

The concurrent statement

$$\textbf{cobegin } S1; S2; \ldots ; Sn \textbf{ coend}$$

can then be regarded as a single operation $S$ with the following effect

$$\text{``}P\text{''} \; S \; \text{``}R\text{''}$$

where

$$P \equiv P1 \; \& \; P2 \; \& \ldots \& \; Pn$$
$$R \equiv R1 \; \& \; R2 \; \& \ldots \& \; Rn$$

As Hoare (1971b) puts it: "Each *Si* makes its contribution to the common goal." The previous result can also be stated as follows: *Disjointness is a sufficient condition for time-independent behavior of concurrent processes.*

The usefulness of disjoint processes is of course, limited. In some cases, concurrent processes must be able to access and change common variables. I will introduce language constructs suitable for process interactions of this kind later in this chapter.

In the following we will derive a sufficient condition for time-independent behavior of concurrent interacting processes. To do this, it is first necessary to formulate the requirement of time-independence in a slightly different way using the concept—the history of a computation.

### 3.2.4. The History Concept*

Consider a *program* which is connected to its *environment* by a single *input variable x* and a single *output variable y*. During the execution of the program, the input variable $x$ assumes a sequence of values determined by the environment:

$$x := a0; \, x := a1; \ldots ; x := am;$$

and the output variable $y$ assumes another sequence of values determined by the program and its input:

$$y := b0; \, y := b1; \ldots ; y := bn;$$

Together, the *input sequence* $X = (a0, a1, \ldots , am)$ and the *output sequence* $Y = (b0, b1, \ldots , bn)$ define the *history* of a computation. For analytical purposes, the history can be represented by an array in which

---

*You may wish to skip this section and the following one on first reading. They illustrate a more formal analysis of time-independent behavior. The practical utility of this approach has yet to be demonstrated.

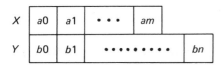

**Fig. 3.7** The history of a computation with two variables, $x$ and $y$.

each row defines the sequence of values assumed by a given variable, as shown in Fig. 3.7.

A history is simply a listing of the sequences of input and output values observed during a computation. It is a time-independent representation that says nothing about the precise time at which these values were assigned to the variables.

When a computation involves several variables, the history array contains a row for each of them. We can divide the complete history into the *input history* and the *output history*. Sometimes we will include the history of internal variables in the output history.

A program is *functional* if the *output history* $Y$ of its execution always is a *time-independent function* $f$ of its *input history* $X$:

$$Y = f(X)$$

A functional program produces identical output histories every time it is executed with the same input history, independent of its speed of execution.

As an example, let us again look at Algorithm 3.1 in which an input sequence

$$f = (1, 2, \ldots , m)$$

is copied to an (initially empty) output sequence $g$.

Figure 3.8 shows the sequence of assignments made initially during the execution of this algorithm.

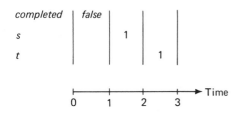

**Fig. 3.8** The initial sequence of assignments made during the copying of a sequence of records.

From these values (and the ones assigned during the rest of the computation), we derive the history shown in Fig. 3.9.

The input history defines the sequence of assignments to the variable $s$; the output history comprises the variables *completed* and $t$.

Notice that the rows in a history array are not necessarily of the same

| completed | false | true | | |
|-----------|-------|------|-----|---|
| s | 1 | 2 | $\cdots$ | m |
| t | 1 | 2 | $\cdots$ | m |

Fig. 3.9 The history of the copying of a sequence of records.

length because the number of assignments may be different for each variable.

Notice also that the elements in a given column of a history array do not necessarily define values assigned at the same time. A comparison of Figs. 3.8 and 3.9 immediately shows that all values in the leftmost column of the history array were assigned at different times. When a program contains concurrent statements, the sequence in which assignments to disjoint variables are made depends on the relative rates of the processes.

So, in general there are many different sequences in which a given history can be produced in time. The functional requirement only says that when the sequence of values is known for each input variable, it must be possible to predict the sequence of values for each output variable, independent of the rate at which they will be produced.

In some cases, we are still interested in observing actual rates of progress. For this purpose, time is regarded as a discrete variable which is increased by one each time an assignment to at least one of the variables considered has been completed.

These instants of time are indicated explicitly in Fig. 3.8. In a history array, an instant of time is defined by a line which crosses each row exactly once. Such a *time slice* defines the extent of the history at a particular instant.

Figure 3.10 shows the previous history with two successive time slices $t1$ and $t2$, which define the extent of the history after the first assignments to the variables *completed* and $s$.

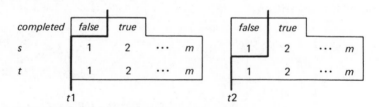

Fig. 3.10 A history with two successive time slices, $t1$ and $t2$.

A history $H1$ is called an *initial part* of another history $H2$ if $H1$ is *contained* in $H2$. More precisely, $H1$ and $H2$ must have the same number of rows, and each row in $H1$ must be equal to an initial part of the corresponding row in $H2$; but some rows in $H1$ may be shorter than the corresponding rows in $H2$. This relationship is denoted

$$H1 \leqslant H2$$

During a computation, every time slice $t$ defines an initial part $H(t)$ of the final history $H$.

We will use the history concept to prove an important theorem by Patil (1970).

### 3.2.5. A Closure Property

Consider again a program which communicates with its environment by means of a set of distinct input and output variables. We will observe the execution of the program in two cases: In the first case, the environment supplies an input history $X$, and the program responds by returning an output history $Y$:

$$X \to Y$$

In the second case, the observed input/output relationship is:

$$X' \to Y'$$

So far, nothing has been said about whether the program is functional. If we repeat the execution with the input history $X'$ the program may possibly produce a different output history, $Y'' \neq Y'$.

But suppose we only consider programs which satisfy the following requirement: If during its execution, a program is supplied with two different input histories $X$ and $X'$, where $X$ is contained in $X'$, then the same relationship will hold between the corresponding output histories $Y$ and $Y'$:

$$X \leqslant X' \text{ implies } Y \leqslant Y'$$

This is called the *consistency requirement*. It is a sufficient condition for functional behavior. If a consistent program is executed twice with the same input, it delivers the same output in both cases because

$$X = X' \text{ implies } X \leqslant X' \ \& \ X' \leqslant X$$
$$\text{implies } Y \leqslant Y' \ \& \ Y' \leqslant Y$$
$$\text{implies } Y = Y'$$

Intuitively, the consistency requirement means that it is possible, at every instant in time, to predict a portion $Y$ of the *final output* from the *observed input* $X$. If a program in execution is supplied with more input $X' \geqslant X$, the additional input cannot affect the output $Y$ predicted earlier, but can only extend it to $Y' \geqslant Y$.

$X$ and $X'$ refer to the input *produced* by the environment. This is not necessarily the same as the input *consumed* by the program. The environment may assign new values to input variables, due to *erroneous synchronization*, before previous values have been consumed by the program. In that case, it is impossible to predict the final output from the observed input. So the program is not consistent.

The consistency requirement is also violated if concurrent processes can enter a *deadlock* state in which they are unable to respond to further input under circumstances which depend on their speed of execution (see Section 2.6.1).

We now introduce an additional requirement of consistent programs: Since the output is a function of the input, a program in execution cannot produce an output value until the corresponding input value is present. This cause-and-effect relationship can be expressed as follows: Suppose we observe an input history at successive instants in time

$$X(0), X(1), \ldots , X(t), \ldots , X$$

where $t$ indicates the earliest time at which an initial part $X(t)$ of the input is available. Let the final input and output histories be $X$ and $Y$, respectively. Now it is clear that an initial input history $X(t)$ must be contained in the final input history:

$$X(t) \leqslant X$$

Because the program is consistent, it is possible to predict part of the output history from the initial input history $X(t)$. But in a physical system it takes a finite time to produce this output; so the earliest moment at which some or all of this output can be available is the next instant of time $t + 1$ where the output history is $Y(t + 1)$. The output $Y(t + 1)$, which is predicted from an initial part of the input, must itself be an initial part of the final output $Y$. So we have

$$Y(t + 1) \leqslant Y$$

If we combine these two physical conditions, we get the so-called *dependency requirement*:

$$X(t) \leqslant X \text{ implies } Y(t + 1) \leqslant Y$$

In the following, we will consider programs for which the consistency and dependency requirements hold unconditionally. They are called *unconditionally functional programs*. We will prove the important *closure property*, which states that *any interconnection of a finite number of unconditionally functional programs is unconditionally functional as a whole.*

A system $S$ consisting of a finite number of components $S1, S2, \dots ,$ $Sn$ can always be partitioned successively into smaller systems consisting of two components each:

$$\begin{aligned}
S &= (S1, S2') \\
S2' &= (S2, S3') \\
&\dots \\
Sn\text{-}1' &= (Sn\text{-}1, Sn)
\end{aligned}$$

It is therefore sufficient to show that the interconnection of two unconditionally functional programs, $S1$ and $S2$, also is an unconditionally functional program $S$. The general theorem follows by induction.

The input and output histories of $S$ are called $X$ and $Y$, as shown in Fig. 3.11. $X$ in turn consists of two separate input histories, $X1$ and $X2$ for $S1$ and $S2$, respectively. Similarly, $Y$ consists of two separate output histories, $Y1$ and $Y2$ for $S1$ and $S2$, respectively. The histories of internal output produced by $S1$ for $S2$, and vice versa, are called $J$ and $K$.

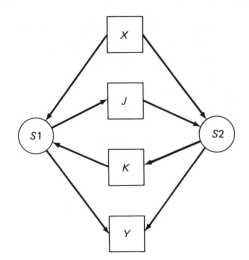

Fig. 3.11 Two programs $S1$ and $S2$, connected to each other and to a common environment by means of input/output sequences $X$, $Y$, $J$, and $K$.

We will study the combined system $S = (S1, S2)$ when it is supplied with two different input histories $X$ and $X'$ where

$$X \leqslant X'$$

and delivers the output histories $J, K, Y$ and $J', K', Y'$.

Consider first subsystem $S1$ and observe its input history $X, K$ and the

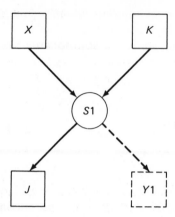

Fig. 3.12 Program $S1$ of the system shown in Fig. 3.11.

corresponding output history $J$ as shown in Fig. 3.12. (The output history $Y1$ is ignored for the moment.)

Suppose the following holds at time $t$:

$$X(t) \leqslant X' \,\&\, K(t) \leqslant K'$$

This means that at time $t$ during the first execution, the initial input history to $S1$ is contained in its final input history of the second execution.

Now since $S1$ is unconditionally functional, it satisfies the dependency requirement; so we have

$$X(t) \leqslant X' \,\&\, K(t) \leqslant K' \text{ implies } J(t+1) \leqslant J'$$

By applying similar reasoning to subsystem $S2$, we find that

$$X(t) \leqslant X' \,\&\, J(t) \leqslant J' \text{ implies } K(t+1) \leqslant K'$$

These results can be combined into the following:

$$X(t) \leqslant X' \,\&\, J(t) \leqslant J' \,\&\, K(t) \leqslant K'$$
$$\text{implies } J(t+1) \leqslant J' \,\&\, K(t+1) \leqslant K'$$

We already assumed that $X \leqslant X'$, so $X(t) \leqslant X'$ holds at any instant of time. Consequently, if the initial histories, $J(t)$ and $K(t)$, at time $t$ are contained in the final histories, $J'$ and $K'$, then this is also the case at time $t+1$. This is trivially true at time $t=0$ where $J(t)$ and $K(t)$ are empty. So it holds throughout the execution that

$$X \leqslant X' \text{ implies } J \leqslant J' \,\&\, K \leqslant K'$$

But since the subsystems satisfy the consistency requirement, this in turn means that

$$X \leqslant X' \text{ implies } Y \leqslant Y'$$

So the combined system $S$ also satisfies the consistency requirement. And, for physical reasons, it also satisfies the dependency requirement. (This can be proved formally as well.)

The closure property enables a designer to verify that a large program is functional by a step-wise analysis of smaller program components. The functional behavior is ensured by *local conditions* (the consistency and dependency requirements) which only constrain the relationship between a program component and its immediate environment (represented by input/output variables).

In actual systems, the consistency requirement seldom holds unconditionally. The functional behavior may depend on certain additional requirements; for example, that the input is of a certain type and is not delivered more rapidly than the system is able to consume it. A system which satisfies the consistency and dependency requirements, provided that additional constraints hold, is called *conditionally functional*. For such systems, the closure property holds when the additional constraints hold.

I will conclude the present discussion with some examples of useful systems in which time-dependent behavior is inherent and desired.

### 3.2.6.  Non-functional Systems

I have stressed the importance of designing multiprogramming systems which are functional in behavior. But it must be admitted that some computational tasks are inherently time-dependent.

Consider, for example, *priority scheduling* according to the rule *shortest job next*. This involves decisions based on the particular set of computations which users have requested *at a given time*. If a scheduling decision is postponed a few seconds, the outcome may well be different because new and more urgent requests can be made in the meantime by users. So priority scheduling depends not only on the order in which users input their requests, but also on their relative occurrence in time.

In the *spooling system* shown in Fig. 1.3 there is a time-dependent relationship between the stream of jobs input and the stream of printed output. But the spooling system has one important property which makes the time-dependent behavior tolerable: *It maintains a functional relationship between the input and output of each job.*

The user computations are disjoint; they could be carried out on different machines. But, for economic reasons, they share the same machine. And this can only be done efficiently by introducing a certain

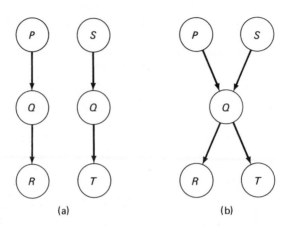

Fig. 3.13 Two disjoint processes (a) without and (b) with a common operation Q.

amount of *time-dependent behavior on a microscopic time scale*. However, *on a macroscopic time scale, the operating system hides the time-dependency from the individual user* and offers him a virtual machine with perfectly reproducible behavior.

Figure 3.13 shows another example of the same principle: (a) shows two disjoint processes consisting of the operations P, Q, R and S, Q, T; (b) shows an equivalent system in which we have taken advantage of the occurrence of *a common operation Q* in both processes. The processes now share a single instance of operation Q, which can receive input from operations P and S and deliver output to operations R and T.

The equivalence of the two systems in Fig. 3.13(a) and (b) is based on the assumption that requests received by Q from P have no effect on the response of Q to requests received from S, and vice versa, and that Q responds to any request within a finite time.

An example of a set of common operations shared by all user computations is a *filing system*, which permits users to create and manipulate data and programs on backing storage and maintain them over a certain period of time.

The system in Fig. 3.13(b) is non-functional if we observe the input and output of the common operation Q because this is a time-dependent merging of data values belonging to independent processes. But the system is still functional if we only observe the relationship between the output from P and the input to R (or that between the output from S and the input to T).

So we come to the conclusion that *functional behavior is an abstraction* just like the concepts operation, process, and state (see Section 2.6.3). Whether or not a system is considered functional depends on the level of description chosen by the observer.

## 3.3. MUTUAL EXCLUSION

Much has been said about the role of disjoint processes and functional behavior in multiprogramming systems. We must now deal with *interacting processes*—concurrent processes which have access to *common variables*.

Common variables are used to represent the state of *physical resources* shared by *competing processes*. They are also used to *communicate* data between *cooperating processes*. In general, we will say that all common variables represent shared objects called *resources*. Interacting processes can therefore also be defined as processes which share resources.

To share resources, concurrent processes must be synchronized. *Synchronization* is a general term for any constraint on the ordering of operations in time. We have already met synchronizing rules which specify a *precedence* or *priority of operations* by constraints of the form "operation *A* must be executed before operation *B*" and "an operation of priority *P* must only be executed when all operations of higher priority have been executed."

In this section, we will discuss process interactions in which the constraint is of the form "operations *A* and *B* must never be executed at the same time." This synchronizing rule specifies *mutual exclusion* of operations in time.

### 3.3.1. Resource Sharing

We begin with an example in which two concurrent processes, *P* and *Q*, share a single physical resource *R*. *P* and *Q* are cyclical processes which every now and then wish to use *R* for a finite period of time, but they cannot use it at the same time.

An example of a resource that can be accessed only by one process at a time is a magnetic tape station. In this case, the requirement of mutual exclusion is dictated by the physical characteristics of the resource: Since we can only mount one tape at a time on a magnetic tape station and access its data strictly sequentially, it is impractical to let several processes use the tape station at the same time. But, as we shall see, there is also a deeper logical reason for the requirement of mutual exclusion of certain operations in time.

We will follow a chain of arguments made by Dijkstra (1965) to illuminate the nature of the mutual exclusion problem.

Let us first try the following approach: The resource *R* is represented by a boolean, indicating whether it is *free* or occupied at the moment. Each process goes through a cycle in which it first *reserves* the resource, then *uses* it, and finally *releases* it again. Before reserving the resource, a process *waits* in a loop until the resource is free. This leads to the following program:

```
var free: boolean;
begin
  free:= true;
  cobegin
  "P" repeat
        repeat until free;
        free:= false;
        use resource;
        free:= true;
        P passive;
      forever
  "Q" repeat
        repeat until free;
        free:= false;
        use resource;
        free:= true;
        Q passive;
      forever
  coend
end
```

This program clearly violates the rules of concurrent statements laid down in Section 3.2.3: Both processes change and refer to the variable *free*. But let us ignore this for the moment.

Initially, *free* is *true*. It is therefore possible for *P* and *Q* to refer to *free* at the same time and find it true. Then, they will both in good faith assign the value *false* to *free* and start using the resource. So this program does not satisfy the condition that the resource can be used by at most one process at a time.

Well, then we must try something else. In the next version, the boolean *free* is replaced by another boolean, *Pturn*, which is *true* when it is *P*'s turn to use the resource and *false* when it is *Q*'s turn:

```
var Pturn: boolean;
begin
  Pturn:= true;
  cobegin
  "P" repeat
        repeat until Pturn;
        use resource;
        Pturn:= false;
        P passive;
      forever
```

(*cont.*)

```
"Q" repeat
       repeat until not Pturn;
       use resource;
       Pturn:= true;
       Q passive;
     forever
   coend
 end
```

There are only two cases to consider: either *Pturn* is *true* or it is *false*. When *Pturn* is *true*, only process *P* can start using the resource and release it again. And when *Pturn* is *false*, only process *Q* can start using the resource and release it again. So mutual exclusion of *P* and *Q* is indeed achieved. But the solution is far too restrictive: It forces the processes to share the resource in a strictly alternating sequence:

$$P, Q, P, Q, \ldots$$

If one of the processes, say *P*, is stopped in its passive state after having released the resource, the other process *Q* will also be stopped when it has released the resource (by means of the assignment *Pturn:= true*) and then tries to reserve it again.

This is quite unacceptable in an installation where *P* and *Q* could be two independent user computations. We must require that a solution to the problem make no assumptions about the relative progress of the processes when they are not using the resource.

Another highly undesirable effect of the previous solution is the waste of processing time in unproductive waiting loops. This is called the *busy form of waiting*.

Our third attempt uses two booleans to indicate whose turn it is:

```
var Pturn, Qturn: boolean;
begin
  Pturn:= false; Qturn:= false;
  cobegin
  "P" repeat
        Pturn:= true;
        repeat until not Qturn;
        use resource;
        Pturn:= false;
        P passive;
      forever                              (cont.)
```

```
"Q" repeat
    Qturn:= true;
    repeat until not Pturn;
    use resource;
    Qturn:= false;
    Q passive;
    forever
coend
end
```

Assignment to variable *Pturn* is only made by process *P*. When *P* does not use the resource, *Pturn* is false, so

> **not** *Pturn* **implies** *P passive*

The two processes are completely symmetrical, so the assertion

> **not** *Pturn* **implies** *P passive*
> **& not** *Qturn* **implies** *Q passive*

must be invariant.

Process *P* waits until *Qturn* is *false* before it uses the resource, so

> *P active* **implies not** *Q turn*
> **implies** *Q passive*

Similar reasoning about process *Q* leads to the conclusion that

> *P active* **implies** *Q passive*
> **&** *Q active* **implies** *P passive*

is invariant.

Mutual exclusion is therefore guaranteed, and it is not difficult to see that stopping one process in its passive state does not influence the progress of the other process. But it is a highly dangerous solution: The processes can make the assignments

> *Pturn*:= *true*       *Qturn*:= *true*

at the same time and then remain indefinitely in their waiting loops waiting for one of the booleans to become *false*. In short, the solution can lead to a *deadlock*.

We learn from our mistakes. The lesson of this one is that when competing processes request the resource at the same time, the decision to *grant* it to one of them must be made within a finite time.

It is possible to continue along these lines and find a correct solution. This was first done by Dekker and described by Dijkstra (1965). Dijkstra solved the general case, in which $n$ processes share a single resource. The solution turns out to be far too complicated and inefficient to be of practical value.

I have described these preliminary, incorrect solutions to make you appreciate the subtlety of the *mutual exclusion* problem and discover a set of criteria that a *realistic solution* must satisfy. Let me repeat these *criteria*:

(1) The resource in question can be used by one process at a time at most.

(2) When the resource is requested simultaneously by several processes, it must be granted to one of them within a finite time.

(3) When a process acquires the resource, the process must release it again within a finite time. Apart from this, no assumption is made about the relative speeds of the processes; processes may even be stopped when they are not using the resource.

(4) A process should not consume processing time when it is waiting to acquire the resource.

For the moment, we will leave the problem there and consider another instance of it in which interacting processes are cooperating rather than competing.

## 3.3.2. Data Sharing

The second example of process interaction is taken from an actual system that supervises an industrial plant. Among other things, this real-time system measures the consumption of energy and the production of materials in the plant continuously and reports it to management every few hours.

Consumption and production are measured in discrete units (kilowatt-hours and product units) and recorded in pulse registers connected to a computer. The computer is multiplexed among a number of concurrent processes. A cyclical process $P$ inputs and resets the pulse registers every few seconds and adds their values (0 or 1) to a corresponding number of integer variables. Another cyclical process $Q$ outputs and resets the integer counters every few hours. Operators can change the frequency of execution of $P$ and $Q$ independently. The processes therefore do not know their relative rates.

Let us assume that the periodic scheduling of processes and the input/output are handled correctly by standard procedures. No generality is lost by considering only one pulse counter $v$. As a first attempt, I suggest the following solution:

```
var v: integer;
begin
  v:= 0;
  cobegin
  "P" repeat
       delay(1);
       v:= v + input;
     forever
  "Q" repeat
       delay(18000);
       output(v);
       v:= 0;
     forever
  coend
end
```

This program too violates the rules of concurrent statements because process $Q$ refers to a variable $v$ changed by process $P$. But again we will ignore this violation for the moment since it expresses the desired interaction between the processes.

The intention is that a value of $v$ output at time $t$ should define the number of pulses accumulated over the past 18,000 seconds, or 5 hours, prior to time $t$.

Now, in most computers, statements such as

$$v:= v + input \qquad output(v)$$

are executed as a sequence of instructions which use registers, say $r$ and $s$, to hold intermediate results:

```
r:= input;      s:= v;
r:= r + v;      output(s);
v:= r;
```

A concurrent statement can therefore be executed as a sequence of instructions interleaved in time. The operating system will ensure that the instructions of each process are executed in the right order, but apart from this, the system may interleave them in many different ways. In the system considered here, the operating system switches from one process to another every 20 msec to maintain the illusion that they are executed simultaneously. The actual interleaving of instructions in time is therefore a time-dependent function of other concurrent processes not considered here.

One possibility is that the instructions of $P$ and $Q$ are interleaved as follows:

$$\textit{``v = pulse count''}$$

P:      $r:= 1;$
Q:      $s:= v;\ output(s);$
P:      $r:= r + v; v:= r;$
Q:      $s:= 0; v:= s;$

$$\textit{``v = 0 \& output = pulse count''}$$

Another possibility is the following:

$$\textit{``v = pulse count''}$$

P:      $r:= 1; r:= r + v;$
Q:      $s:= v;\ output(s);$
Q:      $s:= 0; v:= s;$
P:      $v:= r;$

$$\textit{``v = pulse count + 1 \& output = pulse count''}$$

In the first case, the program measures an input pulse ($r:= 1$), but fails to accumulate it ($v = 0$); in the second case, the program outputs the current pulse count correctly, but proceeds to include it in the count over the next five hours. The result should have been

$$\textit{``v = 1 \& output = pulse count''}$$

or

$$\textit{``v = 0 \& output = pulse count + 1''}$$

depending on when the last pulse was measured.

The penalty of breaking the laws of concurrent statements is time-dependent erroneous behavior. The example shown here illustrates the remark made in Section 3.1.1 about concurrent processes executed simultaneously on several processors or on a single, multiplexed processor: "The logical problems turn out to be the same in both cases; they are caused by our ignorance of the relative speeds of concurrent processes."

It should be evident by now that our present programming tools are hopelessly inadequate for controlling access to physical resources and data shared by concurrent processes. A new tool is needed, and like our previous tools it should be simple to understand, efficient to implement, and safe to use.

### 3.3.3. Critical Regions

The erroneous behavior in the pulse counting program is caused by the interleaving of concurrent statements in time. If we were sure that only one process at a time could operate on the common variable $v$, the previous solution would work.

So let us postulate a language construction which has precisely this effect. I will use the notation

**var** $v$: **shared** $T$

to declare a *common variable v* of type $T$.

Concurrent processes can only refer to and change common variables within structured statements called *critical regions*. A critical region is defined by the notation

**region** $v$ **do** $S$

which associates a statement $S$ with a common variable $v$. This notation enables a compiler to check that common variables are used only inside critical regions.

Critical regions referring to the same variable $v$ exclude one another in time. More precisely, we make the following *assumptions about critical regions* on a variable $v$:

(1)  When a process wishes to enter a critical region, it will be enabled to do so within a finite time.

(2)  At most, one process at a time can be inside a critical region.

(3)  A process remains inside a critical region for a finite time only.

Criterion 3 says that all statements operating on a common variable must *terminate*.

Criterion 2 expresses the requirement of *mutual exclusion* in time of these statements.

Criteria 1 and 2 put the following constraints on the *scheduling* of critical regions associated with a given variable: (a) when no processes are inside critical regions, a process can enter a critical region immediately; (b) when a process is inside a critical region, other processes trying to enter critical regions will be delayed; and (c) when a process leaves a critical region while other processes are trying to enter critical regions, one of the processes will be enabled to proceed inside its region; (d) these decisions must be made within finite periods of time.

Finally, (e) the priority rule used to select a delayed process must be *fair*: It must not delay a process indefinitely in favor of more urgent processes. An example of a fair scheduling policy is *first-come, first-served*, which selects processes in their order of arrival; an unfair policy is *last-come, first-served*, which favors the latest request.

Although we require that scheduling be fair, no assumptions are made about the specific order in which processes are scheduled. This depends entirely on the underlying implementation. As Dijkstra (1971b) puts it: "In the long run a number of identical processes will proceed at the same macroscopic speed. But we don't tell how long this run is." (See also Dijkstra, 1972.)

Critical regions can be implemented in various ways. We are going to consider some of them later.

Critical regions referring to different variables can be executed simultaneously, for example:

> **var** $v$: **shared** $V$; $w$: **shared** $W$;
> **cobegin**
>    **region** $v$ **do** $P$;
>    **region** $w$ **do** $Q$;
> **coend**

A process can also enter nested critical regions:

> **region** $v$ **do**
> **begin** ...
>        **region** $w$ **do** ... ;
>        ...
>    **end**

In doing so, one must be aware of the danger of *deadlock* in such constructions as:

> **cobegin**
> "$P$" **region** $v$ **do region** $w$ **do** ... ;
> "$Q$" **region** $w$ **do region** $v$ **do** ... ;
> **coend**

It is possible that process $P$ enters its region $v$ at the same time as process $Q$ enters its region $w$. When process $P$ tries to enter its region $w$, it will be delayed because $Q$ is already inside its region $w$. And process $Q$ will be delayed trying to enter its region $v$ because $P$ is inside its region $v$. This is a case in which correctness criterion 3 is violated: The processes do not leave their critical regions after a finite time. A method of avoiding this problem will be described later.

The concept *critical region* is due to Dijkstra (1965). The language constructs which associate critical regions with a common variable are my own (Brinch Hansen, 1972b). Similar constructs have been proposed independently by Hoare (1971b).

With this new tool, common variables and critical regions, the solutions to our previous problems become trivial. In the first problem, our only concern was to guarantee mutual exclusion of operations on a physical resource performed by concurrent processes. Algorithm 3.2 solves the problem in the general case of $n$ processes.

*ALGORITHM 3.2   A Resource R Shared by n Concurrent Processes*

```
var R: shared boolean;
cobegin
  "P1" repeat
          region R do use resource;
          P1 passive;
      forever
      . . . . .
  "Pn" repeat
          region R do use resource;
          Pn passive;
      forever
coend
```

The pulse counting problem is solved by Algorithm 3.3.

*ALGORITHM 3.3   A Variable v Shared by Two Concurrent Processes*

```
var v: shared integer;
begin
  v:= 0;
  cobegin
    "P" repeat
          delay(1);
          region v do v:= v + input;
        forever
    "Q" repeat
          delay(18000);
          region v do begin
                    output(v);
                    v:= 0;
                  end
              forever
  coend
end
```

### 3.3.4. Conclusion

Critical regions provide an elegant solution to the resource sharing problem. But how fundamental is this concept? After all, we succeeded in one instance in solving the problem without introducing critical regions in our language. I am referring to the algorithm in Section 3.3.1, which permits a resource to alternate between two processes: $P, Q, P, Q, \ldots$ . This solution may not be ideal, but it does ensure mutual exclusion without using critical regions—or does it?

In the analysis of its effect, I made the innocent statement: "There are only two cases to consider: either *Pturn* is *true* or it is *false*." These are the only values that a boolean variable can assume from a *formal point of view*. But suppose the computer installation consists of several processors connected to a single store as shown in Fig. 2.3. Then, it is quite possible that the operations of processes $P$ and $Q$ can overlap in time. We must now carefully examine what happens in this *physical system* when $P$ and $Q$ try to operate simultaneously on the variable *Pturn*.

Suppose process $P$ initiates the assignment

$$Pturn := false$$

This storage operation takes a finite time. We know that *Pturn* is *true* before the operation is started and that *Pturn* will be *false* when the operation is completed. But there is a transitional period, called the *instruction execution time*, during which the physical state of the storage cell is unknown. It is changing in a time-dependent manner, determined by the characteristics of the electronic circuits and the storage medium used.

If process $Q$ is allowed to refer to the same storage location while the assignment is in progress, the resulting value (or more precisely, the bit combination used to represent the value) is unpredictable. In other words, process $Q$ is performing an undefined operation.

The hardware designer solves this problem by connecting the concurrent processors to a sequential switching circuit called an *arbiter*. The arbiter ensures that, at most, one processor at a time can access a given storage location. It is a hardware implementation of critical regions.

So our reasoning on the effect of the algorithm in Section 3.3.1 was based on the implicit assumption that *load* and *store* operations on a given variable exclude each other in time. The same assumption underlies Dekker's solution to the resource sharing problem.

The load and store operations are proper critical regions at the short grains of time controlled by hardware. But at higher levels of programming, we must guarantee mutual exclusion in larger grains of time for arbitrary statements. The language construct

$$\textbf{region } v \textbf{ do } S$$

is introduced for this purpose.

Mutual exclusion is indeed one of the most fundamental concepts of programming. Whenever we make assertions about the effect of any operation on a certain variable, for example:

> "$A$: **array** 1. .$n$ **of** *integer*"
> *sort*($A$);
> "**for all** $i, j$: 1. . $n$ ($i \leqslant j$ implies $A(i) \leqslant A(j)$)"

it is tacitly understood that this is the only operation performed at that time on this variable. In the above example, it would indeed have been a coincidence if the array $A$ had been sorted if other processes were happily modifying it simultaneously.

In sequential computations, mutual exclusion is automatically achieved because the operations are applied one at a time. But we must explicitly indicate the need for mutual exclusion in concurrent computations.

*It is impossible to make meaningful statements about the effect of concurrent computations unless operations on common variables exclude one another in time.* So in the end, our understanding of concurrent processes is based on our ability to execute their interactions strictly sequentially. Only disjoint processes can proceed at the same time.

But there is one important difference between sequential processes and critical regions: The statements $S1, S2, \ldots, Sn$ of a *sequential process* are *totally ordered* in time. We can therefore make assertions about its *progress* from an initial predicate $P$ towards a final result $R$:

$$\text{"}P\text{" }S1\text{ "}R1\text{" }S2\text{ "}R2\text{" }\ldots\text{ "}Rn\text{-}1\text{" }Sn\text{ "}R\text{"}$$

In contrast, nothing is specified about the ordering of *critical regions* in time—they can be *arbitrarily interleaved*. The idea of progressing towards a final result is therefore meaningless. All we can expect is that each critical region leave certain relationships among the components of a shared variable $v$ unchanged. These relationships can be defined by an assertion $I$ about $v$ which must be true after initialization of $v$ and before and after each subsequent critical region. Such an assertion is called an *invariant*.

When a process enters a critical region to execute a statement $S$, a predicate $P$ holds for the variables accessible to the process outside the critical region, and an invariant $I$ holds for the shared variable accessible inside the critical region. After the completion of statement $S$, a result $R$ holds for the former variables and invariant $I$ has been maintained.

So a critical region has the following axiomatic property:

"*P*"
**region** *v* **do** "*P* & *I*" *S* "*R* & *I*";
"*R*"

## 3.4. PROCESS COOPERATION

The interactions controlled by critical regions are rather indirect—each process can ignore the existence and function of other processes as long as they exclude each other in time and maintain invariants for common variables.

We will now study more *direct interactions* between processes cooperating on common tasks. Such processes are well aware of each other's existence and purpose: Each of them depends directly on data produced by other members of the community.

### 3.4.1. Process Communication

To cooperate on common tasks, processes must be able to *exchange data.* Figure 3.14 shows the situation we will study. A process *P produces* and *sends* a sequence of data to another process *C*, which *receives* and *consumes* them. The data are transmitted between the processes in discrete portions called *messages.* They are regarded as *output* by *P* and as *input* by *C.*

Since either process can proceed at a rate independent of the other's, it is possible that the sender may produce a message at a time when the receiver is not yet ready to consume it (it may still be processing an earlier message). To avoid delaying the sender in this situation, we introduce a

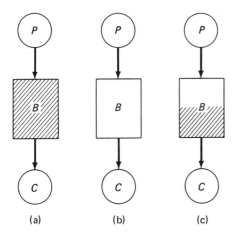

(a)          (b)          (c)

Fig. 3.14 A producer *P* and a consumer *C* connected by a buffer *B* which can either be (a) full, (b) empty, or (c) somewhere in between.

temporary storage area in which the sender can place one or more messages until the receiver is ready to consume them. This storage area is called a *buffer* and designated $B$; its function is to smooth speed variations between the processes and occasionally permit the sender to be ahead of the receiver.

The communication must be subject to two *resource constraints*: (1) the sender cannot exceed the *finite capacity* of the buffer; and (2) the receiver cannot consume messages faster than they are produced.

These constraints are satisfied by the following *synchronizing rule*: If the *sender* tries to put a message in a *full buffer*, the sender will be delayed until the receiver has taken another message from the buffer; if the *receiver* tries to take a message from an *empty buffer*, the receiver will be delayed until the sender has put another message into the buffer.

We also assume that all messages are intended to be received exactly as they were sent—in the same order and with their original content. Messages must not be lost, changed, or permuted within the buffer. These requirements can be stated more precisely with the aid of Fig. 3.15.

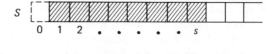

**Fig. 3.15** A message sequence $S$ sent by a producer and the corresponding message sequence $R$ received by a consumer.

The sequence $S$ of messages sent by a producer $P$ and the corresponding sequence $R$ of messages received by a consumer $C$ are shown conceptually as infinite arrays:

$$\textbf{var } S, R\text{: } \textbf{array } 0\text{. .}\infty \textbf{ of } \textit{message}$$

Two index variables $s$ and $r$

$$\textbf{var } s, r\text{: } 0\text{. .}\infty$$

initialized to zero, define the number of messages sent and received at any instant in time:

$s > 0$ **implies** $S(1)$ to $S(s)$ have been sent in that order

$r > 0$ **implies** $R(1)$ to $R(r)$ have been received in that order

Our requirements are the following:

(1) The number of messages received cannot exceed the number of messages sent

$$0 \leqslant r \leqslant s$$

(2) The number of messages sent, but not yet received, cannot exceed the buffer capacity *max*

$$0 \leqslant s - r \leqslant max$$

(3) Messages must be received exactly as they are sent

$$\textbf{for } i: 1 . . r \ (R(i) = S(i))$$

So, all in all, we have the following *communication invariant*:

$$0 \leqslant r \leqslant s \leqslant r + max \ \& \\ \textbf{for } i: 1 . . r \ (R(i) = S(i))$$

I suggest the following notation for a language construct which satisfies this requirement:

**var** $B$: **buffer** *max* **of** $T$

It declares a message buffer $B$, which can transmit messages of type $T$ between concurrent processes. The buffer capacity is defined by an integer constant, *max*.

Messages are sent and received by means of the following standard procedures:

$$send(M, B) \qquad receive(M, B)$$

where $M$ is a variable of type $T$.

Since *send* and *receive* refer to a common variable $B$, we require that these operations exclude each other in time. They are critical regions with respect to the buffer used.

It is worth pointing out that with the synchronizing rules defined, *a sender and a receiver cannot be deadlocked with respect to a single message buffer*. A sender can only be delayed when a buffer is full

$$s = r + max$$

and a receiver can only be delayed when a buffer is empty

$$s = r$$

A situation in which they are both delayed with respect to the same buffer is therefore impossible if the buffer has a non-zero capacity $max > 0$.

It is also interesting to notice that a message buffer (if properly used) is unconditionally functional in the sense defined in Section 3.2.5.

If we observe a message sequence $X$ going into a buffer, we expect that a message sequence $Y = X$ will eventually come out of it. And if we observe two input sequences, $X$ and $X'$, where the former is contained in the latter, then we have trivially that

$$X \leqslant X' \text{ implies } Y \leqslant Y'$$

So a message buffer satisfies the consistency requirement *if all messages sent are eventually received.* And since *send* and *receive* cannot take place at the same time, it takes a finite time for a message to pass through the buffer. So the dependency requirement is also satisfied.

From the closure property we conclude that *a set of unconditionally functional processes connected only by message buffers is unconditionally functional as a whole, provided there are only one sender and one receiver for each buffer, and all messages sent are eventually received.*

It is quite possible, with the synchronizing rules defined here, to connect *several senders and receivers* to a single buffer, as shown in Fig. 3.16. But when this is done, the input to the buffer is a time-dependent merging of messages from $m$ different processes, and the output is a time-dependent splitting of messages to $n$ different receivers. In that case, there is no functional relationship between the output of each producer and the input of each consumer.

The communication primitives, *send* and *receive*, as proposed here will *transmit messages by value*; that is, by copying them first from a sender variable $M$ into a buffer $B$, and then from $B$ into a receiver variable $M'$. This is only practical for *small messages.*

For *larger messages*, the data structures and primitives must be defined such that messages are *transmitted by reference*, that is; by copying an address from one process to another. But in order to satisfy the

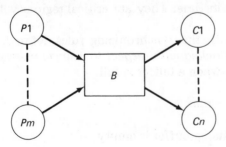

Fig. 3.16 A message buffer $B$ which connects $m$ producers and $n$ consumers.

communication invariant, such a language construct must ensure that at most one process at a time can refer to a message variable.

In the following, I will consider the simplest possible form of process communication—the exchange of timing signals.

### 3.4.2. Semaphores

In some cases, a process is only interested in receiving a *timing signal* from another process when a certain event has occurred. But apart from that, no other exchange of data is required.

An example is Algorithm 3.3 where each process wishes to be delayed until a certain interval of time has elapsed.

This can be regarded as a special case of process communication in which an *empty message* is sent each time a certain event occurs. Since the messages are empty (and therefore indistinguishable), it is sufficient to *count* them. The buffer is therefore reduced to a single, non-negative integer, which defines the number of signals sent, but not yet received.

Such a synchronizing variable is called a *semaphore*. It was first proposed and investigated by Scholten and Dijkstra. A semaphore variable $v$ will be declared as follows:

$$\textbf{var } v: semaphore$$

The corresponding *send* and *receive* primitives will be called

$$signal(v) \qquad wait(v)$$

(Dijkstra originally called them $V$ and $P$.)

Since a semaphore is a common variable for its senders and receivers, we must require that *signal* and *wait* operations on the same semaphore exclude each other in time. They are critical regions with respect to the semaphore.

Following Habermann (1972), a semaphore $v$ will be characterized by two integer components:

$s(v)$        the number of signals sent

$r(v)$        the number of signals received

Initially, $s(v) = r(v) = 0$.

The communication invariant defined in the previous section now becomes:

$$0 \leqslant r(v) \leqslant s(v) \leqslant r(v) + max(integer)$$

It means that: (1) a process can only send or receive some or no signals; (2) signals cannot be received faster than they are sent; and (3) a semaphore can only count to the upper limit of integers set by a given machine.

It is useful to permit an *initial assignment* to a semaphore before process communication begins. So we will introduce a third semaphore component:

$$c(v) \qquad \text{the number of initial signals}$$

and permit an assignment:

$$v := c$$

to be made outside concurrent statements. But within concurrent statements, the only operations permitted on a semaphore $v$ are still *signal* and *wait*.

The *semaphore invariant* now becomes

$$0 \leqslant r(v) \leqslant s(v) + c(v) \leqslant r(v) + max(integer)$$

In most computers, the range of integers is much larger than the number of unconsumed signals that can occur in practice. For example, in a computer with 24-bit words, $max(integer) = 8388607$. We will therefore ignore this constraint in the following and assume that an implementation treats *semaphore overflow* as a programming error.

The *synchronizing rules* of semaphores are the following:

(1) If the operation *wait* $(v)$ is started at a time when $r(v) < s(v) + c(v)$, then $r(v)$ is increased by one and the receiver continues; but if $r(v) = s(v) + c(v)$, then the receiver is delayed in a *process queue* associated with the semaphore $v$.

(2) The operation *signal* $(v)$ increases $s(v)$ by one; if one or more processes are waiting in the queue associated with the semaphore $v$, then one of them is selected and enabled to continue, and $r(v)$ is increased by one. The scheduling of waiting processes must be fair (see Section 3.3.3).

A *critical region*

$$\textbf{var } R: \textbf{shared } T;$$
$$\textbf{region } R \textbf{ do } S;$$

can be implemented by associating a semaphore *mutex*, initialized to one, with the shared variable $R$ and then surrounding the statement $S$ by a pair of *wait* and *signal* operations as shown in Algorithm 3.4.

*ALGORITHM 3.4  Mutual Exclusion Implemented With Semaphores*

```
var R: record content: T; mutex: semaphore end
begin
  with R do mutex := 1;
  cobegin
    with R do
    begin wait(mutex); S1; signal(mutex) end
      . . .
    with R do
    begin wait(mutex); Sn; signal(mutex) end
      . . .
  coend
end
```

To see that this implementation is correct, observe the following: Since the processes always execute a *wait* operation before a *signal* operation on *mutex*, we have

$$0 \leqslant s(mutex) \leqslant r(mutex)$$

When this is combined with the semaphore invariant, the result is

$$0 \leqslant s(mutex) \leqslant r(mutex) \leqslant s(mutex) + 1$$

From the structure of Algorithm 3.4, it is evident that the number of processes $n$ that are inside their critical regions at a given time are those which have passed a *wait* operation at the beginning of these regions, but have not as yet passed a corresponding *signal* operation at the end of the regions. So

$$n(mutex) = r(mutex) - s(mutex)$$

This in turn means that

$$0 \leqslant n(mutex) \leqslant 1$$

In other words, one process at most can be inside its critical region at any time. When no processes are inside their critical regions, we have

$$n(mutex) = 0$$

or

$$r(mutex) = s(mutex)$$

Since $r(mutex) < s(mutex) + 1$, in this situation another process can complete a *wait* operation and enter its critical region immediately.

So the correctness criteria for critical regions are satisfied provided each of the statements $S1$ to $Sn$ terminates.

It is an amusing paradox of critical regions that, in order to implement one, we must appeal to the existence of simpler critical regions (namely, *wait* and *signal*). In the next chapter, which explains an implementation of *wait* and *signal*, I shall appeal to the existence of a *storage arbiter*—a hardware implementation of still simpler critical regions, and so on, ad infinitum. The buck ends at the atomic level, where nuclear states are known to be discrete and mutually exclusive.

At this stage, it is tempting to conclude that there is no need for extending a programming language with a construct for critical regions and common variables. The problem can evidently be solved by *wait* and *signal* operations on semaphores.

This conclusion is indeed valid in a world where programs are known to be correct with absolute certainty. But in practice it is untenable. The purpose of the language construct

**var** $v$: **shared** $T$;
**region** $v$ **do** $S$;

is to enable a compiler to *distinguish between disjoint and interacting processes, and check that common variables are used only within critical regions.*

If we replace this structured notation with semaphores, this will have grave consequences:

(1) Since a semaphore can be used to solve arbitrary synchronizing problems, a compiler cannot conclude that a pair of *wait* and *signal* operations on a given semaphore initialized to one delimits a critical region, nor that a missing member of such a pair is an error. A compiler will also be unaware of the correspondence between a semaphore and the common variable it protects. In short, a compiler cannot give the programmer any assistance whatsoever in establishing critical regions correctly.

(2) Since a compiler is unable to recognize critical regions, it cannot make the distinction between critical regions and disjoint processes. Consequently, it must permit the use of common variables everywhere. So a compiler can no longer give the programmer any assistance in avoiding time-dependent errors in supposedly disjoint processes.

The horrors that this leads to have already been demonstrated (see Section 3.2.2).

As an example of the first problem, consider the programmer who by mistake writes the following:

$$wait(mutex); \qquad signal(mutex);$$
$$S; \qquad\qquad S;$$
$$wait(mutex); \qquad wait(mutex);$$

In the left example, the program will be deadlocked at the end of the "critical" region; in the right example, the program will sometimes permit 3 processes to be inside a "critical" region simultaneously.

The advantage of language constructs is that their correctness can be

**ALGORITHM 3.5**  *Periodic Scheduling of Concurrent Processes*

```
var    schedule: array 1. .n of
                    record deadline, interval: integer end
       start: array 1. .n of semaphore;
       timer: semaphore;
       task: 1. .n; t: integer;
begin
  timer:= 0; initialize(schedule, start);
  cobegin
    repeat "hardware timer"
      t:= interval desired;
      while t > 0 do t:= t -1;
      signal(timer);
    forever

    repeat "scheduler"
      wait(timer);
      for every task do
      with schedule(task) do
      begin
        deadline:= deadline - 1;
        if deadline ≤ 0 then
        begin
          deadline:= interval;
          signal(start(task));
        end
      end
    forever

    repeat "task i"
      wait(start(i));
      perform task;
    forever
  coend
end
```

established once and for all when the compiler is tested. The alternative is to test each critical region separately in all user programs!

It is reasonable to use semaphores in a compiler to implement critical regions. But at higher levels of programming, the main applicability of semaphores is in situations in which processes exchange only timing signals. This is the concept that semaphores represent in a direct, natural manner.

As an example, let us again consider the problem of scheduling a number of processes periodically in a real-time system. In Algorithm 3.3, the periodic scheduling was handled by a standard procedure that delays a process until a certain interval of time has elapsed. We now want to show how this delay can be implemented in terms of semaphores.

For each *task process*, we introduce a record defining the time interval between two successive executions (called the *interval*), the time interval until its next execution (called the *deadline*), and a semaphore on which the process can wait until its next execution *starts*.

The time schedule of all tasks is scanned by a central *scheduling process* every second: In each cycle, the scheduler decreases all deadlines by one and sends a start signal to the relevant tasks.

The scheduling process in turn receives a signal from a *hardware timer* every second.

This scheme is shown in Algorithm 3.5.

### 3.4.3. Conditional Critical Regions

The synchronizing tools introduced so far:

> critical regions
> message buffers
> semaphores

are simple and efficient tools for delaying a process until a special condition holds:

> mutual exclusion
> message available (or buffer element available)
> signal available

We will now study a more general synchronizing tool which enables a process to wait until an *arbitrary condition* holds.

For this purpose I propose a synchronizing primitive *await*, which delays a process until the components of a shared variable $v$ satisfy a condition $B$:

**var** $v$: **shared** T
**region** $v$ **do**
**begin** ... **await** $B$; ... **end**

The *await* primitive must be textually enclosed by a critical region associated with the variable $v$. If critical regions are nested, the synchronizing condition $B$ is associated with the innermost enclosing region.

The shared variable $v$ can be of an arbitrary type $T$. The synchronizing condition $B$ is an arbitrary boolean expression which can refer to components of $v$.

The *await* primitive can for example be used to implement *conditional critical regions* of the form proposed by Hoare (1971b):

| *"Consumer"* | *"Producer"* |
|---|---|
| **region** $v$ **do** | **region** $v$ **do** $S2$ |
| **begin await** $B$; $S1$ **end** | |

Two processes, called the *consumer* and the *producer*, cooperate on a common task. The consumer wishes to enter a critical region and operate on a shared variable $v$ by a statement $S1$ when a certain relationship $B$ holds among the components of $v$. The producer enters a critical region unconditionally and changes $v$ by a statement $S2$ to make $B$ hold.

I will use this example and Fig. 3.17 to explain the implementation of critical regions and the *await* primitive. When a process such as the consumer above wishes to enter a critical region, it enters a *main queue, Qv,* associated with the shared variable $v$. From this queue, the processes enter

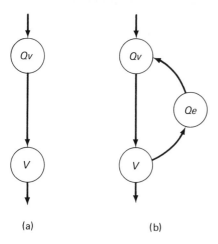

(a)                    (b)

**Fig. 3.17** Scheduling of (a) simple and (b) conditional critical regions $V$ by means of process queues $Qv$ and $Qe$.

their critical regions one at a time to ensure mutual exclusion of operations on $v$.

After entering its critical region, the consumer inspects the shared variable $v$ to determine whether it satisfies the condition $B$: In that case, the consumer completes its critical region by executing the statement $S1$; otherwise, the process leaves its critical region *temporarily* and joins an *event queue*, $Qe$, associated with the shared variable.

Other processes can now enter their critical regions through the main queue, $Qv$. These processes may either complete their critical regions unconditionally or decide to *await* the holding of an arbitrary condition on variable $v$. If their conditions are not satisfied, they all enter the same event queue, $Qe$.

When another process such as the previous producer changes the shared variable $v$ by a statement $S2$ inside a critical region, it is possible that one or more of the conditions expected by processes in the event queue, $Qe$, will be satisfied. Consequently, when a critical region has been successfully completed, all processes in the event queue, $Qe$, are transferred to the main queue, $Qv$, to permit them to *reenter* their critical regions and inspect the shared variable $v$ again.

It is possible that a *consumer* will be transferred in vain between the main queue and the event queue several times before its condition $B$ holds. But this can only occur as frequently as *producers* change the shared variable. This controlled amount of *busy waiting* is the price we pay for the conceptual simplicity achieved by using arbitrary boolean expressions as synchronizing conditions.

In the case of simple critical regions, we expect that all operations on a shared variable maintain an *invariant I* (see Section 3.3.4). Within conditional critical regions, we must also require that the desired invariant is satisfied before an *await* statement is executed. When the waiting cycle of a consumer terminates, the *assertion B & I* holds.

In the following, we will solve two synchronizing problems using first critical regions and semaphores, and then conditional critical regions. This will enable us to make a comparison of these synchronizing concepts.

### 3.4.4. An Example: Message Buffers

We will implement the message buffer defined in Section 3.4.1 and shown in Fig. 3.18.

The buffer consists of a finite number of identical elements arranged in a *circle*. The circle consists of a sequence of *empty* elements that can be filled by a *producer* and a sequence of *full* elements that can be emptied by a *consumer*. The producer and consumer refer to empty and full elements by means of two *pointers*, $p$ and $c$. During a computation, both pointers move clockwise around the circle without overtaking each other.

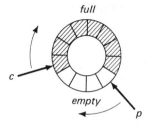

*full*

*c*

*empty*

*p*

**Fig. 3.18** A cyclical message buffer with a producer pointer $p$ and a consumer pointer $c$.

The sequence of messages received

$$R(1), R(2), \ldots , R(r)$$

must be contained in the sequence of messages sent

$$S(1), S(2), \ldots , S(s)$$

Let the buffer and its pointers be declared as follows:

$$buffer: \textbf{array } 0..max-1 \textbf{ of } T;$$
$$p, c: 0..max-1;$$

The desired effect is achieved if the following rules are observed:

(1) During a computation, *pointers* $p$ and $c$ must enumerate the same sequence of buffer elements:

| | | |
|---|---|---|
| $buffer(0):=$ | $S(1);$ | $R(1):= buffer(0);$ |
| $buffer(1):=$ | $S(2);$ | $R(2):= buffer(1);$ |
| . . . . . | | . . . . . |
| $buffer(p-1 \textbf{ mod } max):= S(s);$ | | $R(r):= buffer(c-1 \textbf{ mod } max);$ |

(2) The receiver must not *empty* an element until it has been sent:

$$0 \leqslant r < s$$

(3) The sender must not *fill* an element until it has been received:

$$0 \leqslant s - r < max$$

The solution that uses conditional critical regions is Algorithm 3.6. Initially, pointers $p$ and $c$ are equal and they are moved by the same function $p+1 \textbf{ mod } max$ and $c+1 \textbf{ mod } max$. So, the pointers enumerate the same sequence of buffer elements.

*ALGORITHM 3.6 Process Communication With Conditional Critical Regions*

```
type B = shared record
                buffer: array 0. .max-1 of T;
                p, c: 0. .max-1;
                full: 0. .max;
          end
"Initially p = c = full = 0"

procedure send(m: T; var b: B);
region b do
begin
  await full < max;
  buffer(p):= m;
  p:= (p + 1) mod max;
  full:= full + 1;
end

procedure receive(var m: T; b: B);
region b do
begin
  await full > 0;
  m:= buffer(c);
  c:= (c + 1) mod max;
  full:= full - 1;
end
```

The variable *full* is initially zero. It is increased by one after each *send* and decreased by one after each *receive*. So

$$full = s - r$$

Receiving is only done when $full > 0$ or $s > r$; sending is only done when $full < max$ or $s - r < max$. The solution is therefore correct.

Now, let us solve the same problem with simple critical regions and semaphores: We will use the pointers $p$ and $c$ exactly as before—so condition 1 is still satisfied.

The delay of the receiver will be controlled by a semaphore *full* in the following way:

| | |
|---|---|
| initially: | *full*:= 0 |
| before receive: | *wait(full)* |
| after send: | *signal(full)* |

When the semaphore is used in this way, we evidently have

$$0 \leqslant r \leqslant \textit{number of waits(full)} \ \&$$

$$0 \leqslant \textit{number of signals(full)} \leqslant s$$

The semaphore invariant defined in Section 3.4.2 ensures that, when the initial number of *full* signals has been consumed by *wait* operations, further *wait* operations cannot be completed faster than the corresponding *signal* operations:

$$\textit{number of waits(full)} \leqslant \textit{number of signals(full)} + 0$$

Immediately before a *wait* operation is completed, the stronger condition

$$\textit{number of waits(full)} < \textit{number of signals(full)} + 0$$

holds.

From this we conclude that before a message is received, the condition

$$0 \leqslant r < s$$

holds.

We have chosen to represent the condition $r < s$ by the semaphore *full*. But since timing signals are merely indistinguishable boolean events, we cannot use the same semaphore to represent the other condition, $s - r < max$, which controls sending.

So we must introduce another semaphore, *empty*, and use it as follows:

|  |  |
|---|---|
| initially: | $\textit{empty} := \textit{max}$ |
| before send: | $\textit{wait(empty)}$ |
| after receive: | $\textit{signal(empty)}$ |

By similar reasoning, we can show that before sending the following holds:

$$0 \leqslant s \leqslant \textit{number of waits(empty)} \ \&$$

$$0 \leqslant \textit{number of signals(empty)} \leqslant r \ \&$$

$$\textit{number of waits(empty)} < \textit{number of signals(empty)} + \textit{max}$$

or

$$0 \leqslant s < r + \textit{max}$$

The complete solution is Algorithm 3.7.

*ALGORITHM 3.7  Process Communication With Semaphores*

```
type B = record
            v: shared record
                      buffer: array 0. .max-1 of T;
                      p, c: 0. .max-1;
                   end
          full, empty: semaphore;
        end
"Initially p = c = full = 0 & empty = max"

procedure send(m: T; var b: B);
begin
  with b do
  begin
    wait(empty);
    region v do
    begin
      buffer(p):= m;
      p:= (p + 1) mod max;
    end
    signal(full);
  end
end

procedure receive(var m: T; b: B);
begin
  with b do
  begin
    wait(full);
    region v do
    begin
      m:= buffer(c);
      c:= (c +1) mod max;
    end
    signal(empty);
  end
end
```

This exercise has already given a good indication of the difference between conditional critical regions and semaphores:

(1) A semaphore can only transmit indistinguishable timing signals; it can therefore only be used to count the number of times a *specific event* has occurred in one process without being detected by another process.

Consequently, *it is necessary to associate a semaphore with each synchronizing condition.*

The first algorithm with conditional critical regions uses two synchronizing conditions

$$full > 0 \qquad full < max$$

but only one variable *full.*

In the second algorithm, these conditions are represented by two semaphore variables

$$full \qquad empty$$

(2) Notice also that *within conditional critical regions, the program text shows directly the condition under which a region is executed.* But in the second algorithm, *the association between a semaphore and a synchronizing condition exists only in the mind of the programmer.* He cannot deduct from the statement

$$wait(empty)$$

that *full < max* before sending without examining the rest of the program and discovering that *full < max* when

$$signal(empty)$$

is executed after receiving! *When semaphores are used to represent general scheduling conditions, these conditions can only be deduced from the program text in the most indirect manner.*

One can also explain the difficulty with semaphores in the following way: If a process decided to *wait* on a semaphore inside a critical region, it would be impossible for another process to enter its critical region and wake up the former process. This is the reason that the *wait operations* in Algorithm 3.7 are executed *outside the critical regions.*

However, it is dangerous to separate a synchronizing condition from a successive critical region. The danger is that another process may enter its critical region first and make the condition *false* again. If we *split critical regions* in this way, we must introduce additional variables to represent intermediate states of the form "I expect condition *B* to hold when I enter my critical region." So, while a single variable *full* is sufficient in Algorithm 3.6, we need two variables, *full* and *empty*, in Algorithm 3.7.

The elegance of Algorithm 3.6 makes it tempting to suggest that the language constructs for message buffers suggested in Section 3.4.1 can be replaced by conditional critical regions and common variables. But I wish to point out that the arguments made earlier in favor of the language construct for simple critical regions can also be made for message buffers.

In Section 3.4.1, we found that a system consisting of processes connected only by buffers can be made functional as a whole. But this is only true if the *send* and *receive* operations are implemented correctly and if they are the only operations on the buffers. A compiler is unable to recognize the data structure *B* in Algorithm 3.6 as a message buffer and check that it is used correctly. So when message buffers are used frequently, it may well be worth including them as a primitive concept in a programming language.

We now proceed to the next problem, which is due to Courtois, Heymans, and Parnas (1971).

### 3.4.5. An Example: Readers and Writers

*Problem Definition*

Two kinds of concurrent processes, called *readers* and *writers*, share a single resource. The readers can use the resource simultaneously, but each writer must have exclusive access to it. When a writer is ready to use the resource, it should be enabled to do so as soon as possible.

The first step is to introduce a terminology which enables us to talk about the problem in a meaningful manner. A process must declare its wish to use the resource, and, since the resource may be occupied at that moment, the process must then be prepared to wait for it. A process must also indicate when it has completed its use of the resource.

So any solution to this kind of resource allocation problem must be of the following nature:

> *request resource*;
> *use resource*;
> *release resource*;

All processes must go through such a sequence of events, and I would expect the solution to be symmetrical with respect to the readers and writers. To simplify matters, I will start by solving a simpler problem in which I do not bother to ensure that the writers exclude one another, but only that they exclude all readers, and vice versa. They are thus more symmetrical with the readers.

A process is called *active* from the moment it has requested the resource until it has released the resource again. A process is called *running* from the moment it has been granted permission to use the resource until it has released the resource again.

The state of the system can be characterized by four integers, all initialized to zero:

| | |
|---|---|
| *ar* | the number of active readers |
| *rr* | the number of running readers |
| *aw* | the number of active writers |
| *rw* | the number of running writers |

## Correctness Criteria

A solution to the simplified problem is correct if the following criteria are satisfied:

(1) *Scheduling of waiting processes*: Readers can use the resource simultaneously and so can writers, but the number of running processes cannot exceed the number of active processes:

$$0 \leqslant rr \leqslant ar \ \& \ 0 \leqslant rw \leqslant aw$$

This invariant will be called $W$.

(2) *Mutual exclusion of running processes*: Readers and writers cannot use the resource at the same time:

$$\textbf{not } (rr > 0 \ \& \ rw > 0)$$

This invariant will be called $X$.

(3) *No deadlock of active processes*: When no processes are running, active processes can start using the resource within a finite time:

$$(rr = 0 \ \& \ rw = 0) \ \& \ (ar > 0 \text{ or } aw > 0) \textbf{ implies}$$
$$(rr > 0 \text{ or } rw > 0) \textit{ within a finite time}$$

(4) *Writers have priority over readers*: The requirement of mutual exclusion means that the resource can only be granted to an active writer when there are no running readers ($rr = 0$). To give priority to writers, we make the slightly stronger condition that the resource can only be granted to an active reader when there are no active writers ($aw = 0$).

## Solution With Semaphores

This time we will solve the problem first by means of simple critical regions and semaphores. Two semaphores, called *reading* and *writing*, enable the readers and writers to wait for the resource. They are both initialized to zero. The solution is Algorithm 3.8.

*ALGORITHM 3.8  The Readers and Writers Problem Solved With Semaphores*

```
type T = record ar, rr, aw, rw: integer end

var v: shared T; reading, writing: semaphore;

"Initially ar = rr = aw = rw = reading = writing = 0"


cobegin
  begin "reader"
    region v do
    begin
      ar := ar + 1;
      grant reading(v, reading);
    end
    wait(reading);
    read;
    region v do
    begin
      rr := rr - 1;
      ar := ar - 1;
      grant writing(v, writing);
    end
    . . .
  end

  begin "writer"
    region v do
    begin
      aw := aw + 1;
      grant writing(v, writing);
    end
    wait(writing);
    write;
    region v do
    begin
      rw := rw - 1;
      aw := aw - 1;
      grant reading(v, reading);
    end
    . . .
  end
  . . .
coend
```

A reader indicates that it is active by increasing $ar$ by one. It then calls a procedure, *grant reading*, which examines whether the resource can be granted for reading immediately. Then the reader *waits* until it can use the resource. Finally, it leaves the running and active states by decreasing $rr$ and $ar$ by one and calls another procedure, *grant writing*, which determines whether the resource should now be granted to the writers. The behavior of a writer is quite symmetrical.

The scheduling procedures, *grant reading* and *grant writing*, are defined by Algorithm 3.9.


*ALGORITHM 3.9   The Readers and Writers Problem (cont.)*

```
procedure grant reading(var v: T; reading: semaphore);
begin
  with v do
  if aw = 0 then
  while rr < ar do
  begin
    rr:= rr + 1;
    signal(reading);
  end
end

procedure grant writing(var v: T; writing: semaphore);
begin
  with v do
  if rr = 0 then
  while rw < aw do
  begin
    rw:= rw + 1;
    signal(writing);
  end
end
```

The resource can be granted to all active readers ($rr = ar$) provided no writers are active ($aw = 0$). And it can be granted to all active writers ($rw = aw$) provided no readers are running ($rr = 0$).

I will now outline a correctness proof of this solution. The arguments are explained informally to make them easy to understand, but a purist will not find it difficult to restate them formally as assertions directly in the program text.

Let us first verify that the components of variable $v$ have the *meaning* intended. Since $ar$ and $aw$ are increased by one for each request and decreased by one for each release made by readers and writers, respectively, we immediately conclude that they have the following meanings:

$$ar = number\ of\ active\ readers$$

$$aw = number\ of\ active\ writers$$

It is a little more difficult to see the meanings of the variables $rr$ and $rw$. Consider for example $rr$: It is increased by one for each *signal* on the semaphore *reading* and decreased by one for each release made by a reader, so:

$$rr = number\ of\ signals(reading) - number\ of\ releases\ made\ by\ readers$$

From the program structure, it is also clear that the running readers are those which have been enabled to complete a *wait* on the semaphore *reading* minus those which have released the resource again. So

> *number of running readers =*
>
> > *number of readers which can or has passed wait(reading) –*
> >
> > *number of releases made by readers*

The semaphore invariant ensures that

> *number of readers which can or has passed wait(reading) =*
>
> > *number of signals(reading)*

So we finally conclude that

$$rr = number\ of\ running\ readers$$

and similarly for writers that

$$rw = number\ of\ running\ writers$$

Consider now correctness criteria 1 and 2. We assume that the assertions $W$ and $X$ hold immediately before a request by a reader. This is trivially true after initialization when

$$0 = rr = ar\ \&\ 0 = rw = aw$$

The increase of $ar$ by one inside a request does not change the validity of $W$ and $X$, so we have:

```
"reader request"
region v do
begin "W & X"
        ar:= ar + 1;                                                    (cont.)
```

> "W & X"
> grant reading(v, reading);
> "?"

**end**

The procedure *grant reading* either does nothing (when $aw \neq 0$ or $rr = ar$), in which case $W$ and $X$ still hold, or it increases the number of running readers by one until

$$0 < rr = ar \ \& \ 0 = rw = aw$$

holds. This implies that $W$ and $X$ still hold:

### ? implies W & X

Consider now a reader release. A release is only made by a running process, so we have $rr > 0$ immediately before. Assuming that $W$ and $X$ also hold initially, we have

> "reader release"
> **region** $v$ **do**
> **begin** "W & X & rr > 0"
>     $rr := rr - 1$;
>     $ar := ar - 1$;
>     "??"
>     grant writing(v, writing);
>     "???"
> **end**

Now $W \ \& \ X \ \& \ rr > 0$ is equivalent to $0 < rr \leqslant ar \ \& \ 0 = rw \leqslant aw$ so

$$?? \equiv 0 \leqslant rr \leqslant ar \ \& \ 0 = rw \leqslant aw$$

which in turn implies $W$ & $X$.

The procedure *grant writing* either does nothing (when $rr \neq 0$ or $rw = aw$), in which case $W$ and $X$ still hold, or it increases the number of running writers by one until

$$0 = rr \leqslant ar \ \& \ 0 < rw = aw$$

holds. This implies that $W$ and $X$ still hold:

### ??? implies W & X

By similar arguments, you can show that the invariance of $W$ and $X$ is maintained by a writer request and release.

The next thing we must show is the absence of deadlocks as required by correctness criterion 3. When the resource is not used by any readers, it can be shared by all active writers; and when the resource is neither used nor desired by any writers, it can be shared by all active readers. It is not difficult to show that this invariant

$$D \equiv (rr = 0 \textbf{ implies } rw = aw) \, \&$$

$$(aw = 0 \textbf{ implies } rr = ar)$$

is maintained by the request and release operations defined by Algorithms 3.8 and 3.9.

If we assume that the resource is idle

$$I \equiv rr = 0 \, \& \, rw = 0$$

then we find that

$$I \, \& \, D \textbf{ implies } aw = rw = 0$$

and also that

$$I \, \& \, D \, \& \, aw = 0 \textbf{ implies } ar = rr = 0$$

In other words, a situation in which no process uses the resource ($rr = 0$ & $rw = 0$) is one in which no process desires to do so ($ar = 0$ & $aw = 0$).

This completes the arguments for the correctness of the first solution to the readers and writers problem. You will appreciate that the proof will be far more tedious if it is formalized in detail. Although it is a well-structured program and quite typical of the way in which semaphores can be used, it is not the sort of program which is self-evident at first glance. (Why, for example, need a reader that releases the resource only worry about the scheduling of writers and not about that of other readers?)

*Solution with Conditional Critical Regions*

It is tempting to conclude that the complexity of the previous solution is caused by the intricate scheduling rules of readers and writers. But this is not true. For by using conditional critical regions, it is possible to write down in a few lines a solution so simple that its correctness is almost self-evident. This is Algorithm 3.10.

It is easy to see that

$$rr = number\ of\ running\ readers$$

$$aw = number\ of\ active\ writers$$

*ALGORITHM 3.10  The Readers and Writers Problem Solved
With Conditional Critical Regions*

> **var** $v$: **shared record** $rr, aw$: *integer* **end**
>
> *"Initially rr = aw = 0"*
>
> **cobegin**
>   **begin** *"reader"*
>     **region** $v$ **do**
>     **begin await** $aw = 0; rr := rr + 1$ **end**
>     *read;*
>     **region** $v$ **do** $rr := rr - 1;$
>     . . .
>   **end**
>   **begin** *"writer"*
>     **region** $v$ **do**
>     **begin** $aw := aw + 1;$ **await** $rr = 0$ **end**
>     *write;*
>     **region** $v$ **do** $aw := aw - 1;$
>     . . .
>   **end**
>   . . .
>   **coend**

The variables $ar$ and $rw$ are not used in this program, so we can simply define that these identifiers denote the following:

$$ar = number\ of\ active\ readers$$

$$rw = number\ of\ running\ writers$$

This establishes the meanings of the variables.

The program text also shows that each active process goes through a waiting and running state in that order. Consequently

$$0 \leqslant running\ processes \leqslant running\ and\ waiting\ processes$$

This means that invariant $W$ holds.

Assuming that $W$ and $X$ hold before a reader request, we find

> **region** $v$ **do**
> **begin** *"W & X"*
>     **await** $aw = 0;$
>     *"W & X & aw = 0"*
>     $rr := rr + 1;$
>     *"?"*
> **end**

Now $W$ & $aw$ = 0 implies $rw$ = 0. After the increase of $rr$, we still have $rw$ = 0, which implies that $X$ holds. $W$ has already been shown to be maintained by all requests and releases, so

$$? \text{ implies } W \text{ \& } X$$

And before a reader release, we have

region $v$ do
"$W$ & $X$ & $rr > 0$" $rr := rr - 1$ "??";

Since $X$ & $rr > 0$ implies $rw$ = 0, it is evident that $X$ also holds after the release, and again $W$ is also maintained.

By similar simple arguments, it can be shown that the invariance of $W$ and $X$ is maintained by the writers.

To see that a deadlock cannot occur, consider the idle resource state $rr$ = 0 & $rw$ = 0. If there are active writers, they will be able to run within a finite time since $rr$ = 0. On the other hand, if there are no active writers, but only active readers, the readers will be able to run within a finite time since $aw$ = 0.

The *original problem* differs only from the simplified one by requiring exclusive access by writers to the resource. Both solutions can be adapted immediately to this requirement by forcing the running writers to use the resource inside another critical region

var $w$: shared *boolean*;
. . . . .
region $w$ do *write*;

This solution shows that the mutual exclusion of writers is completely irrelevant to the readers; it can be settled among the writers themselves.


## 3.4.6. A Comparison of Tools

It is time now to compare the two synchronizing methods and consider why the use of semaphores introduces so much complexity for problems of the previous type.

The root of the matter is that any synchronizing concept is an ideal, direct means of expression for a particular type of process interaction, but it fails miserably when applied to a totally different type of interaction.

The conditional critical region

region $v$ do begin await $B$; $S$ end

is the most natural tool in a situation where a process wishes to wait until the components of a shared data structure satisfy a certain condition.

Likewise, a *wait* operation on a semaphore is the most direct way of expressing the wish to wait until a timing signal has been produced.

The difficulty is that the former situation is far more common in realistic systems, and it can only be expressed by means of simple critical regions and semaphores in a most indirect and obscure manner. The programmer must associate a semaphore with each possible scheduling condition $B$ and express himself as follows:

> **region** $v$ **do**
> **if** $B$ **then begin** $S$; *signal(sem)* **end**
>      **else** *indicate request(q)*;
> *wait(sem)*;

And all other processes which might make condition $B$ true inside their own critical regions, such as the following:

> **region** $v$ **do** $R$

must now take responsibility for activating the delayed processes as follows:

> **region** $v$ **do**
> **begin**
>   $R$;
>   **if** $B$ & *request(q)* **then**
>   **begin**
>     *remove request(q)*;
>     $S$; *signal(sem)*;
>   **end**
> **end**

When this indirect way of expression is used to control resources, the programmer is forced to separate the request, grant, and acquisition of resources and introduce additional variables to represent the intermediate states "resource requested, but not yet granted" and "resource granted, but not yet acquired." The former state is represented by the condition *request(q)* and the latter by the relation *waits(sem)* $<$ *signals(sem)*.

To make matters worse, the use of semaphores forces the programmer to make very strong logical connections among otherwise independent processes: Readers must be prepared to schedule writers, and vice versa. A *wait* operation on a semaphore represents a synchronizing condition $B$, which is stated elsewhere in the program at points where the corresponding *signal* operations are carried out. So the programmer must now examine not only the preceding *request* operation, but also all other *release* operations to verify that a *signal* operation is performed only when condition $B$ holds and one or more processes are waiting for it.

### 3.4.7. Event Queues

The conceptual simplicity of simple and conditional critical regions is achieved by ignoring details of scheduling: The programmer is unaware of the sequence in which waiting processes enter critical regions and access shared resources. This assumption is justified for processes that are so *loosely connected* that simultaneous requests for the same resources rarely occur.

But in most computer installations, *resources are heavily used* by a large group of users. In these situations, operating systems must be able to *control the scheduling of resources* explicitly among competing processes.

The scheduling of heavily-used resources can be controlled by associating a synchronizing variable with each process and maintaining explicit queues of requests.

Since our purpose is not to study data structures, I will simply declare a *queue* of elements of type $T$ as follows:

$$\textbf{var } q \colon \textbf{queue of } T$$

and postulate that the standard procedures

$$enter(t, q) \qquad remove(t, q)$$

enters and removes an element $t$ of type $T$ from a given queue $q$ according to the scheduling policy desired.

The boolean function

$$empty(q)$$

determines whether or not a given queue $q$ is empty.

A *queue* differs from a *sequence* in that the elements of the former are not necessarily removed in the same order in which they are entered.

As an example of completely controlled resource allocation, we will solve the following problem: A number of processes share a pool of equivalent resources. When resources are *available*, a process can *acquire* one immediately; otherwise, it must enter a *request* and wait until a resource is *granted* to it.

Algorithm 3.11 is an attempt to solve this problem by means of

*ALGORITHM 3.11   Scheduling of Heavily Used Resources*
                 *With Conditional Critical Regions*

```
type P = 1. .number of processes;
     R = 1. .number of resources;
var v: shared record
               available: sequence of R;
               requests: queue of P;
               turn: array P of boolean;
           end

procedure reserve(process: P; var resource: R);
region v do
begin
  while empty(available) do
  begin
    enter(process, requests);
    turn(process):= false;
    await turn(process);
  end
  get(resource, available);
end

procedure release(resource: R);
var process: P;
region v do
begin
  put(resource, available);
  if not empty(requests) then
  begin
    remove(process, requests);
    turn(process):= true;
  end
end
```

conditional critical regions. Available resources are defined by a sequence of indices of type $R$. Pending requests are defined by a queue of indices of type $P$. A resource unit is granted to process number $i$ by setting an element $turn(i)$ of a boolean array to *true*.

My first objection to this program is that it does not solve the problem correctly, at least not under our present assumptions about critical regions. When a process $A$ tries to reserve a resource unit at a time when none are available, the process enters its own identity in the queue of requests and awaits its *turn*. When another process $B$ releases a resource unit at a time when other processes are waiting for it, the process selects one of the waiting processes, say $A$, and makes its *turn true*. So when process $B$ leaves its critical region (within the *release* procedure), process $A$ will reenter its critical region (within the *reserve* procedure) and find that its *turn* is *true*; process $A$ then completes its critical region by removing the index of an available resource unit.

The trouble is that the programmer does not control the sequence in which processes enter and reenter their critical regions from the main queue, $Qv$ associated with the shared variable $v$ (see Fig. 3.17(b)). Therefore, it is possible that when process $B$ leaves its critical region after a *release*, another process $C$ enters its critical region on the same variable $v$ directly through the main queue and *reserves* the unit intended for process 4. So this algorithm does not give us explicit control over the scheduling of individual processes.

To solve the problem correctly with the present tools, we must introduce a sequence of *resources* that have been *granted to, but not yet acquired by waiting processes*.

However, rather than make this intermediate state explicit in the program, I suggest that *processes reentering their critical regions from event queues take priority over processes entering critical regions directly through a main queue*. This ensures that resources granted to waiting processes remain available to them until they reenter their critical regions.

In other words, we make the scheduling rules of critical regions partially known to the programmer. The proposed priority rule is reasonable because: (1) it simplifies explicit control of scheduling; and (2) it ensures fair scheduling of conditional critical regions in the sense that it gives processes waiting for events a chance to complete their critical regions within a finite time (provided, of course, the events occur).

With this modification Algorithm 3.11 becomes at least logically correct.

My second objection to Algorithm 3.11 is that it is extremely inefficient. The definition of conditional critical regions in Section 3.4.3 implies that all processes waiting for resources will be allowed to reenter their critical regions as soon as a resource is granted to one of them; then, all of them but one will reevaluate their boolean *turn* in vain. This is inevitable because there is only one event queue associated with a given shared variable and because the language does not permit the programmer to identify individual processes and say "please, enable process $A$ to reenter its critical region."

To control scheduling explicitly, a programmer must be able to associate an arbitrary number of event queues with a shared variable and control the transfers of processes to and from them. In general, I would therefore replace my previous proposal for conditional delays with the following one:

The declaration

$$\textbf{var } e\colon \textbf{event } v$$

associates an event queue $e$ with a shared variable $v$ declared elsewhere.

A process can leave a critical region associated with the variable $v$ and join the event queue $e$ by executing the standard procedure

$$await(e)$$

Another process can enable all processes in the event queue $e$ to reenter their critical regions by executing the standard procedure

$$cause(e)$$

The *await* and *cause* procedures can only be called within critical regions associated with the variable $v$. They exclude each other in time.

A consumer/producer relationship must now be expressed as follows:

| *"Consumer"* | *"Producer"* |
|---|---|
| **region** $v$ **do** | **region** $v$ **do** |
| **begin** | **begin** |
|   **while not** $B$ **do** *await*($e$); |   $S2$; |
|   $S1$; |   *cause*($e$); |
| **end** | **end** |

Although less elegant than the previous notation:

| | |
|---|---|
| **region** $v$ **do** | **region** $v$ **do** $S2$ |
| **begin await** $B$; $S1$ **end** | |

the new one still clearly shows that the consumer is waiting for condition $B$ to hold.

We can now control process scheduling efficiently to any degree desired. Algorithm 3.12 is an efficient version of the scheduling of heavily-used resources: It associates an event variable with each process.

One more objection can be made to both Algorithms 3.11 and 3.12: They violate the rules of procedures defined in Section 3.2.3 by their use of side effects on the shared variable $v$. It would have been more honest to pass $v$ explicitly as a parameter to the *reserve* and *release* procedures.

My reason for not doing so is the following: There is no reason that processes calling the *reserve* and *release* procedures should be concerned about the existence and structure of the shared variable $v$ used to

implement these procedures. All that matters to a process is that a call of
*reserve* eventually returns the identity of an available resource, and that a
call of *release* makes a resource available to other processes. Even the
scheduling algorithm used to grant a resource to a particular process is
irrelevant to the user processes in the sense that these processes usually
have little or no influence on this policy.

ALGORITHM 3.12 *Scheduling of Heavily Used Resources With
                Simple Critical Regions and Event Variables*

```
type P = 1. .number of processes;
     R = 1. .number of resources;
var v: shared record
               available: sequence of R;
               requests: queue of P;
               turn: array P of event v;
           end

procedure reserve(process: P; var resource: R);
region v do
begin
  while empty(available) do
  begin
    enter(process, requests);
    await(turn(process));
  end
  get(resource, available);
end

procedure release(resource: R);
var process: P;
region v do
begin
  put(resource, available);
  if not empty(requests) then
  begin
    remove(process, requests);
    cause(turn(process));
  end
end
```

For this reason, processes should not be forced to be aware of the
existence of the shared variable *v* and pass it as a parameter to the
resource scheduling procedures. Indeed, if the variable *v* were accessible to

processes, they might be tempted to operate directly on it within their own critical regions and perhaps override the scheduling rules of the installation or cause the total collapse of service by making the variable $v$ inconsistent with the assumptions made about it by *reserve* and *release*.

So what we need is a language notation which associates a set of procedures with a shared variable and enables a compiler to check that these are the only operations carried out on that variable and ensure that they exclude each other in time. I will not try to bend Pascal in this direction, but will present an example of such a notation in Chapter 7: a simple case of the *class concept* in *Simula 67*.

I will use the term *monitor* to denote a shared variable and the set of meaningful operations on it. The purpose of a monitor is to control the scheduling of resources among individual processes according to a certain policy.

In the previous example, the monitor consisted of a shared variable $v$ and two procedures *reserve* and *release*.

As we shall see in Chapter 4, most computers support the implementation of a *basic monitor*, which controls the sharing of processors, storage, and peripherals among computations at the lowest level of programming.

This section has shown that the monitor concept is equally useful at higher levels of programming and that one generally needs several monitors—one for each shared variable. (One can, of course, combine all shared variables into a single shared data structure. But this becomes an unnecessary bottleneck due to the requirement of mutual exclusion of all operations on it.)

### 3.4.8. Conclusion

We have now considered several methods of process synchronization:

> critical regions
> semaphores
> message buffers
> conditional critical regions
> event queues

I find that they are all *equivalent* in the sense that each of them can be used to solve an arbitrary scheduling problem from a *logical point of view*. But for a given problem, some of them lead to more complicated and inefficient programs than others. So they are clearly *not equivalent* from a *practical point of view*.

Each synchronizing concept is defined to solve a certain kind of problem in a direct, efficient manner:

| *synchronizing problem* | *synchronizing tool* |
| --- | --- |
| mutual exclusion | critical region |
| exchange of timing signals | semaphore |
| exchange of data | message buffer |
| arbitrary conditional delay | conditional critical regions |
| explicit process scheduling | event queues |

If the programmer has a choice, he should select the tool that conceptually corresponds most closely to the synchronizing problem he faces. He will then find that his program becomes not only simple to understand, but also efficient to execute.

The most general synchronizing tool considered is the event queue. But it has the same deficiency as semaphores: It forces the programmer to be explicitly aware of scheduling details. Therefore, it should only be used in situations in which this awareness is necessary to control heavily-used resources.

This concludes the discussion of synchronizing concepts. We will now study the deadlock problem in some detail.

## 3.5. DEADLOCKS

### 3.5.1. The Deadlock Problem

A *deadlock* is a state in which two or more processes are waiting indefinitely for conditions which will never hold.

A deadlock involves circular waiting: Each process is waiting for a condition which can only be satisfied by one of the others; but since each process expects one of the others to resolve the conflict, they are all unable to continue.

We have met the deadlock problem twice: in connection with the banker's algorithm and the mutual exclusion problem (see Sections 2.6.1, 3.3.1, and 3.3.3). In both cases, the occurrence of a deadlock depended on the relative speed of concurrent processes. Deadlocks are serious, time-dependent errors which should be prevented at all costs.

The deadlock problem was first recognized and analyzed by Dijkstra (1965). But it had occurred often enough in earlier operating systems. In 1968, Havender said about *OS/360*: "The original multitasking concept of the operating system envisioned relatively unrestrained competition for resources to perform a number of tasks concurrently .... But as the system evolved, many instances of task deadlock were uncovered."

A similar observation was made by Lynch in 1971: "Several problems remained unsolved with the *Exec II* operating system and had to be avoided by one *ad hoc* means or another. The problem of deadlocks was not at all understood in 1962 when the system was designed. As a result several annoying deadlocks were programmed into the system."

It has been argued that deadlocks are not a problem of program correctness, but an economic issue. An installation may deliberately take the risk of deadlocks if they occur infrequently enough. When they occur, the cheapest way of resolving them is by removing one or more jobs.

The difficulty with this point of view is that no methods are available at the moment for predicting the frequency of deadlocks and evaluating the costs involved. In this situation, it seems more honest to design systems in which deadlocks cannot occur. This is also a vital design objective when you consider how hopeless it is to correct erroneous programs with time-dependent behavior (see Section 3.2.2).

So in the following we will concentrate on methods of *deadlock prevention*.

### 3.5.2. Permanent Resources

Following Holt (1971), we distinguish between *permanent* and *temporary resources*. A permanent resource can be used repeatedly by many processes; a temporary resource is produced by one process and consumed by another. Examples of permanent and temporary resources are physical devices and messages, respectively.

We will first study a system with a fixed number of *permanent resources* of various *types*. Resources of the same type are *equivalent* from the point of view of the processes using them.

A process is expected to make a *request* for resources before it uses them. After making a request, a process is delayed until it *acquires* the resources. The process can now use the resources until it *releases* them again.

So a process follows the pattern:

> *request resources*;
> *use resources*;
> *release resources*;

Coffman (1971) has pointed out that the following *conditions* are *necessary* for the occurrence of a deadlock with respect to permanent resources:

(1) *Mutual exclusion*: A resource can only be acquired by one process at a time.

(2) *Non-preemptive scheduling*: A resource can only be released by the process which has acquired it.

(3) *Partial allocation*: A process can acquire its resources piecemeal.

(4) *Circular waiting*: The previous conditions permit concurrent processes to acquire part of their resources and enter a state in which they wait indefinitely to acquire each other's resources.

Deadlocks are *prevented* by ensuring that one or more of the necessary conditions never hold.

The first possibility is to permit several processes *simultaneous access* to resources (for example, read-only access to common data within disjoint processes). But, in general, processes must be able to get exclusive access to resources (for example, access to common data within critical regions). So, to prevent deadlock by permitting simultaneous access to all resources is unrealistic.

The second possibility is deadlock prevention by *preemptive scheduling*—that is, by forcing processes to release resources temporarily in favor of other processes. It takes a finite time to transfer a resource from one process to another. Preemption therefore leads to a less efficient utilization of resources.

In present computers, preemption is used mainly to multiplex central processors and storage between concurrent processes. As we will see later, the resulting loss in the utilization of equipment can be quite significant unless the frequency of preemption is carefully controlled.

Preemption is impractical for peripheral devices that require mounting of private data media by operators (such as card readers, line printers, and magnetic tape stations).

In *THE* multiprogramming system (Bron, 1971), a line printer is nevertheless subject to preemptive scheduling. But this is done with great restraint: The system will try to print the output of one process consecutively; only if a process threatens to monopolize the printer will the system start to print forms for another process. In practice, very few files are split, but it is doubtful whether this method would be practical for larger installations.

The third possibility is to prevent deadlocks by a *complete allocation* of all resources needed by a process in advance of its execution. This means that the resource requirements of concurrent processes cannot exceed the total capacity of the system.

The success of this method depends on the characteristics of the workload—whether it is possible to find a combination of jobs which can utilize all resources concurrently in a disjoint manner.

The fourth possibility is to prevent deadlocks by a *sequential ordering of requests*, which prevents circular waiting.

The *banker's algorithm* does this by finding a sequence in which concurrent processes can be completed one at a time if necessary. The difficulty with this algorithm is that it is quite expensive to execute at run time.

Consider a system with $m$ resource types and $n$ processes. Algorithm 2.6 determines whether the current situation is *safe* from deadlocks by examining the $m$ resource claims of each process until it finds a process which can be completed. The algorithm repeats this examination until all $n$ processes are eliminated. In the worst case, the algorithm has an *execution time* proportional to

$$m(n + n - 1 + n - 2 + \ldots + 1) = mn(n + 1)/2$$

In *THE* multiprogramming system, 2 resource types (plotters and paper tape punches) and 5 user processes are controlled by a banker. This gives a maximum of 30 iterations for each request. But in a system with 10 resource types and 10 concurrent processes, the maximum is 550 iterations of, say, 1 msec, or 0.55 sec per request!

It is possible to write a more complicated algorithm with an execution time proportional to $mn$ (Holt, 1971). This algorithm avoids repeated examination of the same processes by ordering the claims of each resource type by size and associating with each process a count of the number of resource types requested.

The main problem with the banker's algorithm is that it takes a *very pessimistic* view of the resource requirements: Each process must indicate its maximum resource requirements in advance; and, in determining whether a situation is safe from deadlocks, the banker assumes that each process may request all its resources at once and keep them throughout its execution.

Consider the situation shown in Fig. 2.8(a) where three processes, $P$, $Q$, and $R$, share 10 resources of the same type which at present are allocated as follows:

|  | cash = 2 |  |
| :---: | :---: | :---: |
| Process: | Loan: | Claim: |
| $P$ | 4 | 4 |
| $Q$ | 2 | 1 |
| $R$ | 2 | 7 |

Suppose we have an installation with a single printer which is needed by practically all processes for short periods of time. If the printer is also controlled by the banker, Algorithm 2.6 will decide that in the above situation, it is only safe to grant it to process $Q$ (because $Q$ is the only process which can be completed with certainty). So the printer will remain idle until $Q$ decides to use it even though $P$ and $R$ could use the printer meanwhile.

For this reason, the printer was excluded from the banker's domain in *THE* multiprogramming system, as was the backing store. In doing so, the design group, of course, took a risk of deadlocking the system. Operating experience has shown that a storage deadlock occurs about 5 times per year. It is resolved by manual removal of user jobs.

In the following, I will discuss prevention of deadlocks by a hierarchal ordering of requests.

### 3.5.3. Hierarchal Resource Allocation

In a hierarchal resource system, the request and release of resources of various types are subject to a fixed sequential ordering.

A resource *hierarchy* consists of a finite number of *levels* $L1, L2, \ldots,$ *Lmax*. Each level in turn consists of a finite number of resource types.

Resources needed by a process from a given level must be acquired by a single request.

When a process has acquired resources at a level $Lj$, it can only request resources at a higher level $Lk$, where $k > j$.

Resources acquired at a level $Lk$ must be released before the resources acquired at a lower level $Lj$, where $k > j$.

When a process has released all resources acquired at a given level, it can make another request at the same level.

In short, resources can be partially requested level by level in one direction, and partially released level by level in the opposite direction as shown in Fig. 3.19.

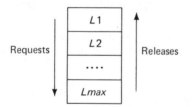

Fig. 3.19 A hierarchy of resources with levels $L1, L2, \ldots, Lmax$. Resources at low levels are requested before resources at high levels. Releases are made in the opposite order of requests.

We assume that a process will release all resources acquired at a given level $Lj$ within a finite time unless it is delayed indefinitely by requests for resources at a higher level $Lk$ where $k > j$.

Under these assumptions, *a deadlock cannot occur in a system with hierarchal resource allocation*. This is easily proved by induction.

Suppose that the resources requested by processes at the level $Lj$ always will be acquired and released within a finite time for $j \geqslant i$. We will then show that this also holds for $j \geqslant i - 1$.

The previous hypothesis is clearly true at the highest level *Lmax*: Processes here can never be delayed by requests for resources at higher levels because such levels do not exist. And, since partial allocation within a level is prevented, processes cannot be deadlocked with respect to resources at level *Lmax*.

Consider now a process $P$ that requests resources at the level $Li-1$. Again, since partial allocation is prevented inside level $Li-1$, processes cannot be deadlocked with respect to resources at that level, provided they are always able to release these resources within a finite time after their acquisition. This release can only be delayed by requests for resources at a higher level $Lj$, where $j \geqslant i$. But, according to our hypothesis, such requests (and subsequent releases) will always be made within a finite time. So requests and releases at level $Li-1$ are also made within a finite time.

It follows by induction that an indefinite delay of requests is impossible at all levels $L1$ to $Lmax$.

An example of hierarchal resource allocation is a *spooling system*, as shown in Fig. 2.2(b). In this case, there is only one level with three resource types: a card reader, a central processor, and a line printer. The system forces each user to use these resources strictly sequentially:

> *request reader;    input;    release reader;*
> *request processor;  execute;  release processor;*
> *request printer;    output;   release printer;*

As another example, consider a common variable $v$ accessed by critical regions. One can regard such a variable as a permanent resource for which a request and release are made upon entry to and exit from each critical region. From the previous theorem, it follows that deadlocks of *nested critical regions* can be prevented by a hierarchal ordering of common variables $v1, v2, \ldots, vmax$ and critical regions:

> **region** $v1$ **do**
> **region** $v2$ **do**
> $\ldots \ldots$
> **region** $vmax$ **do**
> $\ldots \ldots$ ;

We now turn to deadlock prevention for temporary resources. The discussion will be restricted to systems with hierarchal process communication.

### 3.5.4. Hierarchal Process Communication

We will consider a system of processes connected only by message buffers. Associated with each buffer is one or more senders and one or more receivers.

It has already been shown in Section 3.4.1 that senders and receivers cannot be deadlocked with respect to a single message buffer. But, if we connect a circle of processes by message buffers, it is possible for them to wait indefinitely for messages from each other.

To avoid this circularity, we will again resort to a hierarchal system. Consider a system in which a fixed number of *processes* are organized as a *hierarchy* with the levels $L1$, $L2$, ... , $Lmax$. In this hierarchy, processes at lower levels, called *masters*, can supply processes at higher levels, called *servants*, with *messages* ("requests"). Servants can return *answers* ("replies") to their masters in response to messages.

So messages are sent in only one direction, and answers are sent in only the opposite direction.

Even though the system is hierarchal, there is still a danger of deadlocks. Figure 3.20 shows a situation in which two chains of buffers lead from a master $P$ to a servant $S$. (A directed branch from a process node $P$ to another process node $Q$ indicates that $P$ and $Q$ are connected by a buffer, with $P$ as a sender and $Q$ as a receiver.)

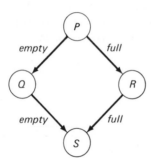

Fig. 3.20 Four processes—$P$, $Q$, $R$, and $S$—connected by unidirectional buffers shown as directed branches.

The danger here is that $P$ may be unable to send to $R$ and $R$ unable to send to $S$ because the buffers which connect them are both full; and, at the same time, $S$ may be unable to receive from $Q$, and $Q$ unable to receive from $P$ because the buffers which connect them are both empty. So we have a deadlock in which

$P$ waits for $R$ to receive,
$R$ waits for $S$ to receive,
$S$ waits for $Q$ to send, and
$Q$ waits for $P$ to send

This shows that when several communication paths lead from one process to another, a deadlock can occur even for *monologues* consisting only of messages.

A deadlock can also occur for *conversations* consisting of messages and answers. Figure 3.21 shows a master $P$ and a servant $Q$. It is possible that $P$ and $Q$ will be unable simultaneously to send a message and an answer, respectively, because both buffers are full. Or they may be unable to

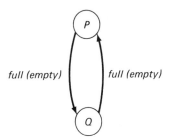

full (empty)   full (empty)

Fig. 3.21 Two processes $P$ and $Q$ connected by bidirectional buffers shown as directed branches.

receive a message and an answer at the same time because both buffers are empty. So we have a deadlock in which

$P$ waits for $Q$ to receive (or send), and
$Q$ waits for $P$ to receive (or send)

The ground rule of deadlock prevention is: Do not try to send a message or answer unless someone will eventually receive it; and do not try to receive a message or answer unless someone will eventually send it.

We will therefore make the following *basic assumption*: When a master $M$ sends a message to a servant $S$, the latter will eventually receive it, and (if required) send an answer, unless it is delayed indefinitely by one of its own servants.

Under this assumption, *a deadlock cannot occur in a system with hierarchal process communication*. This is again proved by induction.

Suppose that messages sent to processes at any level $Lj$ always will be received, consumed, and (if required) answered within a finite time for $j \geq i$. We will then show that this also holds for $j \geq i - 1$.

According to our basic assumption, the previous hypothesis is true for any process $Pj$ at the highest level, $j = max$, because there are no servants to delay it.

Consider now a process $Pi-1$ at the level $Li-1$. Thanks to the basic assumption, $Pi-1$ will satisfy the hypothesis if it is not delayed indefinitely by a servant $Pj$ at a higher level $Lj$, where $j \geq i$. There are two possibilities of such delays:

(1) $Pi-1$ may be *unable to send a message* to a servant $Pj$ because a buffer is full. But according to the hypothesis, the servant $Pj$ at level $Lj$ (where $j \geq i$) will eventually receive one of the messages and enable $Pi-1$ to continue.

(2) $Pi-1$ may be *unable to receive an answer* from a servant $Pj$ because a buffer is empty. Again, according to the hypothesis, the servant at level $Lj$ (where $j \geq i$) will eventually receive the corresponding message and produce the answer which enables $Pi-1$ to continue.

So messages sent to processes at the level $Li-1$ will always be received, consumed, and (if required) answered within a finite time. It follows by induction that this holds at all levels, $L1$ to $Lmax$.

The following conditions are sufficient to ensure that the basic assumption about process communication holds:

(1) There must be constant agreement between senders and receivers about where the next message or answer will be delivered.

(2) Inside each process, all operations (other than *send* and *receive*) that produce and consume messages or answers must terminate.

(3) Messages and answers must be complete in the following sense: When a process has received a message or an answer, it needs no further data from the sender to produce the corresponding answer or next message.

(4) A message requiring an answer must only be sent when there is an empty buffer element in which the answer can be delivered immediately.

In *THE* multiprogramming system, the latter requirement is satisfied by a strict alternation between messages and answers exchanged by two processes: When a message is sent, the corresponding answer buffer is always empty, and vice versa.

In the *RC 4000* system, the same is achieved by permitting two processes to exchange a message and an answer in the same buffer element (Brinch Hansen, 1970).

The above conditions are well-suited to step-wise system construction: They can be verified by examining each process and its senders and receivers separately.

Hierarchal process communication was first studied by Habermann (1967) in connection with *THE* multiprogramming system.

The previous results also apply to conditional critical regions if the words *message* and *answer* are understood in an abstract sense: A producer *sends* a message (or an answer) by making a condition $B$ true and causing an event; a consumer *receives* it by awaiting the event and making the condition false again.

This concludes our analysis of concurrent processes.


## 3.6. LITERATURE

No student of multiprogramming can afford to miss the monograph in which Dijkstra (1965) gave the field a firm foundation by his analysis of critical regions, semaphores, message buffers, and deadlocks.

A discussion of the use of message buffers for a step-wise construction of multiprogramming systems is found in the paper by Morenoff and

McLean (1967). The *RC 4000* scheme for process communication is unusual in the sense that it considers the sending of a message and the return of an answer between two processes as a single interaction (Brinch Hansen, 1970).

The paper by Hoare (1971b) contains a proposal for a restricted form of conditional critical regions. It also clearly states the requirements of a well-structured language notation for concurrent processes and resource sharing.

The survey by Coffman, Elphick, and Shoshani (1971) is an excellent guide to the literature on deadlocks.

I also recommend that you study the synchronizing concept *coroutines* invented by Conway (1963) and illustrated by Knuth (1969). I have not included it here because it is mainly suited to a strictly interleaved execution of processes on a single processor. As such, it is a highly efficient and conceptually simple tool for the *simulation* of concurrent processes.

In recent years, some efforts have been made to formalize the concepts of concurrent computations. The monograph of Bredt (1970) summarizes the works of Adams, Karp and Miller, Luconi, and Rodriguez. These researchers have primarily studied the functional behavior and equivalence of various computational models.

BREDT, T. H., "A survey of models for parallel computing," Stanford University, Palo Alto, California, Aug. *1970*.

BRINCH HANSEN, P., "The nucleus of a multiprogramming system," *Comm. ACM 13*, 4, 238-50, April *1970*.

COFFMAN, E. G., ELPHICK, M. J., and SHOSHANI, A., "System deadlocks," *Computing Surveys 3*, 2, pp. 67-78, June *1971*.

CONWAY, M. E., "Design of a separable transition-diagram compiler," Comm. *ACM 6*, 7, pp. 396-408, July *1963*.

DIJKSTRA, E. W., "Cooperating sequential processes," Technological University, Eindhoven, The Netherlands, *1965*. (Reprinted in *Programming Languages*, F. Genuys, ed., Academic Press, New York, New York, 1968).

HOARE, C. A. R., "Towards a theory of parallel programming." *International Seminar on Operating System Techniques*, Belfast, Northern Ireland, Aug.-Sept. *1971b*.

KNUTH, D. E., *The Art of Computer Programming*, Volume 1, Chapter 1. Addison-Wesley, Reading, Massachusetts, *1969*.

MORENOFF, E. and McLEAN, J. B., "Inter-program communications, program string structures and buffer files," *Proc. AFIPS Spring Joint Computer Conf.*, pp. 175-83, *1967*.

# 4

# *PROCESSOR MANAGEMENT*

This chapter explains how concurrent processes and synchronizing primitives can be implemented on a computer with one or more processors and a single internal store. It concludes with an evaluation of the influence of these abstractions on the real-time characteristics of the system.

## 4.1. INTRODUCTION

The previous chapter introduced language constructs for describing concurrent processes and their interactions. We will now consider how concurrent processes and synchronizing primitives can be implemented on present computers.

The sharing of a computer installation by a group of users is an economic necessity. It leads to a situation in which resources become scarce—there are not enough physical processors and storage to simultaneously execute all processes requested by users. The available resources can be shared among the processes either by executing them one at a time to completion or by executing several of them in rapid succession for short periods of time. In both cases, each processor must pause every now and then and decide whether to continue the execution of its present process or switch to some other process instead. The rule according to which this decision is made is called a *scheduling algorithm*.

To make the scheduling problem manageable, it is usually considered at several levels of abstraction. The view of scheduling presented here recognizes two main levels:

At the lower level, which may be called *hardware management* or *short-term scheduling*, the objective is to allocate physical resources to processes, as soon as they become available, to maintain good utilization of the equipment. This level of programming simulates a virtual machine for each process and a set of primitives which enable concurrent processes to achieve mutual exclusion of critical regions and communicate with one another.

At the higher level of scheduling, which may be called *user management* or *medium-term scheduling*, the aim is to allocate virtual machines to users according to the rules laid down by the installation management. Typical tasks at this level are the establishment of the identity and authority of users; the input and analysis of their requests, the initiation and control of computations, the accounting of resource usage, and the maintenance of system integrity in spite of occasional hardware malfunction.

The decision to allocate a resource to a process inevitably favors that process (at least temporarily) over other processes waiting for the same resource. In other words, all levels of scheduling implement a *policy* towards users and their computations. This is important to realize because policies are among the first things installation managers will wish to modify to satisfy users. Consequently, policies should be clearly separated from the logical aspects of scheduling such as processor synchronization and store addressing.

The present chapter on *processor management* discusses the short-term problems of scheduling concurrent processes on a limited number of processors connected to an internal store of practically unlimited capacity.

Chapter 5 on *store management* considers the short-term problems of allocating an internal store of limited capacity to concurrent processes using a larger, slower backing store.

Chapter 6 on *scheduling algorithms* analyzes the effect of various medium-term policies on the average response times to user requests.

## 4.2.  SHORT-TERM SCHEDULING

The aim of the following discussion is to explain how concurrent processes are scheduled on a computer with one or more *identical processors* connected to a *single internal store*, as shown in Fig. 2.3. The number of concurrent processes can exceed the number of processors, but the store is assumed to be large enough to satisfy all concurrent processes at any time.

We will take a "bottom-up" approach and show:

(1) how a *basic monitor* can be implemented by means of a storage arbiter and simple machine instructions;

(2) how this monitor can be used to implement *scheduling primitives*, which initiate and terminate processes and transmit timing signals between them; and

(3) how these primitives in turn can be used to implement *concurrent statements, critical regions, message buffers*, and more *general monitors.*

The algorithms in this chapter are written in Pascal at a level of detail that clarifies the main problems of process scheduling and suggests efficient methods of implementation. These algorithms represent the *machine code* that a compiler would produce to implement the concurrent statements and synchronizing constructs defined in Chapter 3.

### 4.2.1. Process Descriptions

Figure 4.1 shows the process states which are relevant at the short-term level of scheduling. Initially, a process is *terminated* or non-existent. When a process is initiated, it enters a queue of processes which are *ready* to run. When a processor becomes available, the process becomes *running*. In the running state, a process may *terminate* itself or *wait* on a timing signal. In the latter case, the process will return to the ready state when the signal is produced by another process.

Also shown in Fig. 4.1 is a list of the primitives which cause the transitions between the states. The following explains how these scheduling primitives are implemented.

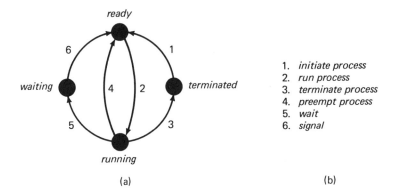

1. *initiate process*
2. *run process*
3. *terminate process*
4. *preempt process*
5. *wait*
6. *signal*

(a)                                       (b)

Fig. 4.1 The possible process states (a) and the primitives (b) that cause the transitions between them.

Our starting point is the trivial case in which each processor is dedicated to perpetual execution of a single process. In other words, only the *running* state is relevant.

We assume that all processes are represented in the common store by an array called the *process table*. An entry in this table is called a *process description*. It defines the initial values of the processor *registers* (including the instruction counter) for a given process.

> type $P$ = 1. .*maximum number of processes*;
>   *process description* = **record**
>                       *register state*: $R$;
>                       **end**
> **var** *process table*: **array** $P$ **of** *process description*;

Each processor has a register containing the index of the process it runs. The *instruction execution cycle* of a processor is as follows:

> **var** *process*: $P$; *registers*: $R$; *store*: $T$;
> **repeat**
>   *execute instruction*(*registers*, *store*);
> **forever**

The details of instruction execution are irrelevant here.

The next step is to consider a dynamic system in which processes are initiated by other processes and terminated by themselves after a finite time.

The number of processes can now vary. So we introduce a sequence called *terminated*, which contains the indices of process descriptions not used at the moment:

> **var** *terminated*: **sequence of** $P$;

It is possible that the number of processes sometimes exceeds the number of processors. So we must also introduce a queue of processes that are *ready* to run when a processor becomes available:

> **var** *ready*: **queue of** $P$;

When a running process terminates itself, its processor can be assigned to a process in the *ready* queue. It is possible for several processors to become available simultaneously and try to refer to process descriptions in the *ready* queue at the same time. Consequently, we must ensure *mutual exclusion* of operations on process descriptions and the *ready* queue; otherwise, the results of process initiation and termination will be unpredictable.

Critical regions have been implemented in hardware for many years on computers in which program execution and input/output can proceed simultaneously. A sequential switching circuit, called an *arbiter*, guarantees that at any instant in time either the central processor or a peripheral device, but not both, can access the internal store to read or write a single word. If processors try to overlap their access, the arbiter enables one of them to proceed and delays the rest for the few microseconds it takes to access the store. This technique has been called *cycle stealing* or *interleaving*.

So the machine instructions *load* and *store* are implemented as critical regions:

> **var** *store*: **shared array** *index* **of** *word*;
> *address*: *index*; *register*: *word*;

> **region** *store* **do** *register*:= *store(address)*;
> **region** *store* **do** *store(address)*:= *register*

We will now assume that, apart from this hardware scheduling of access to single store words, the computer also includes another arbiter to which all processors are connected. This device along with two machine operations *enter region* and *leave region* is a hardware implementation of critical regions performed on process descriptions and queues. These will be the only critical regions which use the busy form of waiting. To make this tolerable, the duration of such regions must be short.

On top of this, we will construct primitives that enable processes to establish other critical regions that use the non-busy form of waiting.

As an intermediate tool, we will first implement a basic monitor concept which in turn can be used to implement specific operations on process descriptions and queues.

### 4.2.2.　A Basic Monitor

Process descriptions and scheduling queues will be maintained by a *basic monitor* which can be called by running processes.

A calling process is identified by the process register in its processor.

A *monitor call* is made by loading the relevant parameters in registers and then executing a machine instruction:

> *monitor call(entry)*

which has the following effect:

> **enter region**
> *process table(process).register state*:= *registers*;
> **case** *entry* **of** . . . **end**

It enters a critical region, stores the register values of the calling process in its description, and jumps to a monitor procedure.

The basic monitor will always complete a call by executing a machine instruction:

$$monitor\ exit(candidate)$$

which has the following effect:

> $process := candidate$;
> $registers := process\ table(process).register\ state$;
> **leave region**

It assigns the value of a variable *candidate* to the process register, loads the other registers from the corresponding process description, and leaves the critical region.

We will use the following notation to define a basic monitor procedure $Q$, which operates on a shared variable $v$ consisting of process descriptions and queues:

> **var** $v$: **shared** $V$;
>
> **procedure** $Q(. . .)$;
> **var** $candidate$: $P$;
> **region** $v$ **do**
> **begin**
>   $S$; $continue(candidate)$;
> **end**

The value of the register which identifies a calling process is defined by a standard function *process*:

$$function\ process: P$$

This simplified monitor concept will now be used to implement scheduling primitives for concurrent processes.

### 4.2.3.  Process Implementation

Once the system has been started, there must be at least one running process which can accept requests from users and initiate their processes. So we assume that one of the processors initially runs this *basic process*.

The other processors will initially run *idling processes* which continue to call the basic monitor until other processes (initiated by the basic process) are ready to run:

> *"idling process"*
> **repeat** *run process* **forever**

It is important that the idling is done by processes outside the monitor. This permits the basic process to enter the monitor and initiate new processes.

The basic monitor procedure *run process*, called by an idling process, is defined by Algorithm 4.1. It examines the *ready* queue: If that queue is empty, the idling process continues; otherwise, one of the *ready* processes continues.

*ALGORITHM 4.1   The Scheduling of a Ready Process*

```
const idling = min(P);
var v: shared
        record
            process table: array P of process description;
            terminated: sequence of P;
            ready: queue of P;
        end

function process: P;

procedure select(var candidate: P; ready: queue of P);
begin
   if empty(ready) then candidate:= idling
                   else remove(candidate, ready);
end

procedure run process;
var candidate: P;
region v do
begin
   select(candidate, ready);
   continue(candidate);
end
```

As an example of process initiation, consider a *concurrent statement* which is both preceded by and followed by sequential statements:

$$
\begin{aligned}
&S0; \\
&\textbf{cobegin } S1; S2; \ldots ; Sn \textbf{ coend} \\
&Sn{+}1;
\end{aligned}
$$

This construct is implemented as follows: The process that executes statement $S0$ initiates the concurrent processes $S1, S2, \ldots, Sn$ by calling a monitor procedure, *initiate process*, $n$ times and then calling another monitor procedure, *delay process*, which delays it until all the concurrent processes are terminated. When the delayed process continues, it executes statement $Sn+1$:

> $S0$;
> **for every** $Si$ **do** *initiate process*(*initial state*);
> *delay process*;
> $Sn+1$;

The parameter to *initiate process* defines the initial register values of a new process.

To implement these monitor procedures, a *process description* is extended to contain the following components:

*register state*    defines the register values of the given process.

*parent*    defines the process which initiated the given process.

*children*    defines the number of processes initiated by the given process, but not yet terminated.

*delayed*    defines whether or not the given process is delayed until all its children have been terminated.

The monitor procedure *initiate process* is defined by Algorithm 4.2. It initializes a process description and enters its index in the *ready* queue. Finally, it increases the number of children of the calling process by one and continues that process.

The monitor procedure *delay process* is defined by Algorithm 4.3. If the number of children of the calling process is greater than zero, the calling process is delayed and its processor is allocated to another process; otherwise, the calling process continues.

Each of the children processes $S1, S2, \ldots, Sn$ within a concurrent statement executes a statement $Si$ and calls a monitor procedure, *terminate process*:

> $Si$;
> *terminate process*;

This monitor procedure is defined by Algorithm 4.4. It releases the description of the calling process and decreases the number of children of its parent by one: If the number of children becomes zero and the parent is delayed, the parent is then continued; otherwise, the processor is allocated to another process.

*ALGORITHM 4.2*　*The Initiation of a Child Process*

```
type process description = record
                              register state: R;
                              parent: P;
                              children: integer;
                              delayed: boolean;
                          end

procedure initiate process(initial state: R);
var new: P;
region v do
begin
  get(new, terminated);
  with process table(new) do
  begin
    register state:= initial state;
    parent:= process;
    children:= 0;
    delayed:= false;
  end
  enter(new, ready);
  with process table(process) do
  children:= children + 1;
  continue(process);
end
```

*ALGORITHM 4.3*　*The Delay of a Parent Process*

```
procedure delay process;
var candidate: P;
region v do
begin
  with process table(process) do
  if children > 0 then
  begin
    delayed:= true;
    select(candidate, ready);
  end
  else candidate:= process;
  continue(candidate);
end
```

*ALGORITHM 4.4  The Termination of a Child Process*

```
procedure terminate process;
var candidate: P;
region v do
begin
  candidate:= process table(process). parent;
  put(process, terminated);
  with process table(candidate) do
  begin
    children:= children – 1;
    if children = 0 & delayed then
    delayed:= false else
    select(candidate, ready);
  end
  continue(candidate);
end
```

### 4.2.4. Semaphore and Event Implementation

The basic monitor can also be used to implement primitives for process interaction. Since the basic monitor uses the busy form of waiting (in interactions with the arbiter), these primitives should be as simple as possible.

As an example, we will implement the *wait* and *signal* operations for a fixed number of *semaphores*. The semaphores are represented by an array inside the basic monitor. Each semaphore consists of two components:

The first component is an integer *counter*, which defines the number of signals sent, but not yet received. Its initial value defines the initial number of signals. It is increased by one when a *signal* operation has been completed and decreased by one when a *wait* operation has been completed.

To satisfy the *semaphore invariant*, which states that signals cannot be received faster than they are sent, the *wait* and *signal* operations must ensure that the *counter* remains greater than or equal to zero (see Section 3.4.2).

The second component is a queue of processes *waiting* to receive signals not yet sent. Initially, this queue is empty.

The monitor procedure *wait* is defined by Algorithm 4.5. If the semaphore *counter* is greater than zero, it is decreased by one and the calling process continues; otherwise, the calling process is delayed.

The monitor procedure *signal* is also defined by Algorithm 4.5. If one or more processes are *waiting* in the semaphore queue, one of them is transferred to the *ready* queue; otherwise, the semaphore counter is increased by one. The calling process continues in any case.

*ALGORITHM 4.5   The Semaphore Operations Wait and Signal*

```
var v: shared record
            . . .
        semaphore: array S of
                record
                    counter: integer;
                    waiting: queue of P;
                end
    end

procedure wait(s: S);
var candidate: P;
region v do
begin
  with semaphore(s) do
  if counter > 0 then
  begin
    counter:= counter - 1;
    candidate := process;
  end else
  begin
    enter(process, waiting);
    select(candidate, ready);
  end
  continue(candidate);
end

procedure signal(s: S);
var candidate: P;
region v do
begin
  with semaphore(s) do
  if not empty(waiting) then
  begin
    remove(candidate, waiting);
    enter(candidate, ready);
  end
  else counter:= counter + 1;
  continue(process);
end
```

The *wait* and *signal* operations can be used to implement arbitrary *critical regions* which use the non-busy form of *waiting* as defined by Algorithm 3.4.

Algorithm 4.6 shows the implementation of *event* variables and the operations *await* and *cause* event. An event variable consists of two

ALGORITHM 4.6.  *The Event Operations Await and Cause*

```
          var v: shared record
                      . . .
                  event: array E of
                          record
                              reentry: S;
                              delayed: queue of P;
                          end
          end

          procedure await(e: E);
          var candidate: P;
          region v do
          begin
            with event(e) do
            begin
              enter(process, delayed);
              with semaphore(reentry) do
              if not empty(waiting) then
              begin
                remove(candidate, waiting);
                enter(candidate, ready);
              end
              else counter := counter + 1;
            end
            select(candidate, ready);
            continue(candidate);
          end

          procedure cause(e: E);
          var candidate: P;
          region v do
          begin
            with event(e) do
            with semaphore(reentry) do
            while not empty(delayed) do
            begin
              remove(candidate, delayed);
              enter(candidate, waiting);
            end
            continue(process);
          end
```

components: a queue of processes waiting for an event and an index of a semaphore on which these processes must wait to reenter their critical regions after the occurrence of an event.

The *await* procedure enters the calling process in an event queue and performs a *signal* operation on the associated semaphore to enable another process to enter its critical region.

The *cause* procedure transfers all processes from an event queue to an associated semaphore queue. As defined here, the processes are transferred one at a time from one queue to the other; however, in practice, the whole event queue would be detached from the event variable and linked to the semaphore queue in one operation. The calling process, which is still inside its critical region, continues.

The four primitives, *wait*, *signal*, *await*, and *cause*, permit the implementation of *conditional critical regions* as defined in Section 3.4.7. And conditional critical regions in turn can be used to implement other synchronizing tools such as *message buffers* and arbitrary *monitors*, as shown by Algorithms 3.6 and 3.12.

Without going into further detail, it should be clear that the synchronizing concepts defined in Chapter 3 can be built on top of the basic monitor.

There is just one problem that remains: How can we preempt running processes which threaten to monopolize processors? This is discussed in the following section.

### 4.2.5. Processor Multiplexing

In the previous discussion, we assumed that once a process has started to run, it continues to do so until it explicitly releases the processor again (by a *terminate*, *delay*, *wait*, or *await* operation). This is called *non-preemptive scheduling*. It makes sense when one can rely on processes to terminate themselves within a reasonable period of time after their initiation. This assumption may be justified in dedicated systems with highly reliable programs, but in general it is not realistic. In most cases, it must be possible to force a process to terminate; otherwise, a programming error might cause it to run forever.

Even when programs are reliable, it is still valuable to be able to interrupt the execution of a process temporarily to allocate its processor to a more urgent process and continue the interrupted process later when the more urgent one terminates. This is called *preemptive scheduling with resumption*. It is the subject of the following discussion.

In the design of Algorithms 4.1 to 4.6, we made the implicit assumption that running processes take priority over ready processes: A process in the *ready* queue is only run when a running process releases its processor. This is quite acceptable as long as the number of processes does not exceed the number of processors, because in that case, there is always an idle processor ready to run a process when it is activated by some other process. But, when the number of processes exceeds the number of processors, scheduling must reflect the policy of management towards user processes rather than their random order of arrival in the *ready* queue.

As a first improvement, we can assign a *fixed priority* to each process and keep the scheduling queues ordered accordingly. Whenever a process is activated by another process, the basic monitor should compare the priorities of the two processes and continue the more urgent one after transferring the other one to the *ready* queue.

The priorities divide the processes into a finite number of *priority groups* numbered 1, 2, ... , *n*, with small integers denoting high priority. In a given queue, processes are scheduled in their order of priority; processes of the same priority are scheduled in their order of arrival in the queue.

A queue *q* of elements of type *T* divided into *n* priority groups can be declared as follows:

$$\textbf{type } priority = 1..n$$
$$\textbf{var } q: \textbf{queue } priority \textbf{ of } T$$

The standard procedure

$$enter(t, p, q)$$

enters an element *t* of type *T* with the priority *p* in a queue *q*.

The standard procedure

$$remove(t, p, q)$$

removes the most urgent element *t* of type *T* from a queue *q* and assigns its priority to a variable *p*.

We also need two boolean functions that determine whether or not a given queue *q* is empty or holds an element which is more urgent than another one with a given priority *p*:

$$empty(q) \qquad urgent(p, q)$$

The priority of a process can be defined when it is initiated.

A further refinement is to permit *dynamic priorities*, priorities that change in time. It would be ideal if each processor could evaluate the priorities of its running process and all ready processes after each instruction executed to determine which process should run next. This is, of course, impractical: Processors would then spend more time evaluating priorities than running processes. This is the basic dilemma of preemptive scheduling: Preemption is necessary to give fast response to urgent processes, but the amount of processor time required to evaluate priorities and switch from one process to another sets a practical limit to the frequency of preemption.

A reasonable compromise is to let priorities remain fixed over the intervals of time considered at the short-term level of scheduling, but permit them to vary slowly over the intervals of time considered at the medium-term level of scheduling. In other words, priorities can only change after reasonable periods of useful execution.

To achieve this effect, each processor is supplied with a timing device. A *timer* is a counter that is decreased at a constant rate; when it becomes zero, a signal is set in a register, and the timer starts another period of counting:

```
var interrupt: shared boolean;
    timer: integer;

repeat
    timer:= interval desired;
    repeat
      timer:= timer - 1;
    until timer = 0;
    region interrupt do interrupt:= true;
forever
```

The timing signal, which is called an *interrupt*, is examined by a processor in each *instruction execution cycle* without any noticeable effect on its speed of execution:

```
var interrupt: shared boolean;
    process: P; registers: R; store: T;

repeat
    region interrupt do
    if interrupt then
    begin
      interrupt:= false;
      monitor call(preempt process);
    end
    execute instruction(registers, store);
forever
```

The processor responds to an interrupt by resetting the interrupt register to *false* and calling a basic monitor procedure, *preempt process*.

The monitor can now preempt the running process, rearrange the *ready* queue according to a dynamic scheduling algorithm, and resume the most urgent process:

```
procedure preempt process;
var candidate: P;
region v do
begin
  enter(process, ready);
  rearrange(ready);
  remove(candidate, ready);
  continue(candidate);
end
```

This form of scheduling, which leads to *frequent preemption* and *resumption* of running and ready processes, is called *processor multiplexing*. A simple form of processor multiplexing is the *round-robin* algorithm described in Section 1.2.4.

The purpose of an interrupt is to replace a complicated scheduling algorithm with the simplest possible algorithm: The evaluation of a single boolean after each instruction execution. An interrupt is a signal to a processor from its environment that indicates that priorities should be reevaluated.

Although the previous *instruction execution cycle* looks plausible, it is actually highly dangerous. Suppose a processor is inside a critical region

**enter region . . . leave region**

executing a basic monitor procedure. In the middle of this, an interrupt may cause the processor to try to reenter the monitor:

```
. . .
entry := preempt process;
enter region
. . .
```

The result is a *deadlock* of the processor.

This problem is solved by introducing two states of execution inside a processor: the *enabled state*, in which interrupts are honored, and the *inhibited state*, in which interrupts are ignored. Interrupts are inhibited and enabled upon entry to and exit from the basic monitor, respectively. This version of a central processor and a monitor call and exit is defined by Algorithms 4.7 and 4.8.

If a computer has only a *single processor* which is multiplexed among

*ALGORITHM 4.7*   *The Instruction Execution Cycle of a*
                         *Processor With Interrupts*

```
var interrupt: shared boolean; enabled: boolean;
    process, initial process: P;
    registers: R; store: T;

begin
  region interrupt do
  begin
    interrupt:= false;
    enabled:= true;
    process:= initial process;
    registers:= process table(process).register state;
  end
  repeat
    region interrupt do
    if interrupt & enabled then
    begin
      interrupt:= false;
      monitor call(preempt process);
    end
    execute instruction(registers, store);
  forever
end
```

*ALGORITHM 4.8*   *A Monitor Call and Exit*

```
"monitor call(entry)"
  enter region
  enabled:= false;
  process table(process).register state:= registers;
  case entry of ... end

"monitor exit(candidate)"
  process:= candidate;
  registers:= process table(process).register state;
  enabled:= true;
  leave region
```

concurrent processes, the operations *enter region* and *leave region* serve no purpose. But the ability to inhibit interrupts is still necessary to ensure that monitor calls exclude one another in time.

So far, we have only considered short-term scheduling of *central processors.* Interrupts are also used to control short-term scheduling of *peripheral devices.* Input/output between peripherals and internal storage can be initiated by machine instructions executed within the basic monitor. The peripherals signal the completion of data transfers by interrupts, which enable the basic monitor to continue processes waiting for input/output.

So in practice, several interrupts are connected to a central processor:

> **type** *index* = 1..*m*;
> **var** *interrupt*: **shared array** *index* **of** *boolean*;

It is therefore necessary to extend the monitor procedure *preempt process* with an identification of the interrupt which caused the monitor call:

> **procedure** *preempt process*(*cause*: *index*)

Since the processors are identical and use the same monitor, it is irrelevant which processor a given interrupt occurs on.

### 4.2.6. Timing Constraints

Short-term scheduling as discussed here is an implementation of the well-structured concepts of multiprogramming defined in Chapter 3. Above this level of programming, the number of physical processors and the use of interrupts are as irrelevant as the logic circuits used to implement an adder.

But while we gain conceptual clarity from this abstraction, we also lose control of the finer details of scheduling at higher levels of programming. So the scheduling decisions taken at the short-term level determine the rate at which a computer is able to respond to *real-time events.*

To get an idea of how serious this problem is, we will assume that each processor has 8 registers and that a store word can be accessed in 1 $\mu$sec. An outline of the machine code required to implement scheduling primitives on a typical computer shows roughly the following execution times:

| | |
|---|---|
| *hardware level* | |
| store access (per word) | 1 $\mu$sec |
| *basic monitor level* | |
| interrupt | 20 $\mu$sec |
| *process level* | |
| wait or signal | 0.05-0.25 msec |
| arbitrary critical region | 0.1 -0.5  msec |

Process initiation and termination within a concurrent statement require about 0.5 msec per process (when store allocation time is ignored!).

It is evident that the better the abstractions become, the more we lose control of short-term scheduling. Within the basic monitor, it is possible to respond to about 50,000 events per second. Above this level, guaranteed response time to real-time events is increased by a factor between 12 and 25.

Although these figures are acceptable in most environments, there are certainly applications which require response to more than 2000-4000 events per second (for example, speech recognition).

If priorities are dynamic, the scheduling decisions made after a timer interrupt will take at least 0.25 msec for the simplest algorithm (such as round-robin). So it is unrealistic to change priorities more frequently than, say, every 10 msec (which means that 2.5 per cent of the processor time is used to control processor multiplexing). If processors are multiplexed at this rate among ready processes by simple round-robin scheduling, guaranteed response by processes to real-time events is suddenly reduced to a multiple of 10 msec, or less than 100 events per second!

It was this drastic reduction of real-time response caused by short-term scheduling that I had in mind when I made the statement in Section 4.1 that "all levels of scheduling implement a *policy* towards users and their computations. This is important to realize because policies are among the first things installation managers will wish to modify to satisfy users."

These figures can no doubt be improved somewhat by additional hardware support. Nevertheless, the decisions made at the short-term level of scheduling cannot always be ignored at higher levels of programming, so a realistic designer must also be prepared to change this part of the system for certain applications.

### 4.2.7. Conclusion

Our intellectual inability to analyze all aspects of a complex problem in one step forces us to divide the scheduling problem into a number of decisions made at different levels of programming. The criteria for a successful decomposition of the scheduling problem are not well-understood at the moment.

The danger of the abstraction achieved by short-term scheduling is that the decisions which determine the efficiency of hardware utilization and the rate at which the system is able to respond to external events are made at a very low level of programming, which is hard to influence at higher levels precisely because it hides the physical characteristics of the system.

Practical experience with operating systems has shown that some short-term policies—in particular those which involve store multiplexing—can have a disastrous effect on the system as a whole and make any attempt to control the mode of operation at the management level futile. Part of the answer to this problem is that there must be a strong interaction between the various levels of scheduling. A reasonable approach is to let the medium-term scheduler *assign priorities* that are used by the short-term scheduler to select candidates for available resources. At the same time, the short-term scheduler can influence the decisions of the medium-term scheduler by *collecting measurements* of the actual utilization of resources and the waiting times of processes.

## 4.3. LITERATURE

The thesis by Saltzer (1966) is an excellent analysis of short-term scheduling. Saltzer made a clear distinction between the *hardware* and *user management* levels of scheduling. The recognition of the *ready*, *running*, and *waiting* states is also due to him. Saltzer implemented basic critical regions by means of two instructions, *lock* and *unlock* (which correspond to *enter region* and *leave region*). Other process interactions were handled by a fairly restrictive set of primitives, *block* and *wakeup*, which enable a process to delay itself until another process wakes it up.

Wirth (1969) explains the implementation and application of the scheduling primitives *initiate process*, *terminate process*, *wait* and *signal* (which he calls *fork*, *join*, *P*, and *V*) in the algorithmic machine language *PL 360*. He points out the danger of forcing programmers to think in terms of interrupts instead of well-structured primitives.

In the *Venus* operating system described by Liskow (1972), processor multiplexing is handled almost exclusively by hardware: *wait* and *signal* are available as machine instructions that maintain process queues ordered by priority.

A paper by Lampson (1968) contains an interesting proposal to centralize all scheduling decisions in a single, microprogrammed computer to which all external interrupts are connected. The scheduler can send a single interrupt to each of the other processors indicating that they should preempt their running processes and resume ready processes of higher priority. The use of small processors to perform specific operating system tasks may well turn out to be more economical for multiprogramming than the use of a system consisting of identical processors, each of medium or large size.

Hoover and Eckhart (1966) describe the influence of extreme real-time requirements in a telephone switching system on the choice of a short-term scheduling strategy. Their scheduler differs from those which preempt less urgent processes unconditionally in favor of more urgent processes in the following way: The scheduler periodically examines all ready processes; a scheduling *cycle* is divided into a number of *phases*, each dedicated to non-preemptive execution of processes of a given priority. In each cycle, all priority levels are served at least once, and high priority is achieved by dedicating several phases to a given class of processes. In this way, excessive delay of processes of lower priority is avoided. This strategy is realistic when the processing time of each process is short compared to the response times required.

Brinch Hansen (1970) describes the *RC 4000* multiprogramming system, which includes a set of scheduling primitives called *create*, *start*, *stop*, and *remove process*. These primitives, implemented by a monitor, enable processes to schedule other processes according to any strategy desired at the medium-term level. This design is described and commented on in detail in Chapter 8.

BRINCH HANSEN, P., "The nucleus of a multiprogramming system," *Comm. ACM 13*, 4, pp. 238-50, April *1970*.

HOOVER, E. S. and ECKHART, B. J., "Performance of a monitor for a real-time control system," *Proc. AFIPS Fall Joint Computer Conf.*, pp. 23-25, Nov. *1966*.

LAMPSON, B. W., "A scheduling philosophy for multiprocessing systems," *Comm. ACM 11*, 5, pp. 347-60, May *1968*.

LISKOW, B. H., "The design of the Venus operating system," *Comm. ACM 15*, 3, pp. 144-59, March *1972*.

SALTZER, J. H., "Traffic control in a multiplexed computer system," *MAC-TR-30*, Massachusetts Institute of Technology, Cambridge, Massachusetts, July *1966*.

WIRTH, N., "On multiprogramming, machine coding, and computer organization," *Comm. ACM 12*, 9, pp. 489-98, Sept. *1969*.

# 5

# *STORE MANAGEMENT*

This chapter describes techniques of sharing an internal store of limited capacity among concurrent computations, with and without the use of a larger, slower backing store. It summarizes current store technology and explains the influence of recursive procedures, concurrent processes, and dynamic relocation on store addressing. It concludes with an analysis of placement algorithms and store multiplexing.

Concurrent processes share two vital resources: processors and storage. Processor management has already been discussed. The subject of this chapter is *store management*—the techniques used to share an internal store of limited capacity among concurrent computations.

Store management decisions are made at all levels of programming. We will again distinguish between two main levels: medium-term and short-term store management.

*Medium-term store management* implements the service policy towards users. It maintains a queue of programs and data on a backing store and decides when computations are initiated and terminated. It also preempts and resumes computations during their execution to satisfy more urgent user requests immediately.

*Short-term store management* transfers programs and data between a backing store and an internal store and assigns processors to them as directed by medium-term management. It tries to utilize the internal store efficiently by: (1) limiting the frequency of data and program transfers; (2) keeping computations in the internal store which can run while others are waiting for input/output; and (3) transferring data and programs to the internal store only when computations actually need them.

In this chapter, we concentrate on short-term store management. To share resources efficiently, a designer must depend on his knowledge of their technology and expected usage. So we begin with two sections on *store technology* and *addressing*. They are followed by two sections on *placement algorithms* and *store multiplexing*, describing how internal storage is assigned to programs and data and how the latter are transferred back and forth between internal store and backing store during execution.

## 5.1. STORE TECHNOLOGY

### 5.1.1. Store Components

A *store* is used to retain data and programs until they are needed during execution. It is divided into a finite set of components called *locations*. Each location can represent any one of a finite set of data *values*. These values are recorded and obtained by *write* and *read* operations.

Following Bell and Newell (1971), we will characterize various store types by the manner in which locations can be accessed efficiently.

A store with *sequential access* consists of locations which can only be accessed in sequential order. The store is positioned at its first location by a *rewind* operation. *Read* and *write* operations access the current location and position the store at its next location:

> **var** *store*: **file of** *V*; *value*: *V*;
>
> *rewind*(*store*);
> *read*(*value*, *store*);
> *write*(*value*, *store*);

Sequential access is used mainly for large files stored on detachable media such as paper tape, punched cards, printed forms, and magnetic tape. It is the cheapest and slowest method of storage.

A store with *direct access* consists of locations which can be accessed in arbitrary order by indexing:

> **var** *store*: **array** *A* **of** *V*; *address*: *A*; *value*: *V*;
>
> *value* := *store*(*address*);
> *store*(*address*) := *value*;

Most computers use two kinds of directly accessible stores:

(1) An *internal store* gives fast, direct access to locations called *words*. It is used to hold data and programs during execution. The store medium is usually fast magnetic cores. Integrated circuits are used to implement a small set of very fast locations called *registers*.

In an internal store, the time required to access a location is independent of the location's physical position. This is called *random access*.

(2) A *backing store* gives slower, direct access to locations consisting of *blocks* of words. It is used to hold data and programs until computations need them in the internal store. The store medium is usually slow magnetic cores or rotating magnetic surfaces such as drums and disks.

In a rotating store, a block can only be accessed when the rotation of the medium brings it under an *access head*. This is called *cyclic access*.

On some disks, the access heads can move linearly across the rotating surface. This is called *sequential-cyclic access*.

The stores mentioned can be characterized more precisely by the following physical properties:

| | |
|---|---|
| *store capacity* | the number of locations |
| *location length* | the number of bits per location |
| *access time* | the average time required to read or write the value of a location |

The figures below are typical for present computers. I have chosen a representative word length of 32 bits and a block length of 1 K words.

| store medium | capacity (K words) | access time (msec/K words) |
|---|---|---|
| integrated circuits | 0.01-1 | 0.1 |
| core | 10-1000 | 1-5 |
| drum | 1000-10,000 | 10-30 |
| disk | 10,000-100,000 | 100-1000 |
| magnetic tape | 10,000-100,000 | 1000-100,000 |

For stores with sequential and cyclic access, the *access time* consists of a *waiting time* required to position an access head in front of a block and a *transfer time* required to transfer the block to or from the store.

| store medium | waiting time (msec) | transfer time (msec/K words) |
|---|---|---|
| drum | 2-10 | 5-20 |
| disk | 100-1000 | 5-20 |
| magnetic tape | 1000-100,000 | 20-100 |

### 5.1.2. Hierarchal Stores

The store in present computers is usually a *hierarchy of store components* of different types. An example is shown in Fig. 5.1. At the bottom of the hierarchy is a fast *internal store* of moderate capacity. Above this level, we find a slower, larger *backing store.* And, on top of this, a still slower and much larger *file store.*

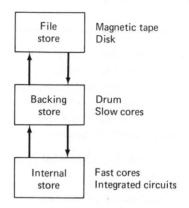

Fig. 5.1. A store hierarchy.

The motivation for this variety of store components is economic: The cost of storage is roughly proportional to the store's capacity and access rate. It would be prohibitively expensive to maintain all user programs and data permanently in an internal store. Instead, users and operating systems try to *distribute programs and data at various levels in the store hierarchy according to their expected frequency of usage.*

An example of hierarchal storage was mentioned in connection with the *SDC Q-32* system (Section 1.2.4): A disk of 4000 K words with an average access time of 225 msec is used to hold data and program files between computations. When a user wishes to execute a program, it is transferred from the disk to a drum of 400 K words with an average access time of 40 msec. From the drum, the program is periodically transferred to a core store of 65 K words to receive short slices of processor time.

Some people have expressed the hope that it may eventually become economical to build internal stores that are an order of magnitude larger than present core stores and therefore eliminate the need for backing stores. I believe that, although internal stores may become as large as that, it will always be economically attractive to use still larger and slower backing stores to hold less frequently used data. The hierarchal structure of stores is not caused by inadequate technology—it is a sound principle for efficient resource utilization.

## 5.2. STORE ADDRESSING

Store management raises three basic questions:

(1) What is the appropriate *unit* of store assignment to computations?

(2) How are these units *placed* in an internal store prior to their use?

(3) How are they *referenced* by computations during execution?

The following discussion of *program segmentation* and *store addressing* gives some of the answers to questions (1) and (3). Subsequent sections on *placement algorithms* and *store multiplexing* deal with question (2).

I assume that programs are written in a well-structured language which enables a compiler and an operating system to take advantage to some extent of predictable store requirements. I also expect a compiler to assign store addresses correctly to programs so that there is no need to check them during execution.

### 5.2.1. Program Segmentation

To the user of a high-level programming language, a *virtual store* consists of *data* identified by textstrings called *identifiers*. It is a mapping of identifiers into values:

$$virtual\ store:\ identifier \rightarrow value$$

To the designer of computer systems, a *real store* consists of *locations* identified by consecutive numbers called *addresses*. It is a mapping of addresses into values:

$$real\ store:\ address \rightarrow value$$

Before a program is executed, locations must be assigned to it in the real store. This so-called *store allocation* defines the intermediate mapping of identifiers into addresses:

$$store\ allocation:\ identifier \rightarrow address$$

Store allocation is performed partly by a compiler, partly by an operating system.

Practical methods of store allocation try to achieve two conflicting goals: (1) to *access* a store as fast as possible during execution; and (2) to *share* it among concurrent jobs.

The fastest access is achieved by a *fixed allocation* of storage to programs at compile time. This enables programs to access locations directly during execution.

But, when a store is shared by jobs requested and terminated at unpredictable times, it is impossible to know the location of available storage in advance of program execution. So sharing requires a *dynamic allocation* of storage at run time.

To make sharing possible and still get reasonably fast access, the following compromise is made:

Programs and data are divided into a few large segments. Each *segment* consists of related data which can be placed anywhere in the store and addressed relative to a common origin, as shown in Fig. 5.2. The origin and number of locations of a segment are called its *base address* and *length*, respectively.

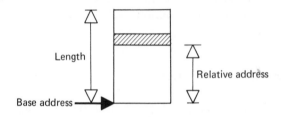

**Fig. 5.2.** A segment identified by a base address and a length, and a location within the segment identified by a relative address.

Base addresses are unique within the entire store, but relative addresses are only unique within segments. They are called *real* and *virtual addresses*, respectively.

The division of programs into segments and the replacement of identifiers by *relative addresses* is done by a *compiler*. When segments are needed during program execution, an *operating system* assigns locations to them and defines their *base addresses*.

The number of base addresses can be kept small if the segments are kept sufficiently large. This makes it practical to store base addresses in directly accessible locations or registers during execution in order to ensure fast access. When a compiled program refers to a segment location by its relative address, a central processor automatically adds the base address of the segment and accesses the location directly.

So efficient sharing of an internal store with direct access requires segmentation of programs at compile time and address mapping at run time:

*virtual store: identifier → virtual address → real address → value*

This is the main idea behind current techniques of store allocation.

Since each instruction requires address mapping, the latter should obviously be made as simple as possible. To cite Wirth (1971b): "The efficiency of a system stands or falls with the efficiency of the address calculations."

We will discuss three independent *computational requirements* which lead to increasingly complicated forms of addressing:

> recursive procedures
> concurrent processes
> dynamic relocation

The first two requirements should be well-known to you, but the third one may be new. So far, we have only considered the need to assign storage to segments immediately *before* execution starts. An extension of this technique is needed when an internal store is multiplexed among several computations by transferring segments back and forth between internal store and backing store: It must now be possible to place segments in different locations and redefine their base addresses *during* execution. This is called *dynamic relocation.*

### 5.2.2. Single-segment Computations

The simplest case is a computation which only requires a single segment.

*Sequential, Non-recursive Computations*

Consider the following program:

> procedure $R$;
>   procedure $S$;
>   begin ... end
> begin ... $S$; ... end
>
>   label $Q$ begin ... $R$; ... end

It consists of a statement $Q$, which calls a procedure $R$; $R$ in turn calls another procedure $S$.

The natural units of segmentation are: (1) the statements which can be compiled into invariant machine code; and (2) the variables declared inside a procedure.

Storage for the *program segment* is needed throughout the computation. Storage for a *data segment* is needed only while the computation is executing the corresponding procedure.

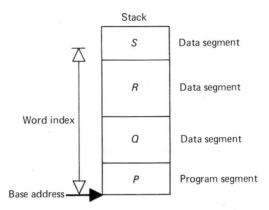

Fig. 5.3. Store allocation for a sequential, non-recursive computation.

Since procedures are called sequentially, storage for data segments will be allocated and released strictly in *last-in, first-out* order. Program and data segments can therefore be combined into a *single segment* which varies in length according to the number of procedures called. A store used in this manner is called a *stack*.

Figure 5.3 shows the extent of the stack when the previous computation is inside procedure $S$. The stack is addressed by word indices relative to its base address.

A slight complication arises if a procedure is called in different contexts, for example:

> **procedure** $S$;
> **begin** ... **end**
>
> **procedure** $R$;
> **begin** ... $S$; ... **end**
>
> **label** $Q$
> **begin** ... $R$; ... $S$; ... **end**

Here, procedure $S$ is called inside both statement $Q$ and procedure $R$. The extent of the stack prior to a call of $S$ is different in each case. But a compiler can calculate the maximum extent of the stack prior to any call of the procedure and can always place its data segment at that point. This is illustrated by Fig. 5.4. In the worst case, a data segment will be allocated permanently for each procedure.

Since the maximum extent of the stack can be determined at compile time, an operating system can regard it as a fixed-length segment at execution time.

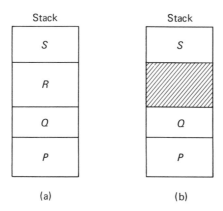

Fig. 5.4.  Store allocation for a nonrecursive procedure $S$
called in different contexts (a) and (b).

So, in general, a sequential, non-recursive computation requires only a single segment of fixed length addressed by word indices. Fast addressing is achieved by keeping the base address in a register.

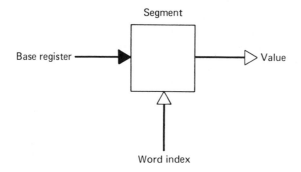

Fig. 5.5.  A virtual store consisting of a single relocatable
segment.

This type of virtual store is shown in Fig. 5.5 using the following symbols:

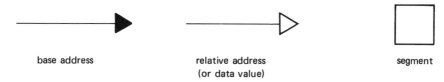

The virtual addresses used by a computation (word indices) are independent of the location of its segment in the store. *Dynamic relocation* therefore only requires a change of the base register value.

Examples of computers of this type are the *IBM 7094 II* (Bell and Newell, 1971), the *CDC 6600* (Thornton, 1964), and the *Atlas* (Kilburn, 1962).

### 5.2.3. Multi-segment Computations

The next case to consider is a computation which requires several segments.

*Sequential, Recursive Computations*

Consider the following program:

> **procedure** $R$;
> **begin** ... **if** $C$ **then** $R$; ... **end**
>
> **label** $Q$ **begin** ... $R$; ... **end**

Procedure $R$ calls itself repeatedly while condition $C$ holds. Each call creates an instance $R1$, $R2$, ... , $Rn$ of the variables declared inside the procedure as shown in Fig. 5.6.

In this case, a compiler cannot predict the extent of the stack prior to an instance of a procedure call. Consequently, programs must be compiled for an array of data segments.

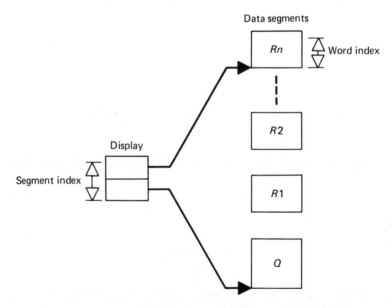

**Fig. 5.6.** Store allocation for a sequential, recursive computation.

At compile time, an identifier is replaced by a *virtual address* consisting of a *segment index* and a *word index*. The segment index is equal to the number of procedures which enclose the identifier in the program text; it is often called the *level of procedure nesting*. The word index is the relative address of a location within the given segment.

At execution time, the currently accessible data segments are defined by an *array of base registers*, the *display*.

When a procedure with segment index $s$ is called, a new display is created. It consists of the entries 0 to $s - 1$ of the previous display and an entry $s$ defining the origin of a new data segment for the procedure called. Upon return from the procedure, the previous display becomes valid again. The displays can be stored as part of the data segments and linked together in their order of creation as shown in Fig. 5.7.

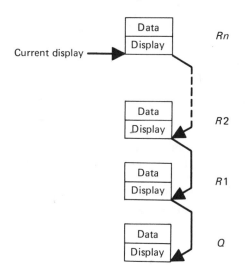

Fig. 5.7.  A stack consisting of data segments and displays
linked in their order of creation.

This brief presentation assumes that you already are familiar with the implementation of recursive procedures. Randell and Russell (1964) explain this in detail in their book on the *KDF 9 Algol 60* compiler.

I conclude that a *sequential, recursive computation* requires a virtual store consisting of segments of fixed length addressed by segment and word indices. This type of store is shown in Fig. 5.8. The segment index is used to select a base address in the current display; this is added to the word index to get the real address of a segment word. Fast access is achieved by keeping the current display (or its most recently used entries) in registers.

It is not clear how many display registers one needs to execute programs efficiently. For example, the *B6700* computer has 32 display registers (Organick and Cleary, 1971). This is much more than most

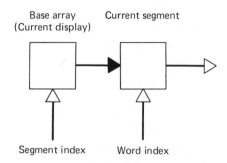

**Fig. 5.8.** A virtual store consisting of
non-relocatable segments.

programs need. Wirth (1971b) reports that a Pascal compiler for the *CDC*
*6400* computer only uses 3 display registers and that Pascal programs are
limited to 5 levels of procedure nesting.

### Concurrent Computations

Consider the following program, which includes concurrent statements,
but no recursive procedures:

> **procedure** $R$;
> **begin** ... **end**
>
> **procedure** $S$;
>   **procedure** $T$;
>   **begin** ... **end**
> **cobegin** $R$; $T$ **coend**
>
> **label** $Q$ **cobegin** $R$; $S$ **coend**

At some point in the execution of this program, the tree of parent and
child processes may look like that shown in Fig. 5.9. The processes are
shown as nodes linked to their parents. Process $S$, for example, is the child
of process $Q$ and also the parent of processes $R2$ and $T$.

Since concurrent processes can create data segments at the same time, it
is necessary to have a separate stack branch for each process. The
computation as a whole therefore builds up a *tree-structured stack*
corresponding to Fig. 5.9.

Although the stack is tree-structured, each process can only access that
part of it which lies on a directed path from the process itself through its
ancestors to the root of the tree. In the previous example, process $T$ can
access its own data and those of processes $S$ and $Q$. So the virtual store of
each process is still a linear array of data segments.

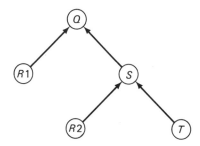

**Fig. 5.9.** A concurrent computation consisting of child processes linked to parent processes.

Each procedure is non-recursive, but can be called by more than one process. (An example is procedure $R$ in the previous program.) This makes it impossible to assign a fixed position in the stack to variables declared within a given procedure. A *display* is therefore needed to define the origins of data segments currently accessible to a given process. When a process is created, a new stack branch and a display are also created. The child display is identical to the parent display.

So the virtual store required by a single process is a linear array of fixed-length segments, as shown in Fig. 5.8. Evidently, it makes no difference whether or not a concurrent computation includes *recursive procedures*—the addressing schemes are the same.

### 5.2.4. Program Relocation

In a concurrent computation, a given variable may be accessible to several processes within various procedures. So the base address of a given data segment may be stored in several displays. If the segment is relocated during execution, it is necessary to follow the chain of displays for each process and change the corresponding base address wherever it is found.

From a practical point of view, it is clearly preferable that relocation of a segment only require an assignment to a single base register. The addressing scheme shown in Fig. 5.8 can therefore only be recommended for non-relocatable segments.

To make *dynamic relocation* practical, the base addresses of all segments belonging to a computation must be kept in a single table called the *segment table*. When a process creates a data segment, its base address is placed in an empty location in the segment table and its index in this table is placed in the current display of the process.

This type of virtual store is shown in Fig. 5.10. Address mapping is now done in three steps: (1) a segment index assigned at compile time is used to select a segment table index from the current display; (2) this index in turn

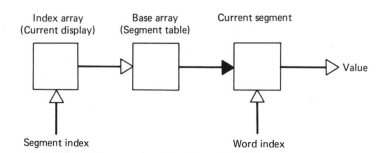

**Fig. 5.10.** A virtual store consisting of relocatable segments.

is used to select a base address from the segment table; and finally, (3) the base address is added to a word index to get a real address.

The length of segment tables varies considerably in present computers:

In the *IBM 360/67* computer, each computation is limited to 16 segments defined by base registers (Comfort, 1965).

The *B5000* computer allows a maximum of 1024 segments within each computation. The segment table is therefore kept in the internal store as an initial part of the stack and only its most recently used entries are kept in registers (Lonergan and King, 1961).

The *B8500* computer keeps the indices and origins of the 16 most recently used segments in a very fast store. When a segment is referenced, an attempt is made to find its base address in this store using its index as a search key. If this search fails, the base address is obtained from the segment table in the slower internal store and entered in the fast store together with its index. Because the fast store associates a value (a base address) with a key (a segment index), it is called an *associative store* (McCullough, 1965).

The *GE 645* computer used in the *Multics* system is rather extreme: It permits a maximum of 256 K segments per computation (Glaser, 1965). The argument originally made in favor of this design was that it makes it possible to assign *unique virtual addresses* to all program and data files in the entire installation and thereby facilitates the sharing of these during execution (Dennis, 1965).

This argument does not seem plausible to me. In practice, dynamic relocation requires that each computation use a separate segment table and assign indices to segments when they are first referenced. And, as Daley and Dennis (1968) point out in a later paper: "An immediate consequence of this is that the same segment will, in general, be identified by *different segment indices* in different computations." Consequently, the range of segment indices need only be large enough to enable a computation to distinguish among the segments it actually uses.

At this point, a general remark about *dynamic relocation* might be helpful: When segments are relocatable during execution, it must be ensured that references to them by computations and their operating systems exclude one another in time.

This can be done by preempting a computation completely while one or more of its segments are being relocated. This method is simple to implement in a *single-processor system* in which at most one process at a time can refer to the store.

Another possibility is to relocate a segment while the computation involved continues to run. This is done in three steps: (1) make the base address invalid; (2) move the segment to its new location; and (3) redefine the base address. If a process refers to the segment during this critical region, its processor will recognize the invalid base address and interrupt the process.

In a *multiprocessor system*, a computation and its operating system may run on different processors. It is also possible that the computation itself consists of concurrent processes which run on different processors, but have access to the same segments. Consequently, dynamic relocation requires that base addresses be kept in store locations or registers accessible to all processors.

It should also be mentioned that *input/output* can interfere with program relocation. Most peripheral devices are built to transfer a block of data to or from an internal store without interruption. Consequently, a segment cannot be relocated before all input/output operations on it are completed.

### 5.2.5. Conclusion

In a survey of store management techniques, Hoare and McKeag (1971c) emphasize that "the designer of software systems should not always strive after the greatest generality and its attendant complexity, but should use his best judgement in selecting the simplest technique which is sufficient for his current purpose."

This is particularly true of store addressing where the price of unnecessary complexity is paid for every instruction executed. To use an addressing scheme that caters to relocatable, concurrent, recursive jobs (Fig. 5.10) in an installation that only runs non-relocatable, sequential, non-recursive jobs (Fig. 5.5) serves no useful purpose, but will certainly complicate the operating system considerably and reduce performance.

## 5.3. PLACEMENT ALGORITHMS

I have described the motivation for program segmentation and have shown how segments are accessed during execution. We must now decide *where* in available internal storage these segments should be placed prior to their use. This decision rule is called a *placement algorithm*.

Placement is complicated by three characteristics of segments: (1) they are created and deleted at unpredictable times; (2) they have different lengths; and (3) they must be placed in a linear store.

### 5.3.1. Contiguous Segments

The most direct approach is to place a segment in contiguous locations in the real store (or more precisely, in locations with contiguous real addresses). When this method is used, the effect of unpredictable creation and deletion is to divide the store into a random pattern of *segments* of different lengths mixed with *holes* of available storage also of different lengths. This is illustrated by Fig. 5.11.

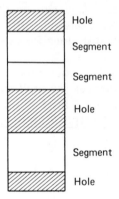

Hole

Segment

Segment

Hole

Segment

Hole

**Fig. 5.11.** Contiguous allocation of segments in a linear store.

If the length of a segment is fixed during its lifetime, the following placement algorithms suggest themselves:

*First fit*: a segment is placed in the first hole large enough to hold it.

*Best fit*: a segment is placed in the smallest hole large enough to hold it.

Intuitively, one would expect the *best fit* algorithm to increase the probability of being able to satisfy subsequent store requests compared to the *first fit* algorithm, which tends to split larger holes into smaller ones. But in simulation experiments Knuth (1969) found that in practice *first fit* appears to be superior. Since it is also the simpler algorithm, it can be recommended. It is used, for example, in the *Master Control Program* for the *B5500* computer (McKeag, 1971a).

If the search for the first hole that fits always starts at one end of the store, the smaller holes tend to accumulate at that end and increase the search time for the larger holes. This effect can be avoided by searching the store cyclically, starting from a different hole each time. The starting point can itself be selected cyclically.

The main problem with contigous segments is that they split the available storage into holes of different lengths. It may therefore be impossible at some point to find a hole for a segment, although it requires less than the total amount of available storage.

The cures that have been used are: (1) dynamic relocation; and (2) complete initial allocation.

*Compacting*

One method of dynamic relocation is to move all segments to one end of the store, thus combining all holes at the other end. This *compacting* technique illustrated by Fig. 5.12 is used in the *Scope* operating system for the *CDC 6600* computer (Wilson, 1971a).

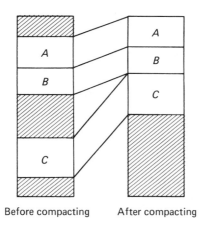

Before compacting          After compacting

**Fig. 5.12.** Compacting of segments.

When a good placement strategy (such as *first fit*) is used, the need for relocation only arises when most of the store is occupied. Knuth (1969) found that 90 per cent of a store could be filled without relocation when segments were small, say 10 per cent of the store capacity each. Measurements made by Batson (1970) on a *B5500* university installation showed that most segments were indeed quite small: Segments were limited to a maximum of 1 K words each, but 60 per cent of them actually contained less than 40 words. When the system was operating in a steady state, the segments in use occupied about 80 per cent of a store of 28 K words.

So, when compacting is needed, a large part of the store (80-90 per cent) must be copied. This can be quite time-consuming: If a word is copied in 2 μsec, 80 per cent of a store of 64 K words can be compacted in about 100 msec.

In a well-designed system, compacting occurs so rarely that the processor time spent on relocation is negligible (except in real-time systems, which must guarantee response to external events in less than 100 msec under all circumstances). But it hardly seems worthwhile to complicate addressing and store allocation just to utilize the last 10-20 per cent of the store in rare circumstances.

The real problem, however, is not processor and store utilization, but the danger of *deadlock*. If nothing is done about it, processes may be unable to continue even though their combined need does not exceed the available storage. Such a system cannot deliver reliable, long-term service. According to McKeag (1971a), a survey of eleven *B5500* installations showed that 9 per cent of all system failures (about one a week) were store deadlocks caused by non-relocatable segments.

*Store Multiplexing*

Segments can also be relocated as part of store multiplexing: Instead of all segments being compacted, some of them are transferred temporarily from the internal store to a backing store and replaced by other segments. This is a good example of *deadlock prevention by preemption* (Section 3.5.2). It is discussed in detail in Section 5.4 on store multiplexing.

*Complete Initial Allocation*

A much simpler method of deadlock prevention is to allocate the *maximum storage* needed by a computation *in advance* of its execution.

A single segment of fixed length is assigned to a *sequential computation*. This segment contains the machine code and a linear stack. During its execution, the sequential computation can create and delete its own data segments in *last-in, first-out* order within the stack, as shown in Fig. 5.3. It can also use recursive procedures as long as the stack does not exceed its maximum extent.

Under special circumstances, complete initial allocation can also be used for *concurrent computations*. The definition of concurrent statements in Section 3.1.2 implies that *parent processes neither create nor delete data segments while child processes exist* (because parents must wait until all their children are terminated). In other words, only the leaves of a stack tree vary in length. In Fig. 5.13(a), the leaves are $C, D, E, G$, and $H$.

Suppose also that *the maximum extent of a stack branch is known before the process using that branch is created*. These two restrictions on concurrent processes make it possible to store a stack tree as *nested segments*, as shown in Fig. 5.13(b).

The spooling system shown in Fig. 1.3 is an example of concurrent processes that use one level of segment nesting. The *RC 4000*

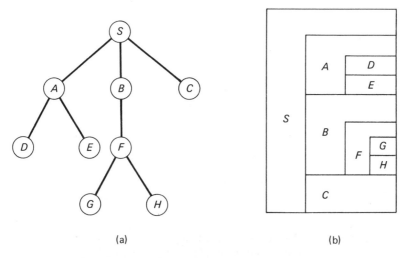

(a)                                                    (b)

Fig. 5.13. A tree of concurrent processes (a) using nested
segments (b).

multiprogramming system (Brinch Hansen, 1970) permits arbitrary nesting
of processes within a single segment.

The disadvantage of using such large contiguous segments is that the
store is utilized less efficiently: A hole may be fairly large, but not large
enough to hold a complete computation.

Finally, it should be mentioned that the deadlock problem of
contiguous segments repeats itself on a more serious time scale on backing
stores.

### 5.3.2. Paged Segments

A system using contiguous segments is constantly fighting "pollution"
of its resources: Gradually, jobs will partition the store into an
unpredictable mixture of non-equivalent holes until drastic measures must
be taken to avoid disaster.

*Paging* is a radical solution to the placement problem. It treats the
stores consistently as pools of equivalent resources. Stores are divided into
*storage units* of equal length, called *page frames*, and segments are divided
into *data units* of the same length, called *pages*. During execution, a page
can be placed in any available page frame. A program still refers to segment
locations by *contiguous virtual addresses*, but in the real store a segment
may be placed in *disjoint page frames* as shown in Fig. 5.14.

Within a segment, a location is identified by *page* and *word indices*. The
page index is used to select the base address of a page frame from a
so-called *page table*; this is added to the word index to get a real address.

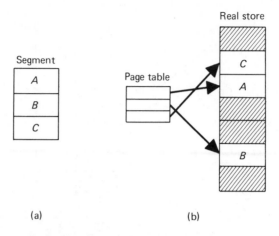

**Fig. 5.14.** A segment (a) consisting of three pages $A$, $B$, $C$,
and its placement (b) in the real store.

One of the aims of segmentation is to make programs insensitive to their placement in the store. It is therefore common to choose the page length as a power of two:

$$p = 2^m$$

where $p$ is the number of words per page and $m$ is a positive integer.

Programs can then use contiguous relative addresses within a segment:

| $n$ bits |
| --- |

relative address

These are interpreted by processors as consisting of a page index (the most significant bits) and a word index (the least significant bits):

| $n$-$m$ bits | $m$ bits |
| --- | --- |

page index  word index

Notice that there is no difficulty in handling *paged segments* which *vary in length* during their lifetime as long as the total number of pages used does not exceed the number of page frames.

The placement algorithm is now trivial, but this has been achieved only by increasing the complexity of addressing. Figure 5.15 illustrates the difference between contiguous and paged segments in this respect.

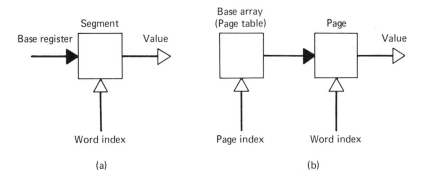

**Fig. 5.15.** Addressing of (a) a contiguous segment, and (b) a paged segment.

Thus, if segments are paged, the symbol Fig. 5.15(a) should be replaced by (b) in Figs. 5.5, 5.8, and 5.10.

The first computer to use paging was the *Atlas*, designed at the University of Manchester in England. It has a core store of 16 K words divided into page frames of 512 words each. An associative store with 32 locations performs fast mapping of page indices into page frames.

Contiguous segmentation leaves about 10 to 20 per cent of an internal store unused. Randell (1969) calls this phenomenon *external fragmentation*—storage wasted *between* segments.

Theoretically, external fragmentation can be avoided altogether by paging. But paging decreases the utilization of storage in other ways: (1) by using additional storage for page tables; and (2) by rounding up storage requests to an integral number of pages. Randell calls this *internal fragmentation*—storage lost *within* segments.

Small pages increase the length of page tables, but reduce the effect of rounding; large pages have the opposite effect. So there must exist a page of medium size that minimizes internal fragmentation.

Let $p$ and $s$ denote the page length and the average segment length in words, respectively. Then a segment requires a page table with approximately $s/p$ entries of one word each, and wastes roughly $p/2$ words within its last page (the latter approximation is only justified when $p \ll s$).

When all page frames are occupied, the fraction of storage lost by internal fragmentation is therefore:

$$f = \frac{1}{p} + \frac{p}{2s} \tag{5.1}$$

By setting $\frac{df}{dp} = 0$, we find the *optimum page length* $p_0$ and the *minimum internal fragmentation* $f_0$:

$$p_0 = \sqrt{2s} \qquad\qquad (5.2)$$

$$f_0 = \sqrt{\frac{2}{s}} \qquad\qquad (5.3)$$

Conversely, there is an *optimum segment length* $s_0$ for a given page length $p$. Table 5.1 shows $s_0$ and $f_0$ for various page lengths $p$, which are powers of two.

TABLE 5.1.   The optimum segment length $s_0$
and the minimum internal fragmentation $f_0$
for various page lengths $p$.

| $p$ (words) | $s_0$ (words) | $f_0$ (per cent) |
|:---:|:---:|:---:|
| 8 | 32 | 25 |
| 16 | 128 | 13 |
| 32 | 512 | 6 |
| 64 | 2 K | 3 |
| 128 | 8 K | 1.6 |
| 256 | 32 K | 0.8 |
| 512 | 128 K | 0.4 |
| 1024 | 512 K | 0.2 |

The general trend is that store fragmentation decreases when segments (and pages) increase in length.

The average segment length measured in the *B5500* installation at the University of Virginia was about 50 words. So, if we were to place each data segment created by a procedure call in a separate set of page frames, the best choice would be a page length of 8 words. This would make the internal fragmentation approximately 25 per cent.

An alternative is to assign a single large segment to each process and let the process create and delete its own data segments within it, as shown in Fig. 5.3. Small user programs in a *B5500* installation typically occupy 2 to 3 K words of core store each (McKeag, 1971a). For $s = 2500$, the best page length would be $p = 64$ words. Putting this into equation (5.1) gives $f = 3$ per cent.

So, while contiguous segments should be small to reduce external fragmentation, paged segments should be large to reduce internal fragmentation.

User programs of 2 to 3 K words are probably exceptionally small. Other installations have measured typical programs of 16 to 32 K words each (see for example, Arden and Boettner, 1969). In this case, a page length of 256 words would minimize store fragmentation.

Most computers, however, use larger pages of 512 words (*Atlas*) or 1024 words (*IBM 360/67* and *GE 645*) to reduce the processing time needed to initiate and complete page transfers between a backing store and an internal store.

Figure 5.16 shows the effect of large pages on store fragmentation for various segment lengths. It also shows the minimum fragmentation that can be achieved by an optimum choice $p_0$ of the page length for a given segment length.

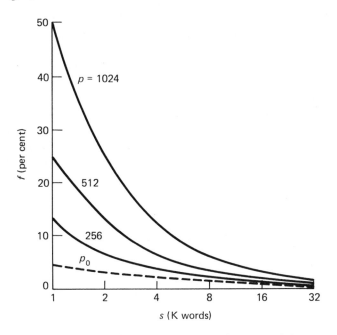

**Fig. 5.16.** Store fragmentation $f$ as a function of the average segment length $s$ for various page lengths $p$.

With pages of 1 K words, store fragmentation is 2 to 6 per cent for segments of 8 to 32 K words. Although this exceeds the theoretical minimum of 1 to 2 per cent, it is still better than the 10 to 20 per cent wasted by contiguous segments.

Randell (1969) reaches the opposite conclusion, that internal fragmentation is more serious than external fragmentation. But his assumption is that the average segment only occupies 1 K words. As I pointed out earlier, internal fragmentation can be reduced by allocating much larger segments for complete computations.

Finally, it is worth mentioning that paging has been successfully

implemented by program alone on at least two small machines: the *GIER*
(Naur, 1965) and the *Electrologica X8* (McKeag, 1971b).

### 5.3.3.  Conclusion

Contiguous placement is well-suited to segments of fixed-length, which
are small compared to the internal store. It simplifies addressing, but
complicates placement. Complete initial allocation of storage or dynamic
replacement of segments is necessary to prevent deadlock; the former
method is recommended for nested segments, the latter for disjoint
segments. Compacting is of doubtful value. Contiguous placement seems to
be the most efficient technique for small, sequential computations.

Paging is best suited to large segments that may vary in length during
execution. It complicates addressing, but makes placement trivial. Properly
used, paging appears to utilize storage better than contiguous placement. It
is ideal for concurrent computations if users can specify reasonable storage
limits for every computation (to avoid a deadlock of unrelated computations) without predicting the precise requirements of single processes.

From time to time, it is suggested that it might be worthwhile to use
more than one page length within a given system. It seems to me that this
combines the worst aspects of contiguous and paged placement; the danger
of deadlock and the complexity of addressing.

## 5.4.  STORE MULTIPLEXING

We will finally examine systems which deliberately initiate more
computations than the internal store can hold. In these systems, segments
are kept on a backing store and transferred to an internal store on demand;
when the internal store is full, some of its segments are removed to the
backing store to make room for others. This is called *store multiplexing*.

The medium-term objective of store multiplexing is to give fast
response to short computations by preempting longer ones temporarily.

The short-term objective of store multiplexing is to increase utilization
of the internal store by only keeping available those segments that
computations actually use.

### 5.4.1.  Demand Fetching

We will mainly study store multiplexing among *paged segments*, but the
results apply qualitatively to *contiguous segments* as well. So wherever I
use the word "page" in the following discussion, I might just as well have
used the term "contiguous segment."

I assume that pages are only brought into the internal store when processes refer to them. This is called *demand fetching*.

The presence or absence of a page in the internal store is defined by a boolean in its page table entry. If a page is *present*, a processor can refer to it directly; if a page is *absent*, a reference to it provokes a call of a procedure, which then fetches the page from the backing store.

When the internal store is full, one of the pages already present must be replaced. The *victim* of replacement may be a *copy* of a page on the backing store. In this case, it is simply overwritten in the internal store. But, if the victim contains *original* data, it must be transferred to the backing store before it is replaced by another page in the internal store.

This decision is based on another boolean in the page table entry of the victim: It is set to *false* when the page is placed in the internal store and becomes *true* after an assignment to any of its locations.

In the following, I explain a simplified algorithm for demand fetching of pages from a drum to a core store. I make the following simplifying assumptions:

(1) Each computation can only access a single paged segment.

(2) Each computation is assigned a fixed set of page frames in core and on drum.

(3) Each page is associated with a fixed page frame on drum, but its page frame in core varies during execution.

(4) A computation selects a victim of replacement from its own core page frames.

Algorithm 5.1 shows the data structures used by a computation to describe the state of its pages and page frames.

Pages are identified by indices of type $P$, while page frames in core and on drum are identified by indices of types $C$ and $D$.

The segment of a given computation is defined by a *page table* with an entry for each page.

The page frames assigned to the computation in core are defined by a *core table*, which contains a sequence of *free* page frames (identified by core page frame indices) and a queue of *used* page frames (identified by page indices).

Algorithm 5.1 also shows how a page is accessed: If the page is not present, a victim is selected and the page is transferred to its core frame; then, the page is marked as *present*, but *not original*, and its index is entered in the set of *used* pages.

Algorithm 5.2 defines the selection of a victim: If the computation has a *free* core page frame, that page frame becomes the victim; otherwise, one of the *used* pages is selected, and, if it is an *original*, it is transferred to its frame on drum. Finally, the victim is marked as *not present*.

The criteria for selecting a specific victim for replacement are irrelevant here. We will return to this question later.

*ALGORITHM 5.1   Demand Paging*

```
type C = 1. .number of core page frames;
     D = 1. .number of drum page frames;
     P = 1. .number of pages;

var page table: array P of
              shared record
                      present, original: boolean;
                      core frame: C;
                      drum frame: D;
                  end

    core table: shared record
                      free: sequence of C;
                      used: queue of P;
                  end

procedure access(page: P);
const to core = true;
region page table(page) do
if not present then
begin
  select victim(core frame);
  transfer(core frame, drum frame, to core);
  present:= true;
  original:= false;
  enter(page, used);
end
```

Drum transfers are controlled by a *drum process*. It uses the data structure shown in Algorithm 5.3 which contains a queue of user processes *waiting* for page transfers. When a user process needs a page transfer, it defines the transfer in a *process table* entry and enters its index in the queue. Then, it activates the drum process by causing a *request* event and waits for a *response* event associated with its process table entry.

The index of the calling process is defined by a standard function:

**function** *process: Q*

*ALGORITHM 5.2   Demand Paging (cont.)*

```
procedure select victim(var core location: C);
const to drum = false;
var victim: P;
region core table do
if empty(free) then
begin
  remove(victim, used);
  region page table(victim) do
  begin
    if original then
    transfer(core frame, drum frame, to drum);
    present:= false;
    core location:= core frame;
  end
end
else get(core location, free);
```

*ALGORITHM 5.3   Demand Paging (cont.)*

```
type Q = 1. .number of processes;

var v: shared record
            waiting: queue of Q;
            process table: array Q of
                        record
                            core frame: C;
                            drum frame: D;
                            fetch: boolean;
                            response: event v;
                        end
            request, completion: event v;
        end

procedure transfer
(core location: C; drum location: D; to core: boolean);
region v do
with process table(process) do
begin
  core frame:= core location;
  drum frame:= drum location;
  fetch:= to core;
  enter(process, waiting);
  cause(request);
  await(response);
end
```

The drum process is defined by Algorithm 5.4. It waits until a *request* is made for a page transfer. Then, it removes the index of a calling process and starts a transfer from drum to core, or vice versa. After the *completion* of a transfer, it signals a response to the waiting process and repeats its cycle.

*ALGORITHM 5.4   Demand Paging (cont.)*

```
"Drum process"
var customer: Q;
region v do
repeat
   while empty(waiting) do await(request);
   remove(customer, waiting);
   with process table(customer) do
   begin
      start input output(core frame, drum frame, fetch);
      await(completion);
      cause(response);
   end
forever
```

Demand fetching of contiguous and paged segments was pioneered on the *B5000* and *Atlas* computers, respectively.

### 5.4.2.  Process Behavior

To evaluate the consequences of demand fetching, we need a model of process behavior. We will first study the execution of a single, sequential program which exceeds the capacity of the internal store.

The available store is characterized by three parameters:

$t$     the access time to a word in the internal store
$T$     the access time to a page on the backing store
$s$     the fraction of the program and its data that is
        kept in the internal store

The process is characterized by the following function:

$p(s)$     the average number of page transfers per store reference
           as a function of the available internal store $s$

The effect of demand fetching is to increase the access time per word from $t$ to $t + p(s)T$.

If a process referred evenly to all its pages, the probability of its referring to an absent page would be:

$$p(s) = 1 - s \qquad (5.4)$$

This pattern of *random references* is shown in Fig. 5.17. The access time varies linearly between $t + T$ (when every reference causes a page transfer) and $t$ (when the program is kept entirely in the internal store).

In practice, processes behave quite differently: They tend to refer heavily to a subset of their pages over a period of time. This pattern of *localized references* is also shown in Fig. 5.17. I believe it was first described by Naur (1965).

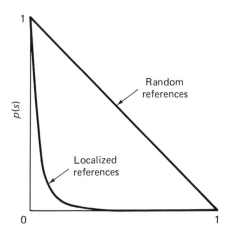

Fig. 5.17. The page transfer probability per store reference $p$ as a function of the fraction of a program $s$ kept in the internal store.

Locality is caused by *sequential execution* of statements stored in consecutive locations, by *repetitive execution* of statements stored within a few pages, and by procedures which operate mainly on *local variables* and parameters also stored within a few pages.

In an analysis of existing programs, Fine (1966) found that a jump from one program page to another occurred after the execution of an average of 100 instructions. During such a sequence of references to the same program page, only a few data pages were referenced.

Locality makes it possible to keep only a fraction of a program internal and still have it executed with tolerable speed. Demand fetching exploits this statistical property of programs.

Measurements of $p(s)$ made by Coffman and Varian (1968b) for various programs suggest that its *tail* can be approximated by

$$p(s) = a \, e^{-bs} \tag{5.5}$$

where

$$0 < a < 1 < b \quad \text{and} \quad a \, e^{-b} T \ll t$$

### 5.4.3. Load Control

The previous model enables us to make certain predictions about the effect of demand fetching on a multiprogramming system. To simplify the argument, I assume that:

(1) the internal store is shared evenly among processes with the same statistical behavior;

(2) the processes run without interruption until they demand page transfers;

(3) the processor utilization is only degraded when all processes are waiting for page transfers; and

(4) the program execution and page transfers overlap in time.

Assumption (1) implies that $s$ and $p(s)$ are identical for all processes; (2) implies that we ignore idle processor time caused by peripheral devices other than the backing store; and (3) and (4), that we ignore the overhead of processor and store multiplexing.

A demand fetching system can be viewed as a *queuing system* in which processes *circulate* between a *ready queue*, waiting for execution, and a *page queue*, waiting for data transfers. This is shown in Fig. 5.18.

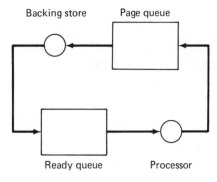

**Fig. 5.18.** Demand fetching viewed as a circular queuing system.

The backing store can *supply* at most one page every $T$ seconds. The processor will *demand* at most one page every $t/p(s)$ seconds. The system can therefore be in one of three possible states:

(1) *Idle backing store*: $p(s) < t/T$.
If pages can be supplied faster than they are demanded, the processes will end up waiting for the slowest server—the processor. This keeps the processor fully utilized and the backing store poorly utilized. Since the backing store is inexpensive compared to the processor, this is not a serious problem.

(2) *Idle processor*: $p(s) > t/T$.
If pages are demanded faster than they can be supplied, the processes will again end up waiting for the slowest server—the backing store. The backing store is now constantly busy and the processor is idle most of the time. This situation, which causes a total collapse of computing service, is called *thrashing*.

(3) *Balanced system*: $p(s) = t/T$.
Between these extremes there is a state in which the processor and the backing store are both fully utilized. This is obviously the most desirable state of operation. The question is: How can an operating system maintain this balance?

The access times, $t$ and $T$, are largely fixed by the hardware, and the reference pattern $p(s)$ is a function of the given program structure. During execution, thrashing can therefore only be avoided by regulating the computational load represented by $s$.

The minimum amount of internal storage that a process needs to prevent thrashing is called its *working set w*. It is determined by the following equation

$$p(w) = \frac{t}{T} \tag{5.6}$$

Using the approximation defined by equation (5.5), we find

$$w = \frac{1}{b} \ln \frac{1}{r} \tag{5.7}$$

where

$$r = \frac{t}{aT}$$

is the so-called *access ratio*. Equation (5.7) shows that the slower the backing store is compared to the internal store, the larger the working set becomes.

A typical numerical example is

$$t = 1 \; \mu\text{sec}$$

$$a = 0.1$$

$$b = 10$$

For disks, drums, and slow core stores, the access ratios and working sets are of the following order of magnitude:

| backing store | $T$ (msec) | $r$ | $w$ (per cent) |
|---|---|---|---|
| disk | 100 | $10^{-4}$ | 96 |
| drum | 10 | $10^{-3}$ | 69 |
| slow core | 1 | $10^{-2}$ | 46 |

The disk is useless as a paging device since practically all pages must be kept internal to maintain high processor utilization. The drum and the slow core store are much better, but still require that $\frac{1}{2}$ to $\frac{2}{3}$ of all pages be kept internal.

In other words, although *demand fetching* simulates a *virtual store* with a capacity as large as the backing store, all computations must be assigned a substantial amount of *real store* to run efficiently.

In our idealized model, the processor is utilized 100 per cent as long as all processes have their working sets in the internal store ($s \geqslant w$). Below the balance point ($s < w$), one process at most is running at a time, while all the others are waiting for page transfers. The running process joins the page queue after an average of $\frac{1}{a} e^{bs} t$ seconds; the processor is then idle until the completion of a page transfer after $T$ seconds enables another process to run. So the *processor utilization* $\eta$ is

$$\eta = r \, e^{bs} \qquad (s \leqslant w \leqslant 1) \tag{5.8}$$

This equation shows that when the internal store $s$ of processes is reduced below their working sets $w$, processor utilization decreases exponentially with $s$. The small access ratio $r = 10^{-4}$ to $10^{-2}$ contributes to the drastic reduction.

The fraction of the working set kept in the internal store is

$$x = \frac{s}{w}$$

By inserting this in equation (5.8) and using equation (5.7), we find

$$\eta = r\, e^{bwx} = r\, e^{x\, \ln(r^{-1})} = r\, e^{\ln(r^{-x})}$$

or

$$\eta = r^{1-x} \qquad (0 \leqslant x \leqslant 1) \tag{5.9}$$

This equation expresses the processor utilization $\eta$ as a function of the access ratio $r$ and the fraction $1 - x$ by which the internal store available to a process is reduced below its working set.

Figure 5.19 illustrates this relationship. The drastic reduction of processor utilization, which characterizes thrashing, is apparent. As an example, suppose an internal store of 128 K words is divided evenly among the working sets of 9 processes. If we now initiate one more process, the internal store of each process is reduced by $\frac{1}{10}$ of its working set. This also reduces processor utilization from 100 per cent to 30 to 65 per cent, depending on the type of backing store used.

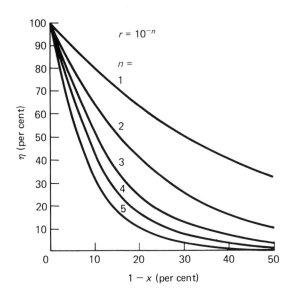

Fig. 5.19. Processor utilization $\eta$ as a function of the fraction $1 - x$, by which the internal store of each process is reduced below its working set for various access ratios $r$.

The only effective remedy against thrashing is to limit the number of processes competing for internal storage. Users cannot easily predict the dynamic behavior of their programs, so the size of their working sets must be evaluated during execution. This can be done as follows: The short-term scheduler starts computations in the order defined by the medium-term scheduler. When thrashing occurs, the short-term scheduler preempts one or more computations with low priorities until a balance point is reached. These computations are resumed when those of higher priority have been completed. This technique is called *load control*.

Variants of load control in paging systems are described by Denning (1968), Oppenheimer and Weizer (1968), DeMeis and Weizer (1969), and Alderson (1971). Wulf (1969) describes an algorithm used to prevent thrashing of contiguous segments in the *B5500* system. In *THE* multiprogramming system, the operator is expected to observe thrashing and reduce the computational load manually.

### 5.4.4. Refinements

Demand fetching systems can be improved in various ways. Here we will briefly evaluate the influence of three factors:

> replacement algorithms
> transfer algorithms
> program structure

*Replacement Algorithms*

When a page must be fetched into a full internal store, one of those already present must be replaced. The rule used to select the victim is called a *replacement algorithm*.

A replacement algorithm should try to minimize the number of page transfers. The *ideal algorithm* would be one that replaces that page which will remain unreferenced for the longest period. But, in practice, the replacement algorithm does not know the future pattern of references; it can only try to predict it from past behavior.

The simplest replacement algorithm is *first-in, first-out*, which is used in the *B5500* system. As Belady (1966) has shown, it performs quite well under most circumstances. But sometimes it has the peculiar effect of increasing the number of page transfers when the internal store available to a computation is increased (Belady, 1969).

The replacement algorithm *least recently used* does not have this defect. If the internal store available to a computation is increased from $f$ to $f + 1$ page frames, the algorithm will maintain the $f + 1$ most recently used pages internally. Since this set includes the $f$ most recently used pages, the number of page transfers cannot be higher than before. Algorithms which have this property are called *stack algorithms*.

*THE* multiprogramming system uses the *least recently used* algorithm. Unfortunately, it is expensive to implement since it requires that a time variable be stored in every page table entry and updated every time the page is referenced. As an approximation to it, some computers associate a boolean with every page: It is set to *true* after every reference and to *false* after a reasonable period of time.

Belady (1966) found that in most cases realizable algorithms, such as *first-in, first-out* and approximations to *least recently used*, cause only 2 to 3 times as many page transfers as the ideal, but unrealizable algorithm. This has been confirmed by Coffman and Varian (1968b).

In our model, the effect of improving the replacement algorithm is roughly to divide the constant $a$ in equation (5.5) by a factor $c$ of 2 to 3. This is again equivalent to multiplying the access ratio $r$ by $c$.

According to equation (5.7), this reduces the working set by the following fraction:

$$\frac{\Delta w}{w} = \frac{\ln c}{\ln \frac{1}{r}} \tag{5.10}$$

For $r = 10^{-4}$ to $10^{-2}$ and $c = 3$, the reduction of $w$ amounts to 12 to 24 per cent.

Figure 5.19 shows that in a thrashing situation, an increase of $r$ by a factor of 3 only improves processor utilization by a few per cent. So a good replacement algorithm cannot by itself prevent thrashing.

*Transfer Algorithms*

For rotating backing stores, the access time $T$ depends to some extent on the order in which page transfers are made. The rule used to select the next page to be transferred to or from the backing store among those waiting to be transferred is called a *transfer algorithm*.

Consider, for example, a drum which can transfer a maximum of $M$ pages during one revolution of $R$ seconds.

If requests for page transfers are honored in *first-come, first-served* order, it will take an average of $R/2$ seconds to position the access head in front of a given page frame and another $R/M$ seconds to transfer the page. So we have

$$T = (\frac{1}{2} + \frac{1}{M}) R \tag{5.11}$$

A better solution is to associate a page queue with each of the $M$ drum sectors and serve them according to the rule *shortest access time next*. This can (at most) reduce the access time $T$ to $R/M$.

The effect of this improvement is to multiply the access ratio $r$ by a constant

$$c = 1 + \frac{M}{2} \qquad (5.12)$$

Thus, if a drum surface is divided into 2 to 8 sectors, $c$ will be 2 to 5. This is comparable to the effect of improving the replacement algorithm.

The same result can be achieved by using $c$ backing store devices simultaneously.

Notice, that the use of *multiprocessors* can only make thrashing more likely by reducing the average time $t$ between references to the internal store.

*Program Structure*

A wise programmer will organize his program to utilize a backing store with sequential or cyclic access efficiently. The principal aim is to divide a large program and its data into smaller parts which are executed and accessed strictly sequentially to avoid random reference to the backing store.

An excellent example is the *GIER Algol* compiler described by Naur (1963). It is divided into 10 parts, each of which performs a single, sequential scanning and transformation of a source program text.

Experiments by Comeau (1967) showed that the number of page transfers in typical programs could be reduced by 50 per cent just by rearranging the program text so that dynamically related procedures would be placed within the same pages.

A simple device to assist the programmer in this task is included in the *RC 4000 Algol* compiler: A standard variable, which can be referenced and reset by an Algol program, is increased by one for each page transfer caused by the program during its execution.

## 5.4.5.  Conclusion

The most important rule of short-term store allocation is to assign reasonable amounts of internal storage to computations to enable them to run efficiently. When thrashing occurs, the computational load on the internal store must be reduced by preemption.

Less important are efficient replacement and transfer algorithms to reduce the frequency and waiting time of page transfers. The programmer can contribute to this reduction by a sensible structuring of program and data.

In the previous analysis we ignored the processor time used to control page transfers. It is worth remembering that in practice, store multiplexing reduces processor utilization even under balanced conditions.

Suppose the internal store consists of a single physical module with an access time $t$ per word. The transfer of a page containing $m$ words therefore "steals" $m$ store cycles from the processor; the initiation and completion of this transfer by the processor consume another $n$ store cycles. Under these circumstances, processor utilization cannot exceed

$$\eta_{max} = 1 - (m + n)\frac{t}{T}$$

For $m = n = 1000$ and $t/T = 10^{-4}$, we find $\eta_{max} = 0.8$.

## 5.5. LITERATURE

The book by Bell and Newell (1971) contains reprints of original papers on the structure of the *IBM 7094 II*, *CDC 6600*, *B5000*, and *Atlas* computers.

Denning (1970) wholeheartedly supports demand paging. Hoare and McKeag (1971c) take a more conservative view of store management.

*THE* multiprogramming system is an example of a demand paging system delicately balanced between input/output processes and user computations. It is described in some detail by McKeag (1971b) and Bron (1971).

BELL, G. and NEWELL, A., *Computer Structures: Readings and Examples*. McGraw-Hill Book Company. New York, *1971*.

BRON, C., "Allocation of virtual store in THE multiprogramming system," *International Seminar on Operating System Techniques*, Belfast, Northern Ireland, Aug.-Sept. *1971*.

DENNING, P. J., "Virtual memory," *Computing Surveys 2*, 3, pp. 153-89, Sept. *1970*.

HOARE, C. A. R. and McKEAG, R. M., "A survey of store management techniques," *International Seminar on Operating System Techniques*, Belfast, Northern Ireland, Aug.-Sept. *1971c*.

McKEAG, R. M., "*THE Multiprogramming System*," The Queen's University of Belfast, Northern Ireland, *1971b*.

# 6

# *SCHEDULING ALGORITHMS*

This chapter analyzes the effect of various medium-term scheduling algorithms on the average response time to user requests in single processor systems.

In this chapter we will study *medium-term scheduling* of a single processor by means of elementary queuing theory.

Medium-term scheduling decisions are made at various levels: at the management level by defining the relative importance of users; at the operator level by running certain types of jobs at prescribed times of day; and at the machine level by the final allocation of resources to jobs.

The ideal objective of scheduling is to minimize the total cost of computer service and user waiting time. In practice, the two problems are often approached separately.

Service time can be reduced by paying attention to the processor time lost by operator intervention, slow peripherals, and resource multiplexing. Changes in this direction usually have a drastic influence on the mode of operation offered to all users. The classical batch-processing system is an example of extreme concern about processor utilization with total neglect of user response time. On the other hand, an interactive system responds instantly to users at a considerable cost of resource multiplexing. A spooling system is somewhere in between: It tries to reduce user waiting time to a few minutes without degrading equipment utilization seriously.

The cost of user waiting time is difficult to evaluate. Programmers may be unable to proceed with their work until the results of program tests are available; the installation may be obliged to pay penalties after certain deadlines; delayed results may lose their value completely in real-time environments; and, finally, impatient customers may turn to a competing system.

The question of which customers an installation wants to favor is a political one. Bright (1962) mentions an early system in which the priority of a job was proportional to the business the user gave the computing center per month! In environments where many people are engaged in program development and testing, it is often assumed that the cost per time unit of waiting for response is the same for all users. In this case, the problem is to minimize the sum of user waiting times. Any job will, during its execution, delay all other jobs following it in the queue, so the important thing is to keep the number of waiting jobs at a minimum. We find therefore that most of the scheduling disciplines considered here give high priority to jobs with short execution times at the expense of jobs with longer ones.

We begin with a summary of the queuing theory needed for our purpose and proceed to derive analytical results for the average waiting times of jobs under the scheduling algorithms *first-come first-served*, *shortest job next*, *highest response ratio next*, and *round-robin*. *Foreground-background* scheduling is discussed informally. The assumptions behind these models are not always in agreement with reality, but they do give valuable insight into the behavior of particular scheduling algorithms and enable the designer to compare their merits qualitatively.

## 6.1. QUEUING SYSTEM MODEL

Figure 6.1 shows a queuing system model of a single processor. Jobs *arrive* at the system when they are submitted for execution. They wait in a *queue* until they can be *served* by the processor and *depart* after completion of their execution.

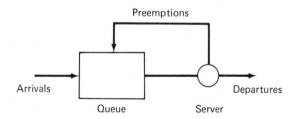

Fig. 6.1. Queuing model of a single processor system.

In a *non-preemptive system*, jobs are executed one at a time to *completion*. The processor will only start the service of a low priority job if no jobs of higher priority are present. But once the processor has selected a job, it is committed to serve that job to completion even if jobs of higher priority arrive during its service. Non-preemptive scheduling has the virtue of simplicity of implementation and good utilization of machinery.

In a *preemptive system*, several jobs can be in various stages of execution. At any moment, the processor is serving a single job; but upon arrival of a job with higher priority, the job in service is *interrupted* and returned to the queue. Service of the higher priority job is then started. The interrupted job will be *resumed* later when no jobs of higher priority are present. Preemptive scheduling gives fast response to urgent jobs at the price of increased complexity and overhead.

In a shared computer system, jobs of varying service time arrive irregularly. From time to time jobs are submitted faster than they can be executed. So a queue is formed even though the processor has sufficient capacity to serve all users in the long run. As Cox (1961) remarks, congestion in a system depends on its *irregularities* and not just on its *average* properties.

In mathematics, irregularities are described in terms of probability distributions. The aim of the following is to use elementary probability theory (for example, see Feller, 1957) to predict average waiting times on the basis of the following knowledge about a single-server queuing system:

the arrival pattern
the service pattern
the scheduling algorithm

### 6.1.1. The Arrival Pattern

The arrival of jobs will be regarded as independent, random events. When jobs are submitted by a large population of independent users, it is reasonable to make the following *assumptions*:

(1) The number of arrivals during a given interval of time depends only on the length of the interval and not on the past history of the system.

(2) For any small time interval $(t, t + dt)$, the probability of a single arrival is $\lambda dt$, where $\lambda$ is a constant, while the probability of more than one arrival is negligible.

These assumptions lead to a *Poisson distribution* of arrivals. (Examples of arrivals which do not follow this pattern are customers who are discouraged by the sight of a long queue and decide not to join it; and jobs that arrive in batches instead of one at a time.)

Under the above assumptions, the probability $P_0(t+dt)$ that no arrivals occur during a time interval of length $t + dt$ is equal to the product of the probability $P_0(t)$ that no arrivals occur during the interval $t$ and the probability $1 - \lambda dt$ that no arrivals occur during the following interval $dt$:

$$P_0(t + dt) = P_0(t)(1 - \lambda\,dt)$$

or

$$\frac{dP_0}{dt} = -\lambda\,P_0(t)$$

which has the solution

$$P_0(t) = e^{-\lambda t} \tag{6.1}$$

since $P_0(0) = 1$.

The time between two successive arrivals is called the *interarrival time*; the constant $\lambda$ is the *arrival rate*.

The probability $dF(t)$ that the interarrival time is between $t$ and $t + dt$ is

$$dF(t) = P_0(t)\,\lambda\,dt = \lambda\,e^{-\lambda t}dt \tag{6.2}$$

The *distribution function* $F(t)$ is defined as the probability that the interarrival time is less than or equal to $t$

$$F(t) = \int_0^t dF(x) = 1 - e^{-\lambda t} \tag{6.3}$$

This equation shows that the interarrival time follows an exponential distribution with the mean value:

$$E(t) = \int_0^\infty t\,dF(t) = \frac{1}{\lambda} \tag{6.4}$$

The expected number of arrivals during a period of time $T$ is $\lambda T$.

Coffman and Wood (1966) measured interarrival times in the *SDC Q-32* system. They found that the assumption of independent arrivals is reasonably justified. The interarrival time distributions all looked more or less exponential, but the observed data showed more short interarrival times than did an exponential curve with the same mean.

A much more satisfactory approximation to the data was obtained with a *hyperexponential distribution*

$$F(t) = 1 - a\,e^{-b\lambda t} - (1 - a)\,e^{-c\lambda t} \tag{6.5}$$

where $1/\lambda$ is the observed mean while $a$, $b$, and $c$ are constants constrained as follows

$$0 < a < 1 \qquad 0 < b < 1 < c$$

By using equation (6.5) to derive the mean $1/\lambda$, we find the relation

$$\frac{a}{b} + \frac{1-a}{c} = 1 \tag{6.6}$$

Figure 6.2 shows the hyperexponential distribution which Coffman and Wood used to fit their average observations. The constants are $a = 0.615$, $b = 0.69$, and $c = 3.5$. The interarrival time is expressed in units of its mean $1/\lambda$, which was actually 23 sec. The figure also shows an exponential distribution with the same mean.

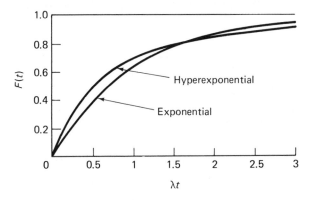

Fig. 6.2. Distribution of normalized interarrival time (after Coffman and Wood, 1966).

The conclusion must be that the assumption of Poisson arrivals is a very crude approximation which underestimates the frequency of short interarrival times. Unfortunately, it is only for completely random (Poisson) and regular arrivals patterns that general mathematical solutions have been obtained.

## 6.1.2.  The Service Pattern

The service times required by jobs will also be regarded as random, independent variables. The assumption is often made that they follow an *exponential distribution*. When this is the case, the probability $dF(t)$ that the service time of a job is between $t$ and $t + dt$ can be expressed as

$$dF(t) = \mu \, e^{-\mu t} \, dt \tag{6.7}$$

The probability $F(t)$ that service time is less than or equal to $t$ is then

$$F(t) = \int_0^t dF(x) = 1 - e^{-\mu t} \qquad (6.8)$$

The constant $\mu$ is called the *service rate*; its reciprocal $1/\mu$ is the mean service time. The variable $\mu t$ measures the actual service time $t$ in units of the mean service time.

The fraction of processor time consumed by jobs with service time not exceeding $t$ is

$$G(t) = \int_0^t \mu x \, dF(x) = 1 - (1 + \mu t) \, e^{-\mu t} \qquad (6.9)$$

The exponential distribution is shown in Figs. 6.3 and 6.4. It characterizes an installation in which most jobs are short. But, although there are very few large jobs, they use a significant amount of the processor capacity.

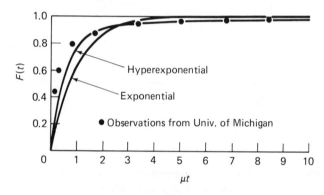

Fig. 6.3. Distribution of normalized service time (after Rosin, 1965).

The mathematical attraction of the exponential distribution is its *memoryless property*, which can be stated as follows:

(1) The probability that a job terminates during a small time interval $dt$ is independent of the amount of service time $T$ consumed by the job before that interval.

(2) If a job is interrupted after $T$ seconds of service, its remaining service time, $t - T$, will be exponentially distributed with the same mean $1/\mu$.

The first assertion is proved by deriving the conditional probability of

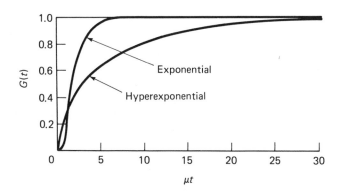

**Fig. 6.4.** The fraction of processor time used by jobs with
service times not exceeding $t$.

job termination during the interval $(T, T + dt)$, assuming that the service
time has exceeded $T$:

$$Prob(\text{remaining service time} \leqslant dt) =$$

$$\frac{Prob(T < t \leqslant T + dt)}{Prob(t > T)} = \frac{\mu\, e^{-\mu T}\, dt}{e^{-\mu T}} = \mu\, dt \qquad (6.10)$$

To prove the second assertion, we need the probability distribution of
the remaining service time, $t - T$, assuming that the service time has
exceeded $T$:

$$Prob(\text{remaining service time} \leqslant \Delta t) =$$

$$\frac{Prob(T < t \leqslant T + \Delta t)}{Prob(t > T)} = \frac{e^{-\mu T} - e^{-\mu(T + \Delta t)}}{e^{-\mu T}}$$

$$= 1 - e^{-\mu \Delta t} \qquad (6.11)$$

The implication of the memoryless property is that a scheduling
algorithm is unable to predict the remaining service time of jobs on the
basis of their elapsed service time. Consequently, priority scheduling must
be based either on *reliable estimates* of service times supplied by users in
advance or on periodic adjustment of priorities during execution as a
function of elapsed service time. The latter technique, which requires
preemption of running jobs, is called quantum controlled scheduling or
*time slicing.*

Rosin (1965) and Walter (1967) analyzed more than 10,000 jobs run at
a batch-processing installation at the University of Michigan. Figure 6.3 shows

some points from these observations. Student runs are excluded from the data to make the distribution more like those found in other service centers engaged in program development and production runs. The average execution time was 1.19 min. This does not include compilation time (0.24 min), loading time (0.14 min), and operating system time (0.18 min).

These results confirm the exponential tendency of service times, but again, as Fife (1966) has pointed out, the distribution is more *hyperexponential*. Figure 6.3 also shows a hyperexponential approximation

$$F(t) = 1 - a\, e^{-b\mu t} - (1 - a)\, e^{-c\mu t} \qquad (6.12)$$

to the observations of Rosin. The constants used are $a = 0.11$, $b = 0.21$, and $c = 1.88$.

The hyperexponential distribution can be interpreted as a mixture of two exponential distributions with different means:

$$F(t) = a\, (1 - e^{-b\mu t}) + (1 - a)\, (1 - e^{-c\mu t})$$

The combined effect is that many jobs of short service time are mixed with a few jobs of extremely long service time. Consequently, the tail of the distribution is prolonged considerably compared to an exponential distribution with the same mean.

This is illustrated most dramatically by the curves in Fig. 6.4, which define the fraction of processor time $G(t)$ demanded by jobs with service times not exceeding $t$:

$$G(t) = \int_0^t \mu x\, dF(x) \qquad (6.13)$$

$$= \frac{a}{b}(1 - (1 + b\,\mu t)\, e^{-b\mu t}) + \frac{1-a}{c}(1 - (1 + c\mu t)\, e^{-c\mu t})$$

When the distribution is exponential, we can ignore the load contributed by jobs with service times greater than 6 times the mean service time. But a hyperexponential distribution forces us to be concerned about jobs with 20 to 30 times the mean service time. Another way of putting this is to say that 80 per cent of all jobs are shorter than the mean service time, but require only 30 per cent of the processor capacity. On the other hand, the 2 per cent longest jobs account for 25 per cent of the load.

As we shall see later, the more dispersed the distribution of service time is, the longer the average waiting times become.

## 6.1.3.  Performance Measures

In a single-server queuing system with Poisson input and an arbitrary service time distribution $F(t)$, the mean number of arrivals during the service time of a single job is

$$\rho = \int_0^\infty \lambda\, t\, dF(t) = \frac{\lambda}{\mu} \tag{6.14}$$

As long as $\rho < 1$, the mean number of arrivals is less than the mean number of departures, and the server can handle the load. But, if $\rho > 1$, the queue will increase indefinitely in time.

The queuing processes considered here will always reach a *steady state* in which the probability distributions are time-independent, provided that the system has been in operation for some time with $\rho < 1$.

If a queuing system is in a steady state over a period $T$, it receives an average of $\lambda T$ jobs, which are served in an average of $\lambda T(1/\mu) = \rho T$ sec. The *utilization factor* $\rho$ thus represents the average fraction of time during which the server is busy.

We will use the following performance measures for a queuing system:

The mean *queue length L* is the mean number of jobs waiting in the system. It does not include the job in service. $L$ is a measure of the backing store capacity required to hold arriving jobs.

The mean *waiting time W* is the mean time spent by a job in the queue.

Little (1961) has proved the following relation between the mean queue length and the mean waiting time in a queuing system in a steady state

$$L = \lambda W \tag{6.15}$$

This theorem says that during the average time $W$ that a job requires to pass from one end of the queue to the other, the average queue length $L$ remains constant due to the number of arrivals $\lambda W$ during that interval.

Two other measures of performance are:

The *waiting ratio W/t* of a job—the ratio of its mean waiting time $W$ to its actual service time $t$.

The *response ratio R/t* of a job—the ratio of its mean response time $R$ to its actual service time. Since $R = W + t$, the response ratio is equal to the waiting ratio plus 1. It represents the degradation of processor speed experienced by a given job as a result of the presence of other jobs and the scheduling algorithm used.

### 6.1.4. A Conservation Law

Scheduling algorithms differ only in their choice of the users to be given preferential treatment. If preemption is used sparingly, the processing capacity is practically uninfluenced by such manipulation of service, and one would expect some overall measure of waiting times to remain constant. In the following, we derive a conservation law that is applicable to a large class of scheduling algorithms with limited preemption.

The conservation law says that for given arrival and service time patterns, a particular weighted sum of average waiting times for all jobs is invariant to the scheduling algorithm used (Kleinrock, 1965). This means that scheduling can only improve the response time of some users at the expense of other users.

We make the following *assumptions* about the queuing system:

(1) It contains a single processor which is constantly available and busy as long as there are jobs in the system.

(2) All jobs remain in the system until their service has been completed.

(3) Preemption (if used) does not degrade processor utilization.

(4) The arrival pattern is a Poisson process.

(5) The service pattern can be arbitrary in non-preemptive systems, but must be exponential in preemptive systems.

(6) Arrival and service times are independent random variables.

(7) The system is in steady state equilibrium.

Assumption (2) implies that preempted jobs are always resumed later and that impatient customers do not withdraw their requests. Assumption (5) and the memoryless property of the exponential distribution ensure that the service pattern is uninfluenced by preemption and resumption.

As a measure of the amount of incomplete work present in the system at a given time $t$, we introduce the *load function* $u(t)$. It is defined as the time it would take the processor to empty the system of all jobs present at time $t$ if no new jobs arrived after that time.

Each arriving job instantly causes the load function to jump by the amount of service time required by that job. Between arrivals, the load function decreases linearly by one second (of processing time) per second (of real time) until it reaches zero.

Since jobs are served continuously to completion with negligible use of preemption, the scheduling algorithm cannot influence the constant rate of decrease of the load between arrivals. So the load function $u(t)$ depends only on the arrival and service patterns, not on the particular scheduling algorithm used.

Let the arrival rate be $\lambda$ and let the service time distribution be $F(t)$ with the mean $1/\mu$. We will now observe the system immediately after the arrival of a job which we will call the "tagged job." At this point, the expected load $U$ is equal to the expected time $W_0$ required to finish the job already in service plus the sum of the expected service times of all waiting jobs.

Consider the group of waiting jobs which have service times between $t$ and $t + dt$. During their expected waiting time $W_t$, the expected number of arrivals within the same group is $\lambda W_t dF(t)$. According to Little's law, equation (6.15), this is also the expected number of jobs waiting in this group. The expected service time required to complete them is therefore $\lambda t W_t dF(t)$. By integrating over the entire range of service times, we find:

$$U = W_0 + \int_0^\infty \lambda t W_t \, dF(t) \qquad (6.16)$$

If the tagged job arrived while a job of service time $t$ was being executed, its expected arrival time would be in the middle of this interval with $t/2$ of the service time to be completed. Since the probability that the tagged job arrived under such circumstances is $\lambda t \, dF(t)$, the mean value of the remaining service time must be:

$$W_0 = \frac{\lambda}{2} \int_0^\infty t^2 \, dF(t) \qquad (6.17)$$

Notice that $W_0$ is independent of the scheduling algorithm. This is intuitively reasonable since the processor can be engaged with a job from any group upon arrival of another job.

Since the load function is independent of the scheduling algorithm, we can find its mean $U$ by considering the simplest possible algorithm *first-come, first-served*. Under this rule, the expected waiting time for any job is equal to the expected amount of unfinished work $U$ present when the job arrives. By substituting $W_t = U$ in equation (6.16) and using equation (6.14), we find

$$U = W_0 + \rho U$$

or

$$U = \frac{W_0}{1 - \rho} \qquad (6.18)$$

Using this result once again in equation (6.16), we find Kleinrock's *conservation law*:

$$\int_0^\infty \lambda t \; W_t \; dF(t) = \frac{\rho W_0}{1 - \rho} \qquad (6.19)$$

It states that the sum of average waiting times for all jobs weighted by the fraction of processor time required by jobs in each group is invariant to the scheduling algorithm. This holds for any queuing system which satisfies assumptions (1) to (7).

The conservation law can also be written as follows:

$$\int_0^\infty t \; W_t \; dF(t) = \frac{\rho}{1 - \rho} \frac{E(t^2)}{2} \qquad (6.20)$$

This shows more clearly that the overall mean waiting time depends on the utilization factor $\rho$ and on the second moment $E(t^2)$ of the service time distribution.

The last factor is particularly interesting: It enables us to evaluate the influence of the shape of the service time distribution on the average waiting times. $E(t^2)$ is a measure of the *dispersion* of service times.

For *hyperexponential service times*, equation (6.12), we find

$$\frac{1}{2} E(t^2) = \frac{d}{\mu^2}$$

where

$$d = \frac{a}{b^2} + \frac{1 - a}{c^2} \qquad (6.21)$$

Using the parameters $a = 0.11$, $b = 0.21$, and $c = 1.88$ (as in Fig. 6.3), we find $d = 2.75$. Freeman (1968) estimates a similar factor of 3.05 for service times observed at the Triangle Universities Computation Center.

If we had used the assumption of *exponential service times*— $a = b = c = d = 1$—the analytical model would have underestimated the average waiting times by a factor of 3. This illustrates the point made earlier that congestion depends on the irregularities of arrival and service times, and not just on their average values.

## 6.2. NON-PREEMPTIVE SCHEDULING

With this background, we will analyze specific scheduling algorithms divided into two main classes: *non-preemptive* and *preemptive*. In preemptive systems, more than one job can be in a state of execution at a given time. This influences the design so much that it seems reasonable to stress the distinction between systems with and without preemption.

Besides this main classification criterion, there are others, for example, whether priorities can be based on reliable *estimates of service time* supplied by users or whether they must be evaluated as a function of the actual behavior of jobs during their execution.

One would expect users to be able to make realistic estimates of the processor time required by non-trivial programs, especially if they are used repeatedly. In a system that gives high priority to jobs with short estimated run times, the normal policy is to terminate jobs which exceed their estimated limits; otherwise, users would soon ruin the scheme. In this situation most users prefer to make a conservative guess. Morris (1967) found that users overestimated their storage requirements by 50 per cent and says that "compute time estimates are much worse than this." Rosin (1965) reports that approximately 6 per cent of all jobs exceeded their time estimates. Finally, Walter (1967) remarks that users tend to estimate "nice" values (0.5, 1, 2, .. min). This may seem discouraging, but Lynch (1967) has shown that even with a partial indication of service time, it is possible to improve response times considerably for small jobs. Over-estimation effectively reduces the loss of processor time caused by termination of unsuccessful jobs.

In systems where the users interact with running programs in an experimental manner, the typical demand of processor time per interaction is only a fraction of a second. Here, it would be unrealistic to expect a user to evaluate his need of computing time; quite often, he is completely unaware of the structure and speed of the programs involved. The reaction of the scheduler to this uncertainty is to allocate processor time piecemeal to jobs to see how long they actually are. Each job is given a finite slice of time. If it completes service during this slice, it departs from the system; otherwise, the scheduler interrupts the job and returns it to the queue with a lower priority. Here it will wait for another time slice. So the choice of preemptive scheduling in interactive systems is a consequence of the uncertainty about service time. The price for this uncertainty is increased overhead of processor and store multiplexing.

Scheduling models also differ in their assumptions about the number of input channels. An interactive system with a small number of user terminals is an example of a system with a *finite input source*. Each user occupies a terminal as long as he is using the system. Normally, he will issue one command at a time, wait for response, think for a while and then make another request. This means that the arrival rate becomes zero in situations where all terminal users are waiting for response. On the other hand, non-interactive systems usually do not limit the rate at which users can submit jobs, so the assumption about an *infinite input source* is valid there.

From a scheduling point of view, the difference between present interactive and non-interactive systems can be characterized by the following list of assumptions:

|  | non-interactive system | interactive system |
|---|---|---|
| preemption: | limited | frequent |
| priority source: | estimated service time | elapsed service time |
| input source: | infinite | finite |

The following is a study of non-preemptive scheduling of Poisson input from an unlimited source with an arbitrary service time distribution based on perfect estimates of service times. It is assumed that the system includes a backing store with direct access and sufficient capacity to hold all waiting jobs and that spooling eliminates idle processor time during program execution.

### 6.2.1. First-come, First-served

The *first-come, first-served* algorithm (FCFS) executes jobs in their order of arrival. It is a discipline that favors the longest waiting job irrespective of the amount of service time demanded by it. The mean waiting time for jobs scheduled by this algorithm has already been derived, equation (6.18). I prefer to repeat it in the present context:

$$W = \frac{W_0}{1 - \rho} \tag{6.22}$$

Using $d = 2.75$, the waiting time $\mu W$ is plotted in Fig. 6.5 for two values of the utilization factor: $\rho = 0.7$, corresponding to a moderate load; and $\rho = 0.93$, representing a fairly heavy load. The latter case is probably the most realistic. Freeman (1968) observed $\rho = 0.92$ as a typical value for the central computer in the Triangle Universities Computation Center.

The sharp increase in waiting time as $\rho$ approaches 1 is evident. If the mean service time is assumed to be 1 minute, jobs wait an average of 6 minutes when $\rho = 0.7$, but 36.5 minutes when $\rho = 0.93$.

Figure 6.5 also shows the waiting ratio $W/t$. If this is taken as a measure of performance, we must conclude that *first-come, first served* scheduling favors the longer-running jobs at the expense of the shorter-running ones. Eighty per cent of all jobs (those shorter than the mean service time) are delayed more than 36.5 times their service time on the average.

The expected number of jobs in the queue is $\lambda W$, or

$$L = \frac{\rho^2}{1 - \rho} d \tag{6.23}$$

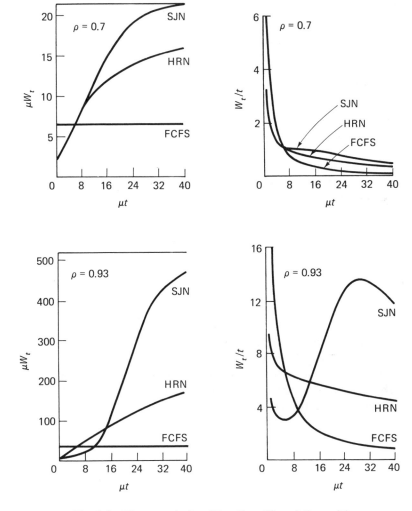

**Fig. 6.5.** The expected waiting time $W_t$ and the waiting
ratio $W_t/t$ as a function of normalized service time $\mu t$ for
the *first-come, first-served* (FCFS), *shortest job next* (SJN),
and *highest response ratio next* (HRN) scheduling
algorithms.

In the present example with $\rho = 0.93$ and $d = 2.75$, this means that an
average of 34 jobs are waiting on the backing store. With an average data
volume of 300 input cards and 500 output lines per job (see Section 1.2.1),
the input and output queues must on the average hold close to 2 million
characters (assuming that the two queues hold the same number of
jobs).

### 6.2.2. Shortest Job Next

Consider now an algorithm that selects the job with the shortest estimated service time as the next one to receive service.

We will derive the mean waiting time $W_t$ for a tagged job with service time $t$, scheduled according to the *shortest job next* algorithm (SJN). $W_t$ is equal to the mean time $U_t$ required to serve all jobs present in the system with service times less than or equal to $t$ when the tagged job arrives, plus the sum of the service times of all jobs that arrive with higher priority during the waiting time $W_t$.

It should be clear from the proof of the conservation law that $U_t$ is simply the mean system load of jobs with service time $x \leqslant t$. So we find from equations (6.14) and (6.18):

$$U_t = \frac{W_0}{1 - \rho_t} \tag{6.24}$$

where

$$\rho_t = \int_0^t \lambda x dF(x) \tag{6.25}$$

During the expected waiting time of the tagged job, the expected number of arrivals of jobs with service times between $x$ and $x + dx$ is $\lambda W_t dF(x)$. If $x < t$, these jobs are served before the tagged one and thus increase its expected waiting time by $\lambda x W_t dF(x)$. All in all, these later arrivals increase $W_t$ by the following amount:

$$\int_0^t \lambda x W_t dF(x) = W_t \rho_t$$

So we find

$$W_t = U_t + W_t \, \rho_t$$

or

$$W_t = \frac{W_0}{(1 - \rho_t)^2} \tag{6.26}$$

This equation was first derived by Phipps (1956).

Using equations (6.13) and (6.25), we can also express $\rho_t$ as follows:

$$\rho_t = G(t) \, \rho$$

where $G(t)$ is the amount of processor time used by jobs with service times not exceeding $t$.

Phipps' equation shows that jobs with a given service time $t$ must pay for the improved service given to all jobs with higher priority. And, whereas waiting times only increase proportionally to $(1 - \rho)^{-1}$ for *first-come, first-served* scheduling, the rate of increase is now $(1 - \rho_t)^{-2}$, which becomes very steep as $\rho_t$ approaches 1.

These points are illustrated in Fig. 6.5, which also gives a direct comparison of the *shortest job next* and the *first-come, first-served* algorithms. Even under heavy load ($\rho$ = 0.93), jobs requiring less than the mean service time of 1 minute now wait less than 4.5 minutes on the average. Jobs between 1 and 10 minutes wait less than 4.5 times their service time. Response is better than *first-come, first-served* for jobs up to 10 minutes. Figure 6.3 shows that this represents 99 per cent of all jobs.

The main difficulty with the *shortest job next* algorithm is the long-running jobs. A glance at Fig. 6.4 shows that the longest 1 per cent of the jobs cannot be ignored because they require 20 per cent of the total processor time. Unfortunately, shorter jobs can effectively prevent longer ones from receiving service. With $\rho$ = 0.93, a job of 30 minutes must wait 6.8 hours before it can start. Furthermore, since preemption is not used, a long-running job, once started, will keep all other jobs waiting for as long as it runs.

### 6.2.3.  Highest Response Ratio Next

*First-come, first-served* and *shortest job next* algorithms both take a rather one-sided view of scheduling. The first algorithm is concerned solely with the actual waiting time of jobs and completely ignores their estimated service time; the other one does exactly the opposite. In the following, we will analyze an algorithm which strikes a balance between these extremes.

The effect of sharing a single processor among many users is to make the response times of jobs considerably longer than their service times. From the point of view of the individual user, the processing rate of the machine appears to be reduced by a factor equal to

$$\frac{\text{response time}}{\text{service time}}$$

This is called the *response ratio* of a job.

It can be argued that all users should experience the same virtual processing speed as a result of their sharing the system. This policy is called *equitable sharing*. It is well-known in preemptive systems with *round-robin* scheduling. For non-preemptive scheduling, the relation between virtual and actual machine speeds suggests an algorithm which selects the job with the *highest response ratio next* (HRN) for service. This algorithm favors short jobs, but it also limits the waiting time of longer jobs: If a job remains in the system long enough, it will eventually achieve a priority so high that it will be served before any other job.

I have analyzed and simulated this algorithm elsewhere (Brinch Hansen, 1971a). Here, I will derive an approximation to the average waiting times of short and long jobs.

Consider first a *short job* with a service time $t$ and an expected waiting time $W_t$. The priority of an extremely short job increases so rapidly in time that it can expect to be served as soon as the job found in service upon its arrival is completed. In other words

$$W_t \rightarrow W_0 \quad \text{as} \quad t \rightarrow 0$$

For short jobs of slightly longer duration, we would expect that the effect of response ratio scheduling is to make the increase of the waiting time approximately proportional to the service time. So we make the assumption that

$$W_t \approx W_0 + k\, t \qquad \text{for small } t$$

where $k$ is a constant.

We will also assume that the service time distribution $F(t)$ is a rapidly decreasing function of the service $t$ with the mean $1/\mu$. More precisely, $F(t)$ must be decreasing so rapidly with $t$ that the error introduced by using the linear approximation of $W_t$ in the conservation law, equation (6.19), is small. So we may assume that

$$\int_0^\infty \lambda t W_t \, dF(t) \approx \int_0^\infty \lambda t (W_0 + k\,t)\, dF(t)$$

or

$$\frac{\rho W_0}{1 - \rho} \approx \rho\, W_0 + 2\, k\, W_0$$

By solving for $k$, we find the approximate mean waiting time for small jobs:

$$W_t \approx W_0 + \frac{\rho^2}{1 - \rho} \frac{t}{2} \qquad \text{for small } t \qquad (6.27)$$

Now consider a very *long job* with service time $t$. Since its priority increases very slowly, it must wait until practically all earlier arrivals have been served. In other words, it must wait at least an amount of time equal to the mean system load $U$ defined by equation (6.18).

In addition, a long job can be delayed by shorter ones arriving later. For

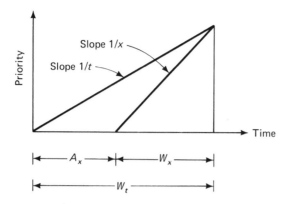

**Fig. 6.6.** Priority diagram of later arrivals.

a job with a service time $x < t$ and an expected waiting time $W_x < W_t$, the latest possible arrival time after the arrival of a long job with the service time $t$ is $A_x$, as shown in Fig. 6.6. If the shorter job arrived later than this, its priority would not reach the priority of the longer job during its expected waiting time $W_x$.

From this diagram, the following relations are derived

$$A_x + W_x = W_t \qquad \frac{W_x}{x} = \frac{W_t}{t}$$

or

$$A_x = W_t \left(1 - \frac{x}{t}\right)$$

The expected number of jobs with service times between $x$ and $x + dx$ arriving during the interval $A_x$ is $\lambda A_x dF(x)$. They will delay the long job by the expected amount $\lambda x A_x dF(x)$. All in all, later arrivals will delay the long job by the amount:

$$W_t \int_0^t \lambda x \left(1 - \frac{x}{t}\right) dF(x)$$

For large values of $t$, this is approximately the same as

$$W_t \int_0^\infty \lambda x \left(1 - \frac{x}{t}\right) dF(x) = W_t \left(\rho - \frac{2 W_0}{t}\right)$$

By adding the delays caused by earlier and later arrivals, we find for very large jobs:

$$W_t \approx \frac{W_0}{1 - \rho} + W_t \left(\rho - \frac{2\,W_0}{t}\right)$$

or

$$W_t \approx \frac{W_0}{(1 - \rho)\left(1 - \rho + \dfrac{2\,W_0}{t}\right)} \qquad \text{for large } t \qquad (6.28)$$

Closer inspection shows that the linear approximation, equation (6.27), is a tangent to the non-linear approximation, equation (6.28), in $t = 2\,W_0/\rho$, where they both have the value $W_t = W_0/(1 - \rho)$. This is the same as the expected waiting time for the *first-come, first-served* algorithm.

I have simulated the *highest response ratio next* algorithm using the hyperexponential distribution of service time shown in Fig. 6.3 (Brinch Hansen, 1971a). The results indicate that it is an excellent approximation to use equation (6.27) for $t \leqslant 2\,W_0/\rho$ and equation (6.28) for $t > 2\,W_0/\rho$. The accuracy of this approximation seems to improve with increasing values of the utilization factor $\rho$.

Notice that for extremely large jobs ($t \to \infty$), the average waiting time approaches the limit of the *shortest job next* algorithm: $W_t = W_0/(1 - \rho)^2$.

The overall mean waiting time is approximately

$$W \approx \int_0^\infty (W_0 + k\,t)dF(t)$$

$$= W_0 + \frac{\rho^2}{1 - \rho}\,\frac{1}{2\mu} \qquad (6.29)$$

which is the value obtained for $t = 1/\mu$ in equation (6.27). The mean queue length is $\lambda W$.

The approximate waiting time is shown in Fig. 6.5 for a hyperexponential distribution of service time with $d = 2.75$. The *highest response ratio next* algorithm is better than the *first-come, first-served* algorithm for jobs up to 5.5 times the average job of 1 min. This represents 96 per cent of all jobs. Jobs that run less than 1 min wait up to 9 min, compared to 4.5 min with the *shortest job next* algorithm and 36.5 min with the *first-come, first-served* algorithm under heavy load, $\rho = 0.93$. Response ratio scheduling is quite effective in limiting the waiting time of longer jobs: a job of 30 min waits an average of 2.4 hours compared to 6.8 hours with the *shortest job next* algorithm. Under response ratio scheduling, sharing is practically equitable for jobs requiring from 2 to 30 min. Over this range of service times, the waiting ratio $W_t/t$ only varies from 7.5 to 5. For $\rho = 0.93$, the average queue has been reduced to 8 jobs, compared to 34 jobs in the *first-come, first-served* system.

All in all, response ratio scheduling is an attractive alternative to *first-come, first-served* and *shortest job next* scheduling in non-preemptive systems. It gives fairly rapid response to small jobs while effectively limiting the delay of longer jobs.

## 6.3.  PREEMPTIVE SCHEDULING

Non-preemptive scheduling can give fast *average response* to short jobs by using priority rules. In doing so, it relies completely on user estimates of service time. The main problem is the long-running jobs, which can monopolize the system for hours while they run to completion.

Preemptive systems, which can interrupt a running job and suspend its service while a job of higher priority is being done, do not have this problem. Preemption makes it possible to achieve *guaranteed response* to short jobs at the price of increased overhead. Preemption complicates the design of an operating system considerably, since the system must now keep track of several jobs that are in various stages of execution.

Although several jobs are in a state of execution simultaneously, a single processor can still only serve one of them at a time. It is therefore uneconomic to let jobs occupy part of the internal store during their idle periods. So preemption must be combined with store multiplexing. When the current job is interrupted, it is transferred to the backing store and the job with the highest priority is placed in the internal store. This exchange of jobs in store is called *swapping*; it is the main source of overhead in preemptive systems.

When reliable estimates of service times are available, preemption can be used to improve the performance of the *shortest job next* algorithm as follows: A running job is interrupted when a job arrives with a service requirement less than the remaining service of the running job. A somewhat simpler scheme to administer is one that limits the number of preempted jobs to one: A job with a service time below a certain threshold is placed in a *foreground queue*, while longer jobs enter a *background queue*. Within each queue service is non-preemptive according to the rule *shortest job next*, but jobs in the foreground queue preempt jobs in the background queue. Hume (1968) suggests a variant of this scheme in which the threshold varies dynamically. In periods of heavy utilization, the threshold moves towards smaller jobs, but when the load diminishes, longer jobs are allowed in the foreground queue. The purpose of this is to guarantee response within 5 min in the foreground queue.

Another scheme for obtaining fast response to non-interactive jobs was used by Irons (1965). His system tries to share a processor equally among all jobs being executed. To accomplish this, it allocates the next time slice to the job with the *shortest elapsed service time*. The time slice is varied in proportion to the amount of swapping time required at any moment to keep the overhead below a preset limit of 10 per cent.

I mention these systems as examples of the use of preemption in non-interactive systems. In the following, however, the discussion is limited to *interactive systems*.

### 6.3.1.  Round-robin Scheduling

We will analyze *round-robin* scheduling of interactive requests. We assume that the number of user terminals $n$ is finite, as shown in Fig. 6.7. A user will input one request at a time, wait for response, and examine the

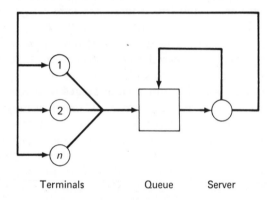

Terminals　　　　　Queue　　　Server

Fig. 6.7.  Queuing model of a single processor with a finite
number of user terminals (compare with Fig. 6.1).

result before making his next request. So the user alternates between a *thinking state*, in which he prepares the next request, and a *waiting state*, in which he waits for response. These states correspond to the interarrival and response times:

| user state | time interval |
| --- | --- |
| thinking | interarrival time |
| waiting | response time |

The interarrival time will include the time used to input a request and output the response at a terminal.

We assume that the interarrival and service times of requests are exponentially distributed with mean values $1/\lambda$ and $1/\mu$. For the *CTSS* system, Scherr (1965) observed a mean interarrival time of 35 sec and a mean service time of approximately 1 sec per request. He found that the day-to-day characteristics of users changed very little. Coffman and Wood

(1966) measured a mean interarrival time of 23 sec in the *SDC Q-32* system. For the same system, Schwartz (1967) reported that approximately 84 per cent of all requests required less than 1.8 sec of processor time. The access time of the internal store was about 2 $\mu$sec in both systems. Shemer (1969) found $1/\lambda = 15$ and $1/\mu = 0.3$ seconds in the *SDS Sigma 7* system with a store access time of 0.85 $\mu$sec.

Here we will use:

$$\text{mean interarrival time} \qquad \frac{1}{\lambda} = 15 \text{ sec}$$

$$\text{mean service time} \qquad \frac{1}{\mu} = 0.5 \text{ sec}$$

as typical values.

In the first analysis of this model, the overhead of swapping is assumed to be negligible. This is probably only realistic in a very large machine which can hold all jobs in its internal store simultaneously. I do not propose it as a realistic model of present interactive systems. It serves as a standard which sets an upper limit to obtainable performance.

Due to the memoryless property of the exponential distribution, we can also ignore the effect of the size of the time quantum used. I am referring to Section 6.1.2, in which it was shown that the remaining service time of jobs which have received $Q$ seconds of service is exponentially distributed with the original mean $1/\mu$, independent of the length of $Q$.

The system can be in $n + 1$ states since $0, 1, 2, \ldots, n$ terminals can be waiting for response. The steady state probabilities of these states are denoted $p_0, p_1, p_2, \ldots, p_n$. We now look at the system during a small time interval $dt$. The state of the system can be changed by an arrival or a departure; the probability of more than one arrival or departure is negligible under the present assumptions. The probability that a job ("request") terminates and departs during this interval is $\mu dt$, according to equation (6.10). The probability that a user in the thinking state generates a request in the same interval is $\lambda dt$ (see Section 6.1.1, assumption 2). So the overall probability of an arrival in state $j - 1$ is $(n - j + 1)\lambda dt$ since $j - 1$ terminals are already waiting for response. Finally, the probability that neither an arrival nor a departure will occur in state $j$ is $1 - ((n - j)\lambda + \mu)dt$. This leads to the following relations between the steady state probabilities:

$$p_0 = p_0 (1 - n\lambda \, dt) + p_1 \mu dt$$

$$p_j = p_{j-1} (n - j + 1) \lambda \, dt + p_j(1 - ((n - j)\lambda + \mu)dt) + p_{j+1} \mu dt$$

$$0 < j < n$$

$$p_n = p_{n-1} \lambda dt + p_n (1 - \mu dt)$$

By solving this set of equations, we find

$$p_j = \frac{n!}{(n-j)!}\left(\frac{\lambda}{\mu}\right)^j p_0 \qquad 0 \leqslant j \leqslant n \tag{6.30}$$

Since the sum of the probabilities is 1

$$p_0 + p_1 + \ldots + p_n = 1$$

the probability that no terminals are waiting is

$$p_0 = \left[\sum_{j=0}^{n} \frac{n!}{(n-j)!}\left(\frac{\lambda}{\mu}\right)^j\right]^{-1} \tag{6.31}$$

We can now use this result to find the expected *response time* $R$. The fraction of time during which a user is thinking is the ratio of the average interarrival time $1/\lambda$ to the *circulation time* $1/\lambda + R$. The circulation time is the average interval between two successive requests from the same terminal. Each of the $n$ terminals generates requests at a rate of $\lambda$ per second provided the user is in the thinking state. So the average *input rate* of requests to the system is

$$n\lambda \frac{\frac{1}{\lambda}}{\frac{1}{\lambda} + R}$$

The average rate at which requests depart from the system is $\mu$ per second when the processor is busy. Since the probability that the processor is busy is $1 - p_0$, the average *output rate* of responses must be

$$\mu(1 - p_0)$$

In the steady state, the average input and output rates are equal, which means that

$$R = \frac{n}{\mu(1 - p_0)} - \frac{1}{\lambda} \tag{6.32}$$

This queuing model was originally used to describe the servicing by a single repairman of $n$ machines which break down individually after a mean of $1/\lambda$ time units and require a mean repair time of $1/\mu$ units each (Cox, 1961). It was later used by Scherr (1965) to describe an interactive computer system with a limited number of terminals.

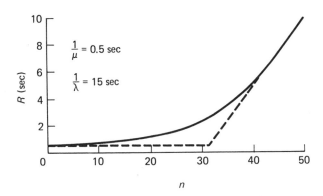

Fig. 6.8. The average response time $R$ as a function of the
number of active terminals $n$.

Figure 6.8 shows the average response time $R$ as a function of the
number of active terminals $n$, assuming that the average user generates a
request for 0.5 sec of processor time after 15 sec of thinking.

Although the response time increases with the overall load, there is no
point at which the system becomes unstable as a system with an infinite
input source does when the utilization factor approaches 1. The present
system is self-regulating because the input rate decreases in proportion to
the number of terminals waiting for response. When all terminals are
waiting, the input rate becomes zero.

As an alternative measure of system *saturation*, Kleinrock (1968) has
proposed the following. Suppose we replace each service time by its average
$1/\mu$ and schedule the arrivals to occur uniformly in time with interarrival
intervals of exactly $1/\lambda$ sec. As long as the system gives immediate response,
each user will require $1/\mu$ sec of processor time every $1/\mu + 1/\lambda$ sec; so the
maximum number of terminals $n*$ is given by

$$n* = \frac{\frac{1}{\mu} + \frac{1}{\lambda}}{\frac{1}{\mu}} = 1 + \frac{\mu}{\lambda} \tag{6.33}$$

When this definition is substituted into equation (6.32), we find

$$\mu R = \frac{n}{1 - p_0} - n* + 1 \tag{6.34}$$

In the example shown in Fig. 6.8, the saturation point $n*$ is
$1 + 15/0.5 = 31$ users. For $n \ll n*$, the response time is short because it is
rare for more than one request to be inside the system. Queuing can

nevertheless occur in this region due to the irregularities of arrival and service times.

In the vicinity of the saturation point, the response time begins to increase sharply. For a large number of terminals $n \gg n^*$, the processor is practically always busy, so $p_0 \approx 0$ and the response time approaches the asymptote

$$\mu R \approx n - n^* + 1 \tag{6.35}$$

In a saturated system, each additional user increases the *response ratio* $\mu R$ by 1.

We will now consider the effect of mixing trivial interactive requests with longer computational requests in a *saturated system*. I define a *trivial request* as one that can be completed during a single time quantum $Q$. The effect of the longer requests is to increase the mean service time to $1/\mu > Q$.

It is important to notice that the *average time quantum* $q$ can be considerably smaller than the *maximum time quantum* $Q$ since the response to requests may be completed in the middle of a quantum. The probability that the quantum will be less than or equal to $t$ is

$$F(t) = \begin{cases} 1 - e^{-\mu t} & t \leqslant Q \\ 1 & t > Q \end{cases} \tag{6.36}$$

The mean value of this truncated exponential distribution is

$$q = \frac{1}{\mu} (1 - e^{-\mu Q}) \tag{6.37}$$

The average response time $R_q$ for a trivial request is approximately equal to the average time quantum $q$ multiplied by the response ratio $\mu R$. So, from equations (6.33) and (6.35), we find

$$R_q = (n - \frac{\mu}{\lambda}) q \tag{6.38}$$

The maximum quantum $Q$ needed by a trivial request depends mainly on the processor speed and the characteristics of interactive programs. The maximum tolerable response time $R_{q\ max}$ and the average thinking time $1/\lambda$ are psychological characteristics of the users. It is therefore reasonable to consider the parameters $Q$, $R_{q\ max}$, and $1/\lambda$ as fixed for a given installation. Consequently, the maximum number of interactive users $n_{max}$ that a system can support is primarily a function of their average service time requirement $1/\mu$:

$$n_{max} = \frac{R_{q\ max}}{q} + \frac{\mu}{\lambda} \qquad (6.39)$$

This relationship is shown in Fig. 6.9 using the values $Q = 0.1$ sec, $R_{q\ max} = 2.5$ sec, and $1/\lambda = 15$ sec.

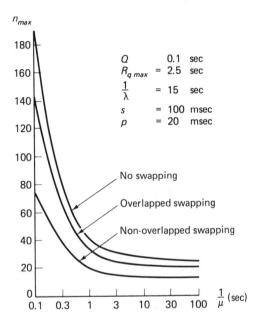

**Fig. 6.9.** The maximum number of interactive users $n_{max}$ as a function of the average service time per request $1/\mu$.

The effect of mixing trivial requests with longer computations ($1/\mu > Q$) is a sharp decrease of $n_{max}$. For $1/\mu > 10\ Q$, we have approximately $n_{max} \approx R_{q\ max}/Q = 25$. At this point, the number of interactive users is determined only by human nature ($R_{q\ max}$) and processor speed ($Q$). And as Simon (1966) aptly remarks, "No scheduling magic can relax this Iron law."

The non-trivial jobs experience a response ratio of 25. Under response ratio scheduling with $1/\mu = 60$ sec, they would be delayed by a factor of 10 at most under heavy loading, as shown in Fig. 6.5. This supports the statement made earlier that interactive systems are able to give fast response to trivial requests, but are not suitable for fast and efficient processing of non-trivial jobs (Section 1.2.4).

We will now include the effect of *swapping* in our analysis. Swapping reduces processor utilization from 100 per cent to a fraction, $\eta$. We can account for this approximately by making the following corrections in the previous equations:

$$\mu \rightarrow \mu\eta \qquad q \rightarrow \frac{q}{\eta}$$

Scherr found that with this correction, the predictions of equation (6.32) were in excellent agreement with actual measurements and simulation of the *CTSS* system. This is very encouraging considering that the introduction of overhead violates the assumption of exponential service times.

The overhead of swapping saturates the system with fewer users and increases the slope of the response curve (Fig. 6.8).

The *CTSS* system uses contiguous segments. Similar response curves have been observed for systems with paged segments (DeMeis, 1969).

The overhead of swapping can be characterized by two parameters: the average *swap time s* required to transfer a job to the backing store and place another job in the internal store; and the average *processor time p* spent on scheduling and swapping during a time quantum.

Suppose, for example, that we have a drum with a waiting time of 10 msec and a transfer time of 5 msec/K words. If an average job consists of a single contiguous segment of 8 K words, the average swap time is $s = 2$ $(10 + 5 * 8) = 100$ msec. (In a paging system, $s$ is the time required to exchange two working sets.)

If the access time to the internal store is 1 $\mu$sec/word, the swapping of 16 K words will require 16 msec of store time. To this must be added the processor time used to control the drum, select the next job, and so on. A reasonable estimate would be an average processor time $p = 20$ msec per time quantum.

In the *CTSS* system studied by Scherr, only one job at a time is placed in the internal store. Swapping and processing are *non-overlapped*, that is, the processor is idle during the swap interval $s$. The processor utilization $\eta$ is therefore

$$\eta = \frac{q}{q + s} \tag{6.40}$$

Figures 6.9 and 6.10 show $n_{max}$ and $\eta$ as a function of the average service time $1/\mu$ using the previous values of $Q$, $R_{q\ max}$, $1/\lambda$, $s$, and $p$. With non-overlapped swapping, processor utilization cannot exceed 50 per cent.

Performance can be improved considerably by using *overlapped swapping* and processing: The internal store is divided into two areas; while a job is processed in one area, another job is swapped into the other area; at the end of a time quantum the roles of the two areas are exchanged. To utilize this technique fully, the machine must be equipped with facilities for dynamic relocation. You can easily see this if you consider cyclical swapping of an odd number of jobs in two areas.

When the average processor time $p + q$ used by the operating system

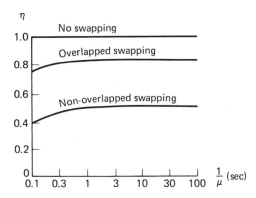

**Fig. 6.10.** Processor utilization $\eta$ as a function of the average service time per request $1/\mu$.

and its current job during a time quantum is less than the average swap time $s$, the system is *swap limited*, and we have

$$\eta = \frac{q}{s} \qquad p \leqslant p + q \leqslant s \qquad (6.41)$$

When the average processor time used during a time quantum exceeds the average swap time, the system is *processor limited*, and we find

$$\eta = \frac{q}{p+q} \qquad p \leqslant s \leqslant p + q \qquad (6.42)$$

The performance of overlapped swapping is also shown in Figs. 6.9 and 6.10. In the processor limited region ($1/\mu > 0.3$ sec), processor utilization is about 83 per cent. The maximum number of users is reduced correspondingly compared to the idealized case with no swapping.

### 6.3.2. Limited Swapping

Even when swapping and program execution overlap each other in time, *round-robin* scheduling still reduces processor utilization considerably (about 20 per cent in the example considered previously). The following is an informal discussion of methods which limit swapping without degrading interactive response to trivial requests.

The following methods will be considered:

> dedicated response programs
> multiple-level scheduling
> improved store management

In his observation of the *CTSS* system, Scherr (1965) found that about 50 per cent of all user requests could be classified as file manipulation, program input, and editing. An interactive system that does not distinguish between these standard tasks and other user tasks will spend a considerable amount of time swapping copies of the same programs for different jobs. An effective solution is to set aside a permanent store area for *dedicated programs* which can respond to the most frequent file handling and editing commands without swapping.

Swapping of non-trivial jobs can be reduced if a job is given a larger and larger time quantum each time it is served, thus decreasing the number of passes the job must make through the scheduling queue. The simplest algorithm uses two priority levels: Upon arrival, a job is placed at the end of a *foreground queue* with *round-robin* service; The job may receive up to $N - 1$ time quanta of $Q$ seconds each in this queue. If the service time exceeds this limit, the job is placed at the end of a *background queue*, which is served either by *round-robin* scheduling with a large quantum or simply by *first-come, first-served* scheduling to completion. The foreground queue preempts the background queue at the end of a time quantum. Background service is only resumed when the foreground queue is empty.

If a background job is served to completion, it can be swapped $N$ times at most. So the average number of swaps per job is

$$K_N = Prob(t > 0) + Prob(t > Q) + \ldots + Prob(t > (N - 1)Q)$$

$$= 1 + e^{-\mu Q} + \ldots + e^{-\mu(N-1)Q}$$

$$= \frac{1 - e^{-\mu N Q}}{1 - e^{-\mu Q}} \tag{6.43}$$

Simple *round-robin* scheduling corresponds to $N \to \infty$. If we choose $NQ = 1/\mu$, then

$$\frac{K_N}{K_\infty} = 1 - e^{-1} = 0.63$$

—a reduction of 37 per cent.

In the *SDC Q-32* system, the simple *round-robin* scheduling with non-overlapped swapping and execution used in the original version was later replaced by *foreground-background* scheduling with three priority levels: At level 1, each request can receive three time quanta, each of 0.6 sec; at level 2, only a single time quantum of 3.6 sec can be obtained; still longer requests are given an unlimited number of time quanta, each of 1.2 sec at level 3. This algorithm reduced average swap time by 50 per cent (Schwartz, 1964 and 1967).

A more complicated *foreground-background* scheduler was proposed by Corbato (1962) and used in the *CTSS* system. In this system, the quantum size increases exponentially with the priority level $i$

$$Q_i = 2^{i-1} Q \qquad i = 1, 2, \ldots, 9$$

where $Q = 0.5$ sec. The initial priority $j$ assigned to a job upon arrival depends on the time $S$ required to swap the job in and out of the internal store as follows

$$S = (2^{j-1} - 1) Q$$

When a job has been pushed down to level $j + k$, the ratio of its swap time to its current time quantum is

$$\frac{S}{Q_{j+k}} = (1 - 2^{-(j-1)}) 2^{-k}$$

This equation shows that a job is always executed for a time greater than or equal to its swap time. Furthermore, the relative swap time of long jobs decreases steadily.

Shorter jobs may delay longer ones excessively. The *CTSS* scheduler compensates for this by moving a job to the next higher priority level when it has waited more than 1 minute for service.

Corbato's scheduler has proved difficult to analyze, but Scherr (1965) has demonstrated its advantage over *round-robin* scheduling by simulation. The introduction of this algorithm, which gives low priority to users with large storage requirements, had a drastic influence on the behavior of users: Within three months the average program size dropped from 9000 to 6000 words! This is an example of the countermeasures that users can and will use to improve their priority. Although this tends to defeat any scheduling algorithm in the long run, it can also be used as an effective means of changing the characteristics of jobs deliberately. When longer jobs are split into shorter ones which can be scheduled individually, the processor time wasted by unsuccessful runs is normally reduced.

Swapping can also be reduced by various methods of *store management*. The solution used in *CTSS* and in Irons's system is to allocate internal store in such a way that the overlapping regions of jobs are minimal. During a swap, only as much of the internal store is transferred to the backing store as is required to make room for the incoming job.

Another possibility is to use as backing store a large, slow core store which is directly addressable in continuation of the smaller and faster internal store. The long-running jobs can be executed efficiently in the internal store, while trivial requests can be executed directly in the slow core store without swapping. This is the approach taken by *Carnegie-Mellon University* on its *IBM 360/67* system (Vareha, 1969).

## 6.4. LITERATURE

Scheduling methods and their countermeasures is the theme of a paper by Coffman and Kleinrock (1968a).

Two excellent papers, Estrin and Kleinrock (1967) and McKinney (1969), survey various analytical models of interactive systems with infinite input sources.

For a much more complete discussion of scheduling, see the book by Conway, Maxwell, and Miller (1967).

COFFMAN, E. G. and KLEINROCK, L., "Computer scheduling methods and their countermeasures," Proc. *AFIPS Spring Joint Computer Conf.*, pp. 11-21, April *1968a*.

CONWAY, R. W., MAXWELL, W. L., and MILLER, L. W., *Theory of Scheduling.* Addison-Wesley, Reading, Massachusetts, *1967*.

ESTRIN, G. and KLEINROCK, L., "Measures, models and measurements for time-shared computer utilities," Proc. *ACM National Meeting*, pp. 85-96, Aug. *1967*.

McKINNEY, J. M., "A survey of analytical time-sharing models," *Computing Surveys 1*, 2, pp. 105-16, June *1969*.

# 7

# *RESOURCE PROTECTION*

This chapter discusses the use of automatic methods to control access to resources. The main techniques considered are the class concept of *Simula 67* and the capability concept.

## 7.1. INTRODUCTION

The last problem that will be discussed in this book is the question of how an installation protects shared resources against unauthorized usage.

The word *resource* covers physical components, processes, procedures, and data structures; in short, any object referenced by computations. Physical resources and processes will always be represented by *data* within the system defining their identity and state as well as the rights of computations to use them, and by *procedures* defining meaningful operations on them. So the protection problem boils down to the following question: How can an installation protect data and procedures against unauthorized usage? I will therefore define *resource protection* as *automatic methods which ensure that data and procedures are accessed properly*.

The protection problem is not well-understood at the moment. Various aspects of it are solved by seemingly *ad hoc* methods in present systems.

Rather than give a detailed description of these, I prefer to give a brief indication of the nature of a more systematic approach. But I can only present fragments of a solution.

Since only users and installation management can define the forms of access they wish to enforce for particular resources, we shall look in vain for a general complete solution to our protection problems. Still, we can hope to solve some aspects of them in a uniform, efficient manner. I will discuss two aspects of protection: *type checking*, which ensures that data are accessed by well-defined operations, and *security checking*, which ensures that these operations are carried out by user computations authorized to do so.

As an example of this distinction, consider a sequential file: The meaningful operations on the file may be *rewind*, *read*, and *write*; but if the file contains valuable (perhaps confidential) data, permission to carry out these operations may not be granted to every computation.

Resource protection is achieved by: (1) identifying a user and establishing his authority to access data; (2) creating an environment which identifies the resources available to his particular computation; and (3) checking that the computation remains within its proper environment.

I shall not discuss the problem of *user identification* in any detail. It is often the weakest part of a protection system since it depends on identification supplied by the users themselves. Many present file systems maintain a *directory* for each user (or group of users) defining his ownership of private files and access rights to public files. A user's identity is often established by quotation of a *password* which is selected by the user himself and can be changed as often as desired. Another technique is to associate access rights with particular *terminals*. Both techniques are used in the Cambridge file system (Fraser, 1971).

In the following, I will concentrate on methods of representing computational environments and checking access to them. Two methods will be described: the use of a *class concept* to check resource access at compile time; and the use of *capabilities* to check resource access at run time.

## 7.2. CLASS CONCEPT

We will first discuss the close relationship between data and operations and use it to define a very important form of protection.

If we consider variables of *primitive types* such as *integer* and *boolean*, it is quite possible that values of different types will be represented by identical bit strings at the machine level. For example both the *boolean* value *true* and the *integer* value 1 might be represented by the bit string

000 ... 001

in single machine words.

So data of different types are distinguished not only by the representation of their values, but also by the operations associated with the types. An *integer*, for example, is a datum subject only to arithmetic operations, comparisons, and assignments involving other data subject to the same restrictions.

Now consider *structured types*. Take for example the variable *b* in Algorithm 3.6. It represents a message buffer that contains a sequence of messages sent, but not yet received. A *static* picture of process communication can be defined by assertions about the relationships of the components of the message buffer. But to understand how and when messages are exchanged *dynamically*, one must also study the *send* and *receive* procedures defined for a message buffer. These operations in turn are only meaningful for the particular representation of the message buffer chosen and can only be understood precisely by studying its type definition.

These examples illustrate the point made by Dahl (1971): "Data and operations on data seem to be so closely connected in our minds, that it takes elements of both kinds to make any concept useful for understanding computing processes."

Simon (1962) has pointed out that the search for state and process descriptions of the same phenomenon is characteristic of problem solving: "These two modes of apprehending structure are the warp and weft of our experience. Pictures, blueprints, most diagrams, chemical structural formulae are state descriptions. Recipes, differential equations, equations for chemical reactions are process descriptions. The former characterize the world as sensed; they provide the criteria for identifying objects, often by modeling the objects themselves. The latter characterize the world as acted upon; they provide the means for producing or generating objects having the desired characteristics.

"The distinction between the world as sensed and the world as acted upon defines the basic condition for the survival of adaptive organisms. The organism must develop correlations between goals in the sensed world and actions in the world of process."

In Section 2.6 on program construction, I have illustrated this alternation between a refinement of data (representing states) and program (representing processes). The essence of this form of problem solving is the following:

When a programmer needs a concept such as process communication, he first postulates a set of operations (in this case, *send* and *receive*) that have the desired effect at his present level of thinking. Later, he chooses a specific representation of a data structure (a message buffer), that enables him to implement the operations efficiently on the available machine.

When the programmer is trying to convince himself of the correctness of a program (by formal proof or testing), he will tacitly assume that these operations (*send* and *receive*) are the only ones carried out on data structures of this type (message buffers).

If other statements in his program are able to operate on message buffers, he cannot make this assumption. The most extreme case is unstructured machine language, which potentially permits each statement to influence any other statement, intentionally or by mistake. This makes program verification an endless task since one can never be sure, when a new component is added to a large program, how this will influence previously tested components.

If, on the other hand, the previous assumption is justified, the programmer can convince himself of the correctness of process communication by studying only the type definition of a message buffer and the procedures *send* and *receive*. Once this program component has been shown to be correct, the designer can be confident that subsequent addition of other components will not invalidate this proof. This makes the task of verification grow linearly with the number and size of components—an essential requirement for the design of large, reliable programs.

According to the previous definition, it is an obvious protection problem to check that data are accessed by operations consistent with their type. To what extent do the structures of present high-level languages enable a compiler to check this?

A decent compiler for an algorithmic language such as *Fortran*, *Algol 60*, or *Pascal* will check the compatibility of data and operations on them for *primitive types* (Naur, 1963). The compiler can do this because the permissible operations on primitive types are part of the language definition.

But in the case of *structured types*, only the most rudimentary kind of checking is possible with these languages. All the compiler can check is that data in assignment statements and comparisons for equality are of the same type. But, since the languages mentioned do not enable the programmer to associate a set of procedures with a type definition, the compiler cannot check whether the operations on a message buffer are restricted to *send* and *receive* procedures as intended by the programmer. This is a serious deficiency of most programming languages available today.

An exception is the *Simula 67* language (Dahl, 1968), an extension of Algol 60 originally designed for simulation. In Simula 67, the definition of a structured data type and the meaningful operations on it form a single syntactical unit called a *class*.*

---

*Readers of the Pascal report by Wirth (1971a) should notice that the Simula class concept is completely unrelated to the Pascal class concept.

I will briefly describe a simplified, restricted form of the Simula 67 class concept in a Pascal-inspired notation.

The notation

$$\text{class } T = v1\colon T1; v2\colon T2; \ldots ; vm\colon Tm;$$

**procedure** $P1(\ \ldots\ )$ **begin** $S1$ **end**

. . .

**procedure** $Pn(\ \ldots\ )$ **begin** $Sn$ **end**

**begin** $S0$ **end**

defines: (1) a data structure of type $T$ consisting of the components $v1$, $v2, \ldots , vm$ of types $T1, T2, \ldots , Tm$; (2) a set of procedures (or functions) $P1, P2, \ldots , Pn$ that can operate on the data structure; and (3) a statement $S0$ that can define its initial value.

A variable $v$ of type $T$ is declared as usual:

$$\text{var } v\colon T$$

Upon entry to the context in which the variable $v$ is declared, storage is allocated for its components $v1, v2, \ldots , vm$, and the initial statement $S0$ is carried out for this variable.

A call of a procedure $Pi$ on the variable $v$ is denoted:

$$v.Pi(\ \ldots\ )$$

Procedure $Pi$ can refer to the components $v1, v2, \ldots , vm$ of $v$, to its own local variables, and to the parameters of the given call. The operations $P1$, $P2, \ldots , Pn$ are the only ones permitted on the variable $v$.

An obvious idea is to represent critical regions by the concept *shared class*, implying that the operations $P1, P2, \ldots , Pn$ on a given variable $v$ of type $T$ exclude one another in time.

The concept *message buffering* is defined as a shared class in Algorithm 7.1. Compare this with Algorithm 3.6. A buffer variable $b$ and a message variable $t$ are declared and accessed as follows:

$$\text{var } b\colon B; t\colon T;$$
$$b.send(t); \ldots b.receive(t);$$

Strictly speaking, assignment to a message parameter $m$ can only be made within the class $B$ if its type $T$ is primitive. But it seems reasonable to retain the simple type definition

$$\text{type } T = \ <\text{type}>$$

to indicate that variables of this type can be accessed directly.

ALGORITHM 7.1    *Representation of a Message Buffer*
*by a Shared Class.*

```
shared class B =
    buffer: array 0..max-1 of T;
    p,c: 0..max-1;
    full: 0..max;

    procedure send(m: T);
    begin
      await full < max;
      buffer(p):= m;
      p:= (p + 1) mod max;
      full:= full + 1;
    end

    procedure receive(var m: T);
    begin
      await full > 0;
      m:= buffer(c);
      c:= (c + 1) mod max;
      full:= full - 1;
    end

begin p:= 0; c:= 0; full:= 0 end
```

The class concept in Simula 67 has several other aspects, among them a mechanism for defining a hierarchy of classes (Dahl and Hoare, 1971). My main purpose here is to show a notation which explicitly restricts operations on data and enables a compiler to check that these restrictions are obeyed. Although such restrictions are not enforced by Simula 67, this would seem to be essential for effective protection.

Many computers support a restricted form of shared class at the machine level of programming. I am referring to the *basic monitor* procedures and data structures which control the sharing of processors, storage, and peripherals at the lowest level of programming, as described in Section 4.2.2. This class concept enforced at run time is implemented as follows: The address mapping performed by a central processor prevents computations from referring directly to data structures belonging to the basic monitor, but permits them to call a well-defined set of monitor procedures. Mutual exclusion in time of such calls is achieved by means of an arbiter and by delaying interrupt response. To prevent computations from bypassing the monitor and referring directly to physical resources, the central processor recognizes two states of execution: the *privileged state*, in which all machine instructions can be executed; and the *user state*, in which certain instructions cannot be executed (those that control program interruption, input/output, and address mapping). The privileged state is entered after a monitor call; the user state is entered after a monitor return.

In Section 1.2.3 I said, "It is now recognized that it is desirable to be able to distinguish in a more flexible manner between many levels of protection (and not just two)." We have seen that it is indeed desirable to be able to enforce a separate set of access rules for each data type used. The class concept is a general structuring tool applicable at all levels of programming, sequential as well as concurrent.

The class concept was introduced here to protect *local* data structures within a program against inconsistent operations. But the concept is applicable also to data structures which are *retained* within the computer after the termination of computations.

One example of retained data structures are those used within an *operating system* to control resource sharing among unrelated computations. These data structures must be accessed only through well-defined procedures; otherwise, the operating system might crash. So an operating system defines a set of standard procedures which can be called by computations. Since these procedures remain unchanged over reasonable periods of time, a compiler should be able to use a description of them to perform type checking of calls of them within user programs in advance of their execution.

We are thus led to the idea of maintaining *data structures defining environments of compilation and execution*. An environment defines a set of retained data structures and procedures accessible to a given computation.

Another example of retained data structures are files stored semipermanently on backing stores. In most present *file systems*, a computation can either be denied access to a given file or be permitted to *read*, *write*, or *execute* it. This seems a rather crude distinction. In most cases, a data file is intended to be used only in a particular manner; for example, a source text of a program is intended to be edited or compiled by a particular compiler; most other operations on it may be entirely meaningless from the user's point of view. To maintain the integrity of a file, its creator should therefore be able to associate it with a set of procedures through which it can be accessed in a meaningful manner. This is possible, for example, in the file system for the *B5500* computer (McKeag, 1971a).

Assuming that this set of procedures remains unchanged over reasonable periods of time, it would again be possible to check the consistency of references to files within user programs at compile time. The basic requirement is that the access rules remain fixed between compilation and execution of programs.

Such a system differs from present ones in two aspects: (1) a program is compiled to be executed in a particular environment; and (2) a compiled program may become invalid if its environment changes. This is acceptable only if most programs are compiled shortly before execution or if they operate in a fairly constant environment. The benefits of this approach would be an early detection of program errors and a more efficient execution because fewer protection rules would have to be checked dynamically.

## 7.3. CAPABILITIES

Certain access decisions can only be made at run time. Consider, for example, a pool of identical resources, say line printers. At compile time we can check that printers are accessed only by well-defined standard procedures. But the sequential nature of printers also makes it necessary to ensure that each of them is used by at most one computation at a time. So at run time we must keep track of the ownership of individual printers.

In general, this means that the system must represent computational environments by data structures at run time. Dennis and Van Horn (1966) have suggested the following technique for doing this: At any moment the access rights of a process are defined by an array of data elements called *capabilities*. Each capability identifies a *resource* accessible to the process and a set of permissible *operations* on it.

One can regard capabilities as parameters associated with a process and made available to standard procedures controlling resources when the process attempts to access these resources. Capabilities are treated differently from other parameters to prevent processes from exceeding their authority.

As an example, the *address mapping* in most computers forces a process to remain within a given set of segments. Each segment is represented by a capability consisting of a *base address* and a *length*, as explained in Chapter 5. Some computers also associate a set of *access rights* with each segment (for example, permission to *read*, *write*, or *execute* it). The safety of this scheme is guaranteed by the inability of processes to refer directly to address maps.

Another example of capabilities is the data structures used within a *monitor* to keep track of resources assigned to individual processes (such as the *loans* granted to customers by the banker in Algorithm 2.6).

The environment of a process changes dynamically as it acquires and releases resources. If we consider local data as resources, we find that, in general, the environment changes every time the process calls a procedure or returns from one.

A process may, for example, access shared data structures inside a monitor procedure, but not outside it. This dynamic change of access rights is supported in a very minimal sense by computers which distinguish between two states of execution: privileged and unprivileged.

A somewhat more flexible scheme is used in *Multics* (Graham, 1968), which distinguishes eight *levels of protection*. The access rights of a process executing at a given level of protection are a subset of the access rights granted at lower levels. Each data and procedure segment is associated with a range of protection levels. A segment can directly access other segments at its own or higher levels, but segments at lower levels can only be accessed through well-defined procedures. A similar system has been implemented on the *HITAC 5020* computer (Motobayashi, 1969).

A practical evaluation of this technique will require publication of performance measures for these systems. The implementation in *Multics* seems to be quite complex (Schroeder, 1972). The scheme requires extensive parameter checking (because addresses can be passed as parameters from higher to lower levels of protection) as well as parameter copying (because segments can be shared with other computations which might modify parameters after the validity checking).

Capabilities are also used in the *RC 4000* system in which a hierarchy of processes share a set of monitor procedures. These procedures enable processes to schedule other processes and communicate with them by means of message buffers. Each process operates in a certain environment defined by capabilities stored within the monitor. A process can invoke operations at other levels of protection by monitor calls (executed in the privileged state) and by messages sent to other processes (executed in the user state with different capabilities).

It is appealing that this system permits both complete isolation and interaction between different levels of protection (represented by different processes). But, in practice, it is cumbersome that these interactions require transmission of messages by value.

In general, the environment of a process is established by another process (an operating system). In the *RC 4000* system, there is initially only one process, the basic operating system. Upon request from terminals, this process will call the monitor and initiate other processes. These are described within the monitor as children of the basic operating system, and these processes in turn can create their own children. Thus, a *process tree* is built.

The question of *process authority* is solved by the simple rule that a process can only schedule its own children and allocate a subset of its own resources to them. Initially, all resources are assigned to the basic operating system at the root of the tree.

When a process receives a message from another process, the monitor supplies the former process with a unique identification of the latter. In theory, this should enable the receiving process to decide whether or not the sending process has the authority to request a given operation. But, in practice, it is difficult to establish the authority of processes because the system does not have a uniform concept of *user authority*.

In most implementations (including the *RC 4000* system), the environment of a process seldom changes. But conceptually, the following viewpoint is more general: When a process calls a procedure, the current environment of the process is replaced by a set of capabilities which apply within that procedure. Upon return from the procedure, the previous set of capabilites apply again. Thus, capabilities become part of the stack of a process.

## 7.4. CONCLUSION

We have considered the use of the class concept at compile time and the use of capabilities at run time to check that resources are accessed properly by computations. The essential properties of these protection mechanisms are the following:

A process operates in an environment which defines the set of resources available to it. These resources consist of data and procedures which are *directly accessible* to the process, and data and procedures which are *indirectly accessible* to it (through calls of directly accessible procedures with directly accessible data as parameters).

Access rights are primarily associated with *procedures* to ensure the consistency of data structures, but the overall authority of a *computation* can be restricted merely by restriction of its *initial environment*.

These relationships between users, procedures, and data should be reflected in the structure of the file system and in the structure of individual programs. Efficient use of these concepts will require a language in which the programmer can express the intended protection rules so they can be recognized and checked automatically.

The machine language interpreted by processors during execution can only represent high-level structure in the crudest manner. Some attempts have been made to refine protection mechanisms at the machine level (as in *Multics*), but, on the whole, I am skeptical about attempts to solve high-level structuring problems by brute force at the lowest levels of programming.

I expect to see many protection rules in future operating systems enforced in the cheapest possible manner by type checking at compile time. However, this will require exclusive use of efficient, well-structured languages for programming.

## 7.5. LITERATURE

The use of the class concept in *Simula 67* for program construction is illustrated in a paper by Dahl and Hoare (1971).

The idea of associating procedures with data structures is also used in the *AED-0* language designed by Ross (1969), but the unrestricted use of pointers in this language makes it impossible to check the correspondence.

The use of capabilities was originally suggested by Dennis and Van Horn (1966) and later developed by Lampson (1969 and 1970).

The security checks in the Cambridge file system are described by Fraser (1971).

The model of computational structures presented by Vanderbilt (1969) is most closely related to the view of protection presented here.

DAHL, O.-J. and HOARE, C. A. R., "Hierarchal program structures," Unpublished draft, *1971*.

DENNIS, J. B. and VAN HORN, E. C., "Programming semantics for multiprogrammed computations," *Comm. ACM 9*, 3, 143-55, March *1966*.

FRASER, A. G., "The integrity of a disc based file system," *International Seminar on Operating System Techniques*, Belfast, Northern Ireland, Aug.-Sept. *1971*.

LAMPSON, B. W., "Dynamic protection structures," *Proc. AFIPS Fall Joint Computer Conf.*, pp. 27-38, *1969*.

LAMPSON, B. W., "On reliable and extensible operating systems," *Infotech State of the Art Proceedings*, *1970*.

ROSS, D. T., "Introduction to software engineering with the AED-0 language," Massachusetts Institute of Technology, Cambridge, Massachusetts, Oct. *1969*.

VANDERBILT, D. H., "Controlled information sharing in a computer utility." *MAC-TR-67*, Massachusetts Institute of Technology, Cambridge, Massachusetts, Oct. *1969*.

# 8

# A CASE STUDY: RC 4000

This chapter describes the philosophy and structure of the *RC 4000* multiprogramming system which can be extended with a hierarchy of operating systems to suit diverse requirements of process scheduling and resource allocation. The system nucleus simulates an environment in which program execution and input/output are handled uniformly as concurrent, cooperating processes. A set of primitives allows dynamic creation and control of a hierarchy of processes as well as communication among them.

We have discussed at length various aspects of concurrent processes and resource management. I will now describe a complete multiprogramming system in some detail to give you an idea of how the various pieces fit together in a coherent design.

The system I have chosen was designed for the *RC 4000* computer manufactured by *Regnecentralen* in Denmark. Work on the system began towards the end of 1967, and a well-documented reliable version of it was running in the spring of 1969. The conceptual part of the design was due to Jørn Jensen, Søren Lauesen, and myself. We spent almost a year with daily discussions trying to formulate objectives, concepts, and overall structure. A presentation of our proposal was written before its implementation. It corresponded closely to the paper published after its completion (Brinch Hansen, 1970). Having reached a clear understanding of the problem, we found that it was an almost trivial task to write and test the system in machine language. It was done in half a year by Leif Svalgaard and myself.

I will first describe the *RC 4000* system as we looked upon it at that time and then take a critical look at it in the light of my present thinking. What follows then is a slightly edited version of the system manual (Brinch Hansen, 1969). The presentation is made as self-contained as possible and will sometimes repeat ideas mentioned in earlier chapters.

## 8.1. SYSTEM OBJECTIVES

The multiprogramming system for the *RC 4000* computer is a tool for the design of operating systems. It allows dynamic creation of a hierarchy of processes in which diverse medium-term strategies of process scheduling and resource allocation can be implemented.

For the designer of advanced information systems, a vital requirement of any operating system is that it allow him to change the mode of operation it controls; otherwise, his freedom of design can be seriously limited. Unfortunately, this is precisely what many operating systems do not allow. Most of them are based exclusively on a single mode of operation such as batch processing, spooling, real-time scheduling, or conversational access.

When the need arises, the user often finds it hopeless to modify an operating system that has made rigid assumptions in its basic design about a specific mode of operation. The alternative—to replace the original operating system with a new one—is in most computers a serious, if not impossible, matter because the rest of the software is intimately bound to the conventions required by the original system.

This unfortunate situation indicates that the main problem in the design of a multiprogramming system is not to define functions that satisfy specific operating needs, but rather to supply a *system nucleus* that can be extended with new operating systems in an orderly manner. This is the primary objective of the *RC 4000* system.

The basic attitude during the designing was to make no assumptions about the particular medium-term strategy needed to optimize a given type of installation, but to concentrate on the fundamental aspects of the control of an environment consisting of cooperating, concurrent processes.

The first task was to assign a precise meaning to the process concept; that is, to introduce unambiguous terminology defining what a process is and how it is implemented on the actual computer.

The next step was to select primitives for the synchronization and transfer of data between concurrent processes.

The final decisions concerned the rules for dynamic creation, control, and removal of processes.

The purpose of the system nucleus is to implement these fundamental concepts: simulation of processes; communication between processes; and creation, control, and removal of processes.

## 8.2. BASIC CONCEPTS

This section opens a detailed description of the *RC 4000* system. A multiprogramming system is viewed as an environment in which program execution and input/output are handled uniformly as cooperating, concurrent processes. The purpose of the nucleus is to bridge the gap between the actual hardware and the abstract concept of multi-programming.

### 8.2.1. Programs and Internal Processes

As a first step, we shall assign a precise meaning to the process concept. We will distinguish between internal and external processes, roughly corresponding to program execution and input/output, respectively.

More precisely, an *internal process* is the execution of one or more interruptable programs in a given store area. An internal process is identified by a unique *process name*. Thus, other processes need not be aware of the actual location of an internal process in store, but can refer to it by name.

Figure 8.1 illustrates the allocation of the internal store to a *monitor* (the system nucleus) and three internal processes, *P*, *Q*, and *R*.

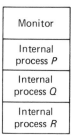

Fig. 8.1. Allocation of store to the monitor and three internal processes.

Later it will be explained how internal processes are created and how programs are placed in their store areas. At this point, it should only be noted that an internal process occupies a contiguous segment with a fixed base address during its lifetime. The monitor maintains a *process description* of each internal process: It defines the name, store area, and current state of the process.

At the short-term scheduling level, processor time is shared cyclically among all active internal processes. Typically, the monitor allocates a maximum *time slice* of 25 msec to each internal process in turn. At the end

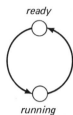

*ready*

*running*

**Fig. 8.2.** The *ready* and *running* states of an internal process.

of this interval, the process is interrupted and its register values are stored in the process description. Following this, the monitor allocates 25 msec to the next internal process, and so on. The queue of internal processes waiting to run is called the *ready queue*. Figure 8.2 shows the *ready* and *running* states of internal processes and the transitions between them.

A sharp distinction is made between the concepts program and internal process. A *program* is a collection of instructions describing a process, and an *internal process* is the execution of these instructions in a given store area.

An internal process such as $P$ can involve the execution of a sequence of programs; for example, editing followed by translation and execution of an object program. Copies of the same program (for example, an Algol compiler) can also be executed simultaneously by two processes, $Q$ and $R$. These examples illustrate the need for a distinction between programs and processes.

### 8.2.2. Documents and External Processes

In connection with input/output, the monitor distinguishes between peripheral devices, documents, and external processes:

A *peripheral device* is an item of hardware connected to a data channel and identified by a device number.

A *document* is a collection of data stored on a physical medium, for example:

> a roll of paper tape
> a deck of punched cards
> a printer form
> a reel of magnetic tape
> an area on the backing store

An *external process* is the input/output of a given document identified by a unique *process name*. This concept implies that once a document has been mounted, internal processes can refer to it by name without knowing the actual device it uses.

For each external process, the monitor maintains a *process description* defining its name, kind, device number, and current state. The *process kind* is an integer defining the type of peripheral device on which the document is mounted.

For each kind of external process the monitor contains a procedure that can start and complete input/output on request from internal processes.

### 8.2.3. Monitor

Multiprogramming and communication between internal and external processes are coordinated by the system nucleus—a *monitor* with complete control of input/output, store protection, and interrupt response. I do not regard the monitor as an independent process, but rather as a software extension of the hardware structure that makes the computer more attractive for multiprogramming. Its function is to implement the process concept and the primitives that processes can call to create and control other processes, and communicate with them.

After system initialization, the monitor resides permanently in the internal store. It is the only program which executes *privileged instructions* in an *uninterruptable* processor state.

So far, I have described the multiprogramming system as a set of concurrent processes identified by names. The emphasis has been on a clear understanding of the relationships between resources (store and peripherals), data (programs and documents), and processes (internal and external).

## 8.3. PROCESS COMMUNICATION

The following explains the monitor procedures for the exchange of data between concurrent processes.

### 8.3.1. Messages and Answers

Two concurrent processes can cooperate by sending messages to each other. A *message* consists of eight machine words. Messages are transmitted from one process to another by means of *message buffers* selected from a common *pool* within the monitor.

The monitor administers a *message queue* for each process. Messages are linked to this queue when they arrive from other processes. The message queue is part of the process description.

Normally, a process serves its queue in *first-come, first-served* order. After the processing of a message, the receiving process returns an *answer* of eight words to the sending process in the same buffer.

Communication between two independent processes requires that they be synchronized during a transfer of data. A process requests synchronization by executing a wait operation; this causes a delay of the process until another process executes a send operation.

The term *delay* means that an internal process is removed temporarily from the ready and running states; the process is said to be *activated* when it is again linked to the ready queue.

The following monitor procedures are available for communication between internal processes:

> *send message(receiver, message, buffer)*
> *wait message(sender, message, buffer)*
> *send answer(result, answer, buffer)*
> *wait answer(result, answer, buffer)*

*Send message* copies a message into an available buffer selected from the pool and delivers it in the queue of a given receiver. The receiver is activated if it is waiting for a message. The sender continues after being informed of the address of the message buffer.

*Wait message* delays the calling process until a message arrives in its queue. When the process is being allowed to proceed, it is supplied with the name of the sender, the contents of the message, and the address of the message buffer. The buffer is removed from the queue and is now ready to transmit an answer.

*Send answer* copies an answer into a buffer in which a message has been received and delivers it in the queue of the original sender. The sender of the message is activated if it is waiting for this particular answer. The answering process continues immediately.

*Wait answer* delays the calling process until an answer arrives in a given buffer. On arrival, the answer is copied into the process and the buffer is returned to the pool. The result specifies whether the answer is a response

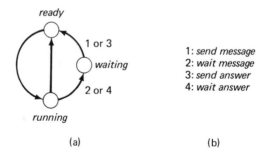

(a)                                    (b)

Fig. 8.3. (a) The process states *ready*, *running*, and *waiting*; and (b) the primitives that cause the transitions between them.

from another process or a dummy answer generated by the monitor in response to a message addressed to a non-existent process.

Figure 8.3 shows the transitions of internal processes between the *ready*, *running*, and *waiting* states. The monitor distinguishes between two possible waiting states for a process: *awaiting message* and *awaiting answer*. In the latter case, the monitor also remembers the buffer in which an answer is expected.

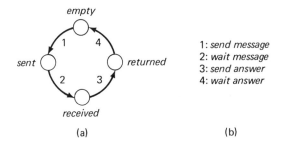

1: *send message*
2: *wait message*
3: *send answer*
4: *wait answer*

(a)                                              (b)

**Fig. 8.4.** (a) The possible states of a message buffer; and
(b) the primitives that cause the transitions between them.

Figure 8.4 shows the life cycle of a message buffer: It begins as an *empty* buffer in the pool. When a message is *sent* in the buffer, it enters the message queue of the receiver. When the message is *received*, the buffer is removed from the queue. When an answer is *returned* in the buffer, it enters the message queue of the original sender. Finally, when the answer is received, the buffer returns to the pool in the *empty* state.

### 8.3.2.  Advantages of Message Buffering

The design of the communication scheme reflects that the multi-programming system is a dynamic environment in which some of the processes may turn out to be black sheep.

The system is dynamic in the sense that processes can appear and disappear at any time. Therefore, in general, a process does not have a complete knowledge of the existence of other processes. This is reflected in the procedure *wait message*, which makes it possible for a process to be unaware of the existence of other processes until it receives messages from them.

On the other hand, once a communication has been established between two processes (by means of a message), they need a common identification of it in order to agree on when it is completed (by means of an answer). So we can properly regard the selection of a buffer as the creation of an identification of a conversation. This also enables two processes to exchange more than one message at a time.

We must be prepared for the occurrence of erroneous or malicious processes in the system (undebugged programs). This is tolerable only if the monitor ensures that no process can interfere with a conversation between two other processes. This is done by storing the identity of the sender and receiver in each buffer, and checking it whenever a process attempts to send or wait for an answer in a given buffer.

Efficiency is obtained by the queuing of buffers, which enables a sending process to continue immediately after delivery of a message or an answer regardless of whether the receiver is ready to process it or not.

To make the system dynamic, it is vital that a process can be removed at any time—even if it is engaged in one or more conversations. When a process is being removed, the monitor leaves all messages from it undisturbed in the queues of other processes. When these processes terminate their actions by sending answers, the monitor simply returns the buffers to the common pool.

The reverse situation is also possible: During the removal of a process, the monitor may find unanswered messages sent to the process. These are returned as dummy answers to the senders. A special instance of this is the generation of a dummy answer to a message addressed to a process that does not exist.

The main drawback of message buffering is that it introduces yet another resource problem since the common pool contains a finite number of buffers. If a process were allowed to empty the pool by sending messages to ignorant processes which do not respond with answers, further communication within the system would be blocked. We have therefore set a limit to the number of messages a process can send simultaneously. By doing this and by allowing a process to transmit an answer in a received buffer, we have placed the entire risk of a conversation on the process that opens it.

### 8.3.3. Event Primitives

The message scheme described so far has certain practical limitations as we shall see later, but it is conceptually consistent. Far more dubious are the following procedures introduced as an *ad hoc* solution to a specific programming problem: the design of that part of an operating system which communicates with operators through terminals. The original motivation was the following:

The communication procedures enable a conversational process to receive messages simultaneously from several other processes. To avoid becoming a bottleneck in the system however, a conversational process must be prepared to be engaged in more than one conversation at a time. As an example, think of a conversational process that engages itself, on request from another process, in a conversation with one of several operators asking him to perform a manual operation (for example, mounting a magnetic tape). If we restrict a conversational process to accepting only one message at a time and to completing the requested action before receiving the next message, the consequence is that other processes (including operators at terminals) can have their requests for response delayed for a long time.

As soon as a conversational process has started a lengthy action by sending a message to some other process, it must be able to receive further messages and start other actions. It will then be reminded later of the completion of earlier actions by means of normal answers.

In general, a conversational process is now engaged in several requests at one time. This introduces a scheduling and resource problem: When the process receives a request, some of its resources (storage and peripherals) can be tied up by already initiated actions. So in some cases the process will not be able to honor new requests before old ones have been completed. In such cases, the process wants to postpone the reception of some requests and leave them pending in the queue, while examining others.

The procedures *wait message* and *wait answer*, which force a process to serve its queue in strict order of arrival and delay itself while its own requests to other processes are completed, do not fulfill the above requirements.

Consequently, we introduce two communication procedures that enable a process to wait for the arrival of the next message or answer and serve its queue in any order:

> *wait event(previous buffer, next buffer, result)*
> *get event(buffer)*

The term *event* denotes a message or an answer. In accordance with this, the queue of a process from now on will be called the *event queue*.

*Wait event* delays the calling process until either a message or an answer arrives in its queue after a given, *previously examined buffer*. The process is supplied with the address of the *next buffer* and a *result* indicating whether it contains a message or an answer. If the *previous buffer address* was zero, the queue is examined from the start. The procedure does not remove any buffer from the queue or in any other way change its status.

As an example, consider an event queue with two pending buffers $A$ and $B$ which arrived in that order:

> *queue = (buffer A, buffer B)*

The monitor calls

> *wait event(0, buffer)*

and

> *wait event(A, buffer)*

will cause immediate return to the process with *buffer* equal to *A* and *B*, respectively. But the call

$$wait\ event(B,\ buffer)$$

will delay the process until another message or answer arrives in the queue after buffer *B* and will then supply the address of the newly arrived buffer *C*.

*Get event* removes a given *buffer* from the queue of the calling process. If the buffer contains a message, the buffer is made ready for the sending of an answer. If the buffer contains an answer, it is returned to the common pool. The copying of the message or answer from the buffer must be done by the process itself before *get event* is called (a shortcut which reveals the *ad hoc* nature of this proposal).

Algorithm 8.1 illustrates the use of event procedures within a conversational process.

The process starts by examining its queue: If it is empty, the process awaits the arrival of the next event. If it finds a message, the process checks

*ALGORITHM 8.1   The Basic Cycle of a Conversational Process*

```
var buffer, previous buffer: B; result: (message, answer);

repeat
  buffer:= 0;
  repeat
    previous buffer:= buffer;
    wait event(previous buffer, buffer, result);
  until result = message & resources available(buffer)
      or result = answer;
  get event(buffer);
  if result = message then
  begin
    reserve resources;
    start action;
    send message to some other process;
    save state of action;
  end else
  begin "result = answer"
    restore state of action;
    complete  action;
    release resources;
    send answer to original sender;
  end
forever
```

whether it has the necessary resources to perform the requested action; if not, it leaves the message in the queue and examines the next event. However, if the process does possess the necessary resources, it accepts the message, reserves the resources, and starts the requested action. As soon as this involves the sending of a message to some other process, the conversational process saves data about the state of the incomplete action and proceeds to examine its queue from the start to engage itself in another action.

Whenever the process finds an answer in its queue, it immediately accepts it and completes the corresponding action. It can now release the resources used and send an answer to the original sender that made the request. After this, it examines the entire queue again to see whether the release of resources has made it possible to accept pending messages.

An example of a process operating in accordance with this scheme is the *basic operating system S*, which creates internal processes on request from typewriter terminals. *S* can be engaged in conversations with several terminals at the same time. It will only postpone an operator request if its store area is occupied by other requests in progress or if it is already in the middle of an action requested from the same terminal.

## 8.4. EXTERNAL PROCESSES

This section clarifies the meaning of the external process concept. It explains the initiation of input/output by means of messages from internal processes, dynamic creation, and removal of external processes, as well as exclusive access to documents by means of reservation and releasing.

### 8.4.1. Input/Output

Consider the situation shown in Fig. 8.5, in which an internal process *P* inputs a data block from an external process *Q* (say, a magnetic tape).

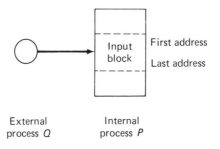

Fig. 8.5. Input from an external process *Q* to an internal process *P*.

*P* starts input by sending a message to *Q*:

*send message*(*Q, message, buffer*)

The message defines an input/output operation and the first and last addresses of a store area within process *P*:

*message*: *operation*
        *first store address*
        *last store address*

The monitor copies the message into a buffer and delivers it in the queue of process *Q*. Following this, the monitor uses the *kind* parameter in the process description of process *Q* to switch to a piece of code common to all magnetic tapes. If the tape station is busy, the message is merely left in its queue; otherwise, input is started to the given store area. On return, program execution continues in process *P*.

When the tape station completes the input by means of an interrupt, the monitor generates an answer and delivers it in the queue of process *P* which in turn receives it by calling

*wait answer*(*result, answer, buffer*)

The answer contains status bits sensed from the device and the actual length of the block input:

*answer*: *status bits*
        *block length*

After delivery of the answer, the monitor examines the queue of the external process *Q* and starts its next operation (unless the queue is empty).

Essentially all external processes follow this scheme, which can be defined by the following algorithm:

```
"external process"
repeat
    wait message;
    if message acceptable then
    begin
        start input output;
        await interrupt;
    end
    produce answer;
    send answer;
forever
```

With low-speed, character-oriented devices, the monitor repeats the input/output for each character until a complete block has been transferred. (While this is taking place, the time between interrupts is, of course, shared among internal processes.) Internal processes can therefore regard all input/output as block-oriented.

## 8.4.2. Mutual Exclusion

The use of message buffering provides a direct way of sharing an external process among a number of internal processes: An external process can simply accept messages from any internal process and serve them in their order of arrival. An example of this is the use of a single typewriter for the output of messages to a main operator.

This method of sharing a device ensures that a block of data is input or output as an indivisible entity. But when sequential media, such as paper tape, punched cards, or magnetic tape, are used, an internal process must have exclusive access to the entire document. This is obtained by calling the following monitor procedure:

$$reserve\ process(name, result)$$

The *result* indicates whether or not the reservation has been accepted.

An external process that handles sequential documents rejects messages from all internal processes except the one that has reserved it. Rejection is indicated by the result of *wait answer*.

During the removal of an internal process, the monitor removes all reservations the process has made. Internal processes can, however, also do this explicitly by means of the monitor procedure:

$$release\ process(name)$$

## 8.4.3. Process Identification

From the operator's point of view, an external process is created when he mounts a document on a device and names it. The name must, however, be communicated to the monitor by means of an operating system—an internal process that controls the scheduling of other internal processes. So it is more correct to say that external processes are created when internal processes assign names to peripheral devices. This is done by means of the monitor procedure

$$create\ peripheral\ process(name, device\ number, result)$$

The monitor has no way of ensuring whether a given document is mounted on a device. There are also some devices, such as the real-time clock, which operate without documents.

The name of an external process can be explicitly removed by a call of the monitor procedure

$$remove\ process(name, result)$$

It is possible to implement an automatic removal of a process name when the monitor detects operator intervention in a device. This is done for magnetic tapes.

### 8.4.4. Replacement of External Processes

The decision to control input/output by means of interrupt procedures within the monitor, instead of using dedicated internal processes for each peripheral device, was made to achieve immediate start of input/output after the sending of messages. In contrast, the activation of an internal process merely implies that it is linked to the ready queue; after activation, several time slices can elapse before the internal process actually starts to execute instructions.

The price paid for the present implementation of external processes is a prolongation of the time spent in the uninterruptable state within the monitor. This limits the system's ability to cope with real-time events—data that are lost unless they are input and processed within a certain time.

An important consequence of the uniform handling of internal and external processes is that it allows one to replace any external process with an internal process of the same name; other processes that communicate with it are quite unaware of this replacement.

Replacement of external processes with internal processes makes it possible to enforce more complex rules of access to documents. In the interest of security one might, for example, want to limit the access of an internal process to one of several files recorded on a particular magnetic tape. This can be ensured by an internal process that receives all messages to the tape and decides whether they should be passed on to it.

As another example, consider the problem of testing a real-time system before it is connected to an industrial plant. A convenient way of doing this is to replace analog inputs with an internal process that simulates relevant values of the actual measuring instruments.

The ability to replace any process in the system with another process is a very useful tool.

(I am still presenting the system as we looked upon it in 1969. Replacement of external processes has indeed been used since, but, as I will point out later, there are severe practical restrictions on its usefulness.)

## 8.5.  INTERNAL PROCESSES

This section explains the creation, control, and removal of internal processes. The emphasis is on the hierarchal structuring of internal processes, which makes it possible to extend the system with new operating systems. The dynamic behavior of the system is explained in terms of process states and the transitions between these.

### 8.5.1.  Scheduling Primitives

Internal processes are *created* on request from other internal processes by means of the monitor procedure:

create process(name, resources, result)

The monitor initializes the process description of the new internal process with its *name* and a set of *resources* selected by the *parent process*. A part of the resources is a store area, which must be within the parent's own area as shown in Fig. 8.6. Also specified by the parent is a protection key, which must be set in all store words of the *child process* before it is started.

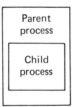

Fig. 8.6. Store allocation to a child process within its parent process.

After creation, the child process is simply a named store area described within the monitor. It has not yet been linked to the ready queue.

The parent process can now *load* a program into the child process by means of an input/output operation. Following this, the parent can *initialize* the *registers* of its child using the monitor procedure:

modify process(name, registers, result)

The register values are stored in the process description until the child process is being started. As a standard convention adopted by parent processes (but not enforced by the monitor), the initial register values inform the child process about its own process description, its parent, and the typewriter terminal it can use for operator communication.

Finally, the parent can *start* the execution of its child by calling:

*start process(name, result)*

which sets the protection keys within the child and links it to the ready queue. The child now shares time slices with other active processes, including its parent.

On request from a parent process, the monitor waits for the completion of all input/output initiated by the child and *stops* it by removing it from the ready or running state:

*stop process(name, buffer, result)*

The purpose of the message buffer will be made clear in Section 8.10.3.

In the stopped state, a child process can either be started again or completely *removed* by the parent process:

*remove process(name, result)*

During the removal, the monitor generates dummy answers to all messages sent to the child and releases all external processes used by it. Finally, the protection keys are reset to the value used within the parent process. The parent can now use the store area to create other child processes.

Figure 8.7 shows the process states and the operations that cause the transitions between them.

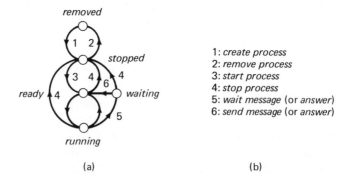

1: *create process*
2: *remove process*
3: *start process*
4: *stop process*
5: *wait message* (or *answer*)
6: *send message* (or *answer*)

(a)                                          (b)

**Fig. 8.7. (a) The states of an internal process; and (b) the primitives that cause the transitions between them.**

According to our philosophy, processes should have complete freedom to choose their own medium-term strategy of child scheduling. The monitor only supplies the essential primitives for the initiation and control of processes. Consequently, the concepts, program loading and swapping, are not part of the nucleus.

However, multiplexing of a common store area among child processes by swapping is possible because the monitor does not check whether internal processes overlap one another as long as they remain within the store areas of their parents. Swapping from a process $A$ to another process $B$ can be implemented in a parent process as follows:

$$stop(A);$$
$$output(A);$$
$$input(B);$$
$$start(B);$$

### 8.5.2. Process Hierarchy

The purpose of the *monitor* is to simulate an environment in which program execution and input/output are handled uniformly as cooperating, concurrent processes. A set of monitor procedures allows dynamic creation and control of processes as well as communication between them.

For a given installation we still need, as part of the system, programs that control medium-term strategies for operator communication, process scheduling, and resource allocation. But it is essential for the orderly growth of the system that these *operating systems* be implemented as other programs. Since the main difference between operating systems and user computations is one of jurisdiction, this problem is solved by arranging the internal processes in a *hierarchy* in which parent processes have complete control over child processes.

This is illustrated in Fig. 8.8. After system initialization, the internal store contains the monitor and an internal process $S$, which is the *basic operating system*. $S$ can create concurrent processes $A, B, C, \ldots$ on request

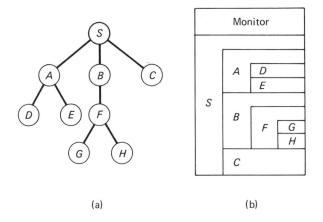

(a)                                                          (b)

Fig. 8.8.  (a) A family tree of internal processes; and (b) the corresponding store allocation.

from terminals. These processes can in turn create other processes $D$, $E$, $F$, . . . . Thus, while $S$ acts as a primitive operating system for $A$, $B$, and $C$, they in turn act as operating systems for their children, $D$, $E$, and $F$.

This *family tree* of processes can be extended to any level, subject only to a limitation of the total number of processes. The maximum number of internal processes is 23, including the basic operating system $S$. The store protection system of the *RC 4000* computer provides mutual protection of 8 independent processes. When this number is exceeded, one must rely on some of the processes being error-free or use swapping to prevent them from being active at the same time.

In this multiprogramming system, all procedures executed in the privileged processor state are implemented within the monitor. The latter embodies a fixed, short-term policy of processor multiplexing. Medium-term scheduling policies can be introduced at higher levels at which each process can control the scheduling and resource allocation of its own children.

The only protection rules enforced by the monitor are the following: A process can only allocate a subset of its own resources (including storage) to its children; and a process can only *modify*, *start*, *stop*, and *remove* its own children.

The structure of the family tree is defined in the process descriptions within the monitor. I emphasize that the only function of the tree is to define the basic rules of process control and resource allocation. Time slices are shared evenly among active processes regardless of their position in the hierarchy, and each process can communicate with all other processes.

For the development of operating systems, the most important properties of the system are the following:

(1) *New operating systems can be implemented as other programs* without modification of the monitor. The Algol and Fortran languages for the *RC 4000* computer contain facilities for calling the monitor and starting concurrent processes. So it is possible to write operating systems in high-level languages.

(2) *Operating systems can be replaced dynamically*, thus enabling an installation to switch among various modes of operation; several operating systems can actually be active simultaneously.

(3) *Standard programs and user programs can be executed under different operating systems* without modification, provided communication between parents and children is standardized.

## 8.6. RESOURCE PROTECTION

This section describes a set of monitor rules that enable a parent process to control the allocation of resources to its children.

In the system, internal processes compete for the following resources:

> processor time
> internal storage and protection keys
> message buffers and process descriptions
> peripheral devices
> backing storage

Initially, the basic operating system $S$ owns all resources. As a basic principle enforced by the monitor, a process can allocate only a subset of its own resources to a child process. These are returned to the parent process when the child is being removed.

## 8.6.1. Processor Allocation

All active processes are allocated *time slices* in a cyclical manner. Depending on the interrupt frequency of the hardware interval timer, the length of a time slice can vary between 1.6 and 1638.4 msec. A reasonable value is 25.6 msec. With shorter intervals, the fraction of processor time consumed by timer interrupts grows drastically; with longer intervals, the delay between the activation and execution of an internal process increases.

In practice, internal processes often start input/output and wait for it in the middle of a time slice. This creates a scheduling problem when internal processes are activated by answers: Should the monitor link processes to the beginning or to the end of the ready queue? Linking processes to the beginning ensures that processes can use peripherals with maximum speed, but there is a danger that a process might monopolize the processor by communicating frequently with fast devices. Linking them to the end prevents this, but introduces a delay in the ready queue which slows down peripherals.

We introduced a modified form of *round-robin* scheduling to solve this problem. As soon as a process leaves the running state, the monitor stores the actual value of the time quantum used by it. When the process is activated again, the monitor compares this quantum with the maximum time slice: As long as this limit is not exceeded, the process is linked to the beginning of the queue; otherwise, it is linked to the end of the queue, and its time quantum is reset to zero. The same test is applied when the interval timer interrupts a running process.

This short-term policy attempts to share processor time evenly among active internal processes regardless of their position in the hierarchy. It permits a process to be activated immediately until it threatens to monopolize the central processor; only then is it pushed into the background to give other processes a chance. This is admittedly a built-in strategy at the short-term level. Parent processes can only control the allocation of processor time to their children in larger portions (on the order of seconds) by means of the procedures *start process* and *stop process*.

For accounting purposes, the monitor collects the following data for each internal process: the time at which the process was created and the sum of time quanta used by it; these quantities are called the *start time* and the *run time*, respectively.

### 8.6.2. Store Allocation

An internal process can only create child processes within its own store area. The monitor does not check whether the store areas of child processes overlap one another. This freedom can be used to implement multiplexing of a common store area among several processes, as described in Section 8.5.1.

The *RC 4000* computer has a rather cumbersome store protection mechanism. Each store word contains a *protection key* of 3 bits. This makes it possible to distinguish between eight different store areas which can be protected against one another.

A *protection register* of eight bits defines the store areas accessible to the running process. In store and jump operations, the protection key of the addressed word is used as an index to select a bit within the protection register. This bit defines whether or not the store word is protected against the running process. An attempt to violate store protection will cause a call of an error procedure within the monitor.

Before the creation of an internal process, the parent must specify the values of the protection register and the protection key to be used by the child. When the child process is started, the monitor sets the corresponding key in all its store words. (This cannot be done during process creation because the store area may be multiplexed among children and their descendants using different keys.)

A parent process can only allocate a subset of its own protection keys to a child but it has complete freedom to allocate identical or different keys to its children. Store areas with these keys remain accessible to the parent after the creation of a child.

### 8.6.3. Message Buffers and Process Descriptions

The monitor has room for only a finite number of message buffers and tables describing internal processes and the so-called area processes (files on the backing store used as external processes). A message buffer is selected when a message is sent to another process; it is released when the sending process receives an answer. A process description is selected when an internal process creates another internal process or an area process and released when the process is removed.

Message buffers and process descriptions only assume an identity when they are used. As long as they are unused, they can be regarded as anonymous pools of resources. Consequently, it is sufficient to specify the maximum number of each resource that an internal process can use: The so-called *buffer claim*, *internal claim*, and *area claim* are defined by the parent when a child process is created. The claims must be a subset of the parent's own claims, which are diminished accordingly; they are returned to the parent when the child is being removed.

The buffer claim defines the maximum number of messages that an internal process can exchange simultaneously with other internal and external processes. The internal claim limits the number of children an internal process can have at one time. The area claim defines the number of backing store areas that an internal process can access simultaneously.

The monitor decreases a claim by one each time a process uses one of its resources, and increases it by one when the resource is released again. So at any moment, the claims define the number of resources that are still unused by the process.

### 8.6.4. Peripheral Devices

A distinction has been made between peripheral devices and external processes. An external process is created when a name is assigned to a device. So it is also true that peripheral devices only assume an identity when they are actually used for input/output. Indeed, the whole idea of naming is to give the operator complete freedom in allocating devices. It would therefore seem natural to control allocation of peripheral devices to internal processes by a complete set of claims—one for each kind of device.

In an installation with remote peripherals however, it is unrealistic to treat all devices of a given kind as a single, anonymous pool. An operating system must be able to force its jobs and operators to remain within a certain geographical *configuration* of devices. The concept configuration must be defined in terms of physical devices, and not in terms of external processes since a parent normally does not know in advance which documents its children are going to use.

Configuration control is exercised as follows: From the point of view of other processes, an internal process is identified by a name. Within the monitor however, an internal process is also identified by a single bit in a machine word. A process description of a peripheral device includes a word in which each bit indicates whether the corresponding internal process is a *potential user* of the device. Another word indicates the *current user* that has reserved the device to obtain exclusive access to a document.

The basic operating system $S$ is a potential user of all peripherals. A parent process can *include* or *exclude* a child as a user of any device, provided the parent is also a user of it:

*include user(child, device number, result)*
*exclude user(child, device number, result)*

During removal of a child, the monitor excludes it as a user of all devices.

All in all, three conditions must be satisfied before an internal process can start input/output:

(1)  The device must be an external process with a unique name.

(2)  The internal process must be a user of the device.

(3)  If the external process controls a sequential document, the internal process must have reserved it.

### 8.6.5.  Privileged Operations

Files on the backing store are described in a catalog, which is also kept on the backing store. Clearly, there is a need to be able to prevent an internal process from reserving an excessive amount of space in the catalog or on the backing store as such. It seems difficult, however, to specify a reasonable rule in the form of a claim that is defined when a child process is created. The main difficulty is that catalog entries and data areas can survive the removal of the process that created them; so backing storage is a resource a parent process can lose permanently by allocating it to its children.

As a half-hearted solution, we introduced the concept *privileged monitor procedures*. A parent process must supply each of its children with a *procedure mask*, in which each bit specifies whether the child is allowed to call a certain monitor procedure. The mask must be a subset of the parent's own mask.

The privileged operations include all monitor procedures that

(1)  change the catalog on the backing store;

(2)  create and remove the names of peripheral devices; and

(3)  change the real-time clock.

## 8.7.  MONITOR FEATURES

This section is a survey of specific monitor features such as real-time synchronization, conversational access, and backing store files. Although these are not essential primitive concepts, they are indispensable features of practical multiprogramming systems.

## 8.7.1.  Real-time Synchronization

Real time is measured by an *interval timer* which interrupts the central processor regularly (normally, every 25 msec). The interval timer is used to control processor multiplexing and to implement an external process that permits the synchronization of internal processes with real time. All internal processes can send messages to this *clock process*. At the end of the time interval specified in the message, the clock process returns an answer to the sender. To avoid a heavy overhead of clock administration, the clock process only examines its queue every second.

## 8.7.2.  Conversational Access

A multiprogramming system encourages a conversational mode of access in which users interact directly with internal processes from typewriter terminals. The external processes for terminals are designed to make this possible.

Initially, all program execution is ordered by operators communicating with the basic operating system. It would be very wasteful if the operating system had to examine all terminals regularly for possible operator requests. Therefore, our first requirement is that terminals be able to activate internal processes by sending messages to them (other external processes are only able to receive messages).

It must of course also be possible for an internal process to open a conversation with a terminal.

And, finally, a terminal should be able to accept messages simultaneously from several internal processes. This will enable an operator to control more than one internal process from the same terminal. This is valuable in a small installation.

In short, terminals should be independent processes that can open conversations with any internal process, and vice versa. A terminal should assist the operator with the identification of the internal processes using it.

An operator opens a conversation by depressing an interrupt key on the terminal. This causes the monitor to assign a line buffer to the terminal. The operator must then identify the internal process to which his message is addressed. Following this, he can input a message of one line, which is delivered in the queue of the receiving process.

A message to the basic operating system $S$ can, for example, be typed as follows:

> **to** $S$
> *new pbh run*

(The word in bold face type is output by the terminal process in response to the key interrupt.)

An internal process opens a conversation with a terminal by sending a message to it. Before the input/output is started, the terminal identifies the internal process to the operator. This identification is suppressed after the first of a series of messages from the same process.

In the following example, two internal processes, *A* and *B*, share the same terminal for input/output. Process identifications are in bold face type:

> **to A**
> *first input line to A*
> *second input line to A*
> **from B**
> **first output line from B**
> **second output line from B**
> **from A**
> **first output line from A**
>
> . . . . .

These processes are unaware of their sharing the same terminal. From the point of view of internal processes, the identification of user processes makes it irrelevant whether the installation contains one or more terminals. (Of course, one cannot expect operators to feel the same way about it.)

### 8.7.3. File System

The monitor supports a semi-permanent storage of files on a backing store consisting of one or more drums and disks. The monitor makes these devices appear to be a single backing store with blocks of 256 words each. This *virtual backing store* is organized as a collection of named *data areas*. Each area occupies a number of consecutive blocks on a single backing store device. A fixed part of the backing store is reserved for a *catalog* describing the names and locations of data areas.

Data areas are treated as external processes by internal processes. Input/output is started by messages sent to the areas specifying the desired operations, internal store areas, and relative block numbers within the data areas. The identification of a data area requires a catalog search. To reduce the number of searches, input/output must be preceded by an explicit creation of an *area process* description within the monitor.

*Catalog Entries*

The catalog is a fixed area on the backing store divided into a number of *entries* identified by unique *names*. Each entry is of fixed length and consists of a *head*, which identifies the entry, and a *tail*, which contains the rest of the data. The monitor distinguishes between entries describing data areas on the backing store and entries describing other things.

An entry is *created* by calling the monitor procedure:

$$create\ entry(name, tail, result)$$

The first word of the *tail* defines the *size* of an area to be reserved and described in the entry; if the size is negative or zero, no area is reserved. The rest of the tail contains nine *optional parameters*, which can be selected freely by the internal process.

Internal processes can *look up*, *change*, *rename*, or *remove* existing entries by means of the procedures:

> *look up entry(name, tail, result)*
> *change entry(name, tail, result)*
> *rename entry(name, new name, result)*
> *remove entry(name, result)*

The catalog describes itself as an area in an entry named *catalog*.

The search for catalog entries is minimized by using a hashed value of names to define the first block to be examined. Each block contains 15 entries so most catalog searches only require the input of a single block unless the catalog has been filled to the brim.

The allocation of data areas is speeded up by keeping a bit table of available blocks within the monitor. In practice, the creation or modification of an entry therefore only requires input and output of a single catalog block.

## Catalog Protection

Since many users share the backing store as a common data base, it is vital that they have means of protecting their files against unintentional modification or complete removal. The protection system used is similar to the store protection system.

The head of each catalog entry is supplied with a *catalog key*. The rules of access within an internal process are defined by a *catalog mask* set by its parent process. Each bit in this mask corresponds to one of 24 possible catalog keys: If a bit is one, the internal process can modify or remove entries (and the associated areas) with the corresponding key; otherwise, the process can only look up these entries. A parent can only assign a subset of its own catalog keys to a child process. Initially, the basic operating system owns all keys.

To prevent the catalog and the rest of the backing store from being filled with irrelevant data, the concept *temporary entry* is introduced. This is an entry that can be removed by another internal process as soon as the internal process that created the entry has been removed. Typical examples are working areas used during program translation and data areas created, but not removed, by erroneous programs.

This concept is implemented as follows: During the creation of an internal process, the monitor increases a *creation number* by one and stores it within the new process description. Each time an internal process creates a catalog entry, the monitor includes its creation number in the entry head indicating that it is temporary. Internal processes can at any time scan the catalog and remove all temporary entries, provided the corresponding creators no longer exist within the monitor.

So, in accordance with the basic philosophy, the monitor only provides the necessary mechanism for the handling of temporary entries and leaves the actual strategy of removal to the hierarchy of processes.

To ensure the survival of a catalog entry, an internal process must call the privileged monitor procedure:

$$permanent\ entry(name, catalog\ key, result)$$

to replace the creation number with a *catalog key*. A process can, of course, only set one of its own keys in the catalog; otherwise, it might fill the catalog with highly protected entries that could be difficult to detect and remove.

### Area Processes

Before it is used for input/output, a data area must be looked up in the catalog and described as an external process within the monitor by a call of the procedure:

$$create\ area\ process(name, result)$$

The area process is created with the same *name* as the catalog entry.

Following this, internal processes can send messages with the following format to the area process:

$$message:\ input\ output\ operation$$
$$first\ store\ address$$
$$last\ store\ address$$
$$first\ block\ number$$

The tables used to describe area processes within the monitor are a limited resource controlled by *area claims* defined by parent processes (see Section 8.6.3).

The backing store is a direct access medium serving as a common data base. To utilize this property fully, internal processes should be able to input simultaneously from the same area (for example, when several copies of an Algol compiler are executed simultaneously). On the other hand, the access to an area must be exclusive during output when its content is undefined from the point of view of other processes.

Consequently, we distinguish between internal processes that are *potential users* of an area process and the single process that may have *reserved* the area for exclusive use. This distinction was also made for peripheral devices (Section 8.6.4), but the rules of access are different here. An internal process is a user of an area process after its creation. This enables the internal process to perform input from the area as long as no other process reserves it. An internal process can reserve an area process if its catalog mask permits modification of the corresponding catalog entry. After reservation, the internal process can perform both input and output.

Finally, it should be mentioned that the catalog is permanently described as an area process within the monitor. This enables internal processes to input and scan the catalog sequentially; for example, during the removal of temporary entries. Only the monitor and the basic operating system can, however, perform output to the catalog. And the basic operating system only does this during system initialization.

## 8.8. BASIC OPERATING SYSTEM

This section illustrates by means of examples the functions of the basic operating system that can create and control the execution of concurrent processes on request from typewriter terminals.

### 8.8.1. Process Control

After system initialization, the internal store contains the monitor and the basic operating system $S$. $S$ enables independent operators to create and control internal processes from typewriter terminals. In addition to this, $S$ can name peripheral devices and keep track of the date and time.

$S$ is the "pater familias" of the family tree of internal processes. Initially, it owns all system resources such as storage, protection keys, peripherals, message buffers, and process description tables. Apart from being a permanent process in the system, $S$ has no special status; it is treated by the monitor like any other internal process. In particular, $S$ does not execute privileged machine instructions or modify process descriptions within the monitor. So it is possible to replace $S$ with another basic operating system during system initialization.

In the following, the creation and control of internal processes from terminals is explained. An operator sends a message to the operating system

*S* by depressing the interrupt key on a terminal and typing the name *S* followed by a command line.

A message, such as the following:

to S
new pbh run

causes *S* to create an internal process with the name *pbh*, load a standard program into it from the backing store, and start its execution. Following this, *S* outputs the response:

ready

In this case, the process was created with a standard set of resources, which enables it to execute systems programs such as the editor, assembler, or Algol compiler. The program loaded into the process was one which will input and interpret further job control statements (the meaning of these is irrelevant to the basic operating system).

The operator can also explicitly specify the resources he wants; for example, the *size* of the store area, the number of *message buffers*, and the *program* to be loaded:

to S
new pbh size 16000 buf 18 prog 0S4000 run

Resources not mentioned (such as the number of area processes) are still given standard values.

Normally, *S* chooses the actual location of storage and the values of protection keys. The operator can, however, specify these absolutely:

to S
new pbh addr 13500 pr 2, 3, 4 pk 2 run

This will assign the *base address* 13500 to the process, set the bits 2, 3, and 4 in its *protection register* to 1, and set the *protection key* to 2 within its store area. But *S* will check that this does not conflict with store and protection keys assigned by it to other processes.

After creation and start, a user process can communicate with the terminal according to its own rules:

from pbh
. . . . .

When the operator wants to stop program execution temporarily within his process, he types:

> to $S$
> *stop*

He can start it again at any time by the command:

> to $S$
> *start*

If the user process sends a message to operating system $S$, the process is stopped by $S$, and the following message is output:

> **from S**
> **pause pbh**

At this point, the operator has the choice of starting the process again or removing it completely from the system:

> to $S$
> *remove*

It is possible to create and control more than one process from the same terminal, for example:

> to $S$
> *new jj run new pbh run*

But in this case the operator must preface subsequent commands with the name of the process he is referring to:

> to $S$
> *proc jj stop*

Actually, the operating system remembers the name of the last process referred to from a terminal. It is therefore only necessary to mention the process name explicitly each time the operator refers to a new process.

After its creation, an internal process is included as a user of a standard configuration defined within $S$; but the operator can also explicitly *include* or *exclude* his process as a user of other devices as well:

> to $S$
> *include* 7, 9, 13 *exclude* 5, 4

where the integers denote device numbers.

After mounting documents, the operator can assign names to peripherals, for example:

**to** *S*
*call 5 = printer, 8 = magtape*

The operating system prints an error message when it is unable to honor a request, for example:

**to** *S*
*new pbh size* 20000 *run*
**no core**

In this situation, the operator can ask *S* to list the *maximum* number of each resource available at present:

**to** *S*
*max*
**max** 18000   18   14   2   6

In this example, the largest available store area has a length of 18,000 locations; whereas the number of message buffers, area process descriptions, internal process descriptions, and protection keys available are 18, 14, 2, and 6, respectively.

Finally, the operating system can output a list of all internal processes created by it. They will be listed in the order in which their store areas follow one another from low toward high addresses. Each process is described by its name, first store address, size of store area, and the protection key set within the area:

**to** *S*
*list*
**jj   12216   10000   3**
**pbh   22216   6000   1**

Commands from a terminal are obeyed in their order of arrival. The monitor permits simultaneous input of messages from all terminals. The basic operating system can, however, only respond simultaneously to a limited number of messages. For each simultaneous conversation, *S* uses a working area to process a command line. When *S* must wait for console output, the current value of its registers and the address of the message buffer involved are stored in a working area before *S* inspects its event queue for other messages or answers. An answer to *S* causes a retrieval of the corresponding working area and a continuation of the interrupted action.

A message to *S* is only processed when a working area is available and all previous messages from the same console have been served (see Algorithm 8.1).

The main function of the basic operating system is to receive requests from typewriter terminals, call the corresponding monitor procedures

> *create process*
> *start process*
> *stop process*
> *remove process*

and transfer programs from the backing store to the internal store.

The operating system obeys these requests unconditionally as long as resources are available. Thus, it is not a realistic operating system, but only a means of activating other operating systems after system initialization.

### 8.8.2.　System Initialization

The system is delivered as a binary paper tape that can be input to the internal store by placing it in a paper tape reader and depressing an *autoload* key on the computer. After loading, the monitor initializes process descriptions of all peripheral devices, links all message buffers to the common pool, assigns all resources to the basic operating system, and starts it.

First, the basic operating system executes a program which can initialize the backing store with catalog entries and binary programs input from paper tape or magnetic tape.

These input tapes consist of *commands* and *programs* with a format such as the following:

> **newcatalog**
> **create** *editor*, 10
> **load** *editor*
> <editor program>
>
> . . . . .
> **end**

The command *newcatalog* causes the creation of an empty catalog on the backing store. This is done by sending output messages to a standard area process called *catalog* defined within the monitor. Only the basic operating system is permitted to use this area process and will only do so during system initialization.

The command *create* makes the basic operating system call the monitor, create a catalog entry named *editor*, and associate a backing store area of 10 blocks with it.

The command *load* is obeyed as follows: First, the basic operating system calls the monitor to create an area process from the catalog entry named *editor*; then, the basic operating system inputs the editor program from the input tape and outputs it to the backing store area; and, finally, the basic operating system calls the monitor to remove the area process again.

Other commands reflect the remaining monitor procedures for files. In this way, the file system can be initialized with a sequence of standard programs. The *end* command terminates the initialization of the catalog. The basic operating system is now ready to receive operator requests from terminals.

If one wishes to load the monitor and the basic operating system without changing an existing catalog, the initializing tape need only contain the commands:

> **oldcatalog**
> **end**

## 8.9. SIZE AND PERFORMANCE

The *RC 4000* is a 24-bit binary computer with typical instruction execution times of 4 $\mu$sec. It permits a practically unlimited expansion of the internal store and a standardized connection of all kinds of peripherals. Multiprogramming is facilitated by program interruption, store protection, and privileged instructions.

The implementation of the system described here makes multiprogramming feasible with a minimum store of 32 K words, backed by a fast drum or disk. The monitor includes external processes for a real-time clock, typewriters, paper tape readers and punches, line printers, magnetic tapes, and files on the backing store. The size of the monitor and the basic operating system is as follows:

|  | words |
| --- | --- |
| primitives | 2400 |
| code for external processes | 1150 |
| process descriptions and buffers | 1250 |
| monitor | 4800 |
| basic operating system | 1400 |
|  | 6200 |

The communication primitives are executed in the uninterruptable state within the system nucleus. The execution time of these sets a limit on the system's response to real-time events:

|  | msec |
| --- | --- |
| *send message* | 0.6 |
| *wait message* | 0.4 |
| *send answer* | 0.6 |
| *wait answer* | 0.4 |

An analysis shows that the 2 msec required by a complete conversation (the sum of the four primitives) are used as follows:

|                         | per cent |
|-------------------------|----------|
| validity checking       | 25       |
| process synchronization | 45       |
| message buffering       | 30       |

The primitives for the creation, start, stop, and removal of processes are implemented in an anonymous internal process within the system nucleus to avoid intolerably long periods in the uninterruptable state. Typical execution times for these are:

|                  | msec |
|------------------|------|
| *create process* | 3    |
| *start process*  | 26   |
| *stop process*   | 4    |
| *remove process* | 30   |

The excessive times for the start and removal of an internal process are due to the peculiar store protection system of the *RC 4000* computer, which requires the setting of a protection key in every store word of a process. If the machine had been equipped with base and limit registers, *start process* and *remove process* would only have taken 2 and 6 msec, respectively.

There were never more than three people involved in the design simultaneously. The total effort of structural design, programming, testing, and documentation was about 4 man-years.

## 8.10.  IMPLEMENTATION DETAILS

The following is an algorithmic definition of a *simplified version* of the monitor procedures for process communication and scheduling. It omits the following details:

> process names
> external processes
> dummy answers
> error reactions
> event primitives
> processor multiplexing
> resource protection (except for message buffers)

I have also simplified the removal of a process as follows: All message buffers sent by a process are immediately returned to the pool upon removal of the process.

The simplified algorithms have not been tested and may contain minor errors. Their main purpose is to illustrate implementation techniques.

### 8.10.1. Process Communication

Algorithm 8.2 shows the *data structure* used within the monitor. *Internal processes* and *message buffers* are represented by two arrays; the *buffer pool*, by a sequence of buffer indices.

ALGORITHM 8.2   *The Monitor Data Structure*

```
type P = 1..max number of processes;
     B = 1..max number of buffers;
     C = array 1..8 of integer;

var v: shared
       record
         process: array P of
                   record
                     state: (removed, started, . . . );
                     claim: 0..max number of buffers;
                     queue: sequence of B;
                     arrival: event v;
                   end
         buffer: array B of
                   record
                     state: (empty, sent, received, returned);
                     content: C;
                     to, from: 0..max number of processes;
                   end
            pool: sequence of B;
         end

  function running: P;
  begin . . . end
```

Each *process description* defines a *state*, a *buffer claim*, a *message queue*, and an event variable on which the given process can await the *arrival* of the next message or answer.

Each *message buffer* contains a *state*, a *content* (message or answer), and an identification of the processes *to* and *from* which the content is sent.

Initially, all process descriptions (except the one representing the basic operating system) are set in the *removed* state with zero claims and empty queues; and all buffers are entered in the pool in the *empty* state with *to* and *from* equal to zero.

A standard function, *running*, identifies the internal process that calls the monitor.

Algorithm 8.3 defines the monitor procedure *send message*. If the receiving process exists and the calling process can claim another message buffer, one is selected from the pool and initialized with the indices of sender and receiver, as well as with the message itself, and the state is set to *sent*. Finally, the index of the buffer is entered in the queue of the receiver and an arrival event is caused (unless the receiver is stopped).

**ALGORITHM 8.3**   *The Monitor Procedure Send Message*

```
procedure send message
(receiver: P; message: C; var index: B);

region v do
begin
  with process(running) do
  if process(receiver).state ≠ removed & claim > 0 then
  begin
    claim:= claim - 1;
    get(index, pool);
    with buffer(index) do
    begin
      state:= sent;
      content:= message;
      to:= receiver;
      from:= running;
    end
    with process(receiver) do
    begin
      put(index, queue);
      if state = started then cause(arrival);
    end
  end
end
```

Algorithm 8.4 defines the monitor procedure *wait message*. As long as the queue of the calling process is empty, it waits for an arrival. Following this, a message buffer is removed from the queue and set in the state *received* after making its content available to the calling process.

*ALGORITHM 8.4   The Monitor Procedure Wait Message*

```
procedure wait message
(var sender: P; message: C; index: B);

region v do
begin
  with process(running) do
  begin
    while empty(queue) do await(arrival);
    get(index, queue);
  end
  with buffer(index) do
  begin
    state:= received;
    message:= content;
    sender:= from;
  end
end
```

Algorithm 8.5 defines the monitor procedure *send answer*. It checks whether the calling process has received a message in the given buffer; if it has, the answer is placed in the buffer and its state is set to *returned*. Finally, an arrival is caused for its original sender (unless it is stopped).

Algorithm 8.6 defines the monitor procedure *wait answer*. It checks whether the calling process has sent a message in the given buffer. As long

*ALGORITHM 8.5   The Monitor Procedure Send Answer*

```
procedure send answer
(answer: C; index: B);

region v do
begin
  with buffer(index) do
  if state = received & to = running then
  begin
    state:= returned;
    content:= answer;
    to:= 0;
    with process(from) do
    if state = started then cause(arrival);
  end
end
```

as no answer has been returned in the buffer, the calling process waits for an arrival. Following this, the buffer claim of the calling process is increased by one, and the buffer is returned to the pool in the *empty* state after having made its content available to the calling process.

*ALGORITHM 8.6　The Monitor Procedure Wait Answer*

> **procedure** *wait answer*
> (**var** *answer*: *C*; **const** *index*: *B*);
>
> **region** *v* **do**
> **begin**
> 　**with** *buffer*(*index*) **do**
> 　**if** *from* = *running* **then**
> 　**begin**
> 　　**while** *state* ≠ *returned* **do**
> 　　*await*(*process*(*running*). *arrival*);
> 　　*state*:= *empty*;
> 　　*answer*:= *content*;
> 　　*from*:= 0;
> 　　*put*(*index*, *pool*);
> 　　**with** *process*(*running*) **do**
> 　　*claim*:= *claim* + 1;
> 　**end**
> **end**

### 8.10.2.　Process Scheduling

More complex are the algorithms which *stop* and *start* processes. To explain this I refer once more to the family tree shown in Fig. 8.8.

Suppose process *B* wants to stop its child *F*. The purpose of doing this is to ensure that all program execution within the store area of process *F* is stopped. Since a part of this area has been assigned to children of *F*, it is necessary to stop not only the *child F*, but also all *descendants* of *F*. However, it is possible that some of these descendants have already been stopped by their own parents. In the present example, process *G* may still be active, while process *H* may have been stopped by its parent *F*. Consequently, the monitor should only stop processes *F* and *G*.

Consider now the reverse situation in which process *B* starts its child *F* again. The purpose is to establish the situation exactly as it was before process *F* was stopped. So the monitor must be very careful to start only those descendants of *F* that were stopped along with it. In our example, the monitor must start processes *F* and *G*, but not *H*; otherwise, we will confuse *F*, which still relies on its child *H* being stopped.

To do this correctly, the monitor must distinguish between processes that are stopped by their *parents* and those stopped by their *ancestors*. The corresponding process states are called *stopped directly* and *stopped indirectly*, respectively.

To identify the descendants which should be stopped or started along with a given child, the monitor must scan the process tree in hierarchal order from the root toward the leaves.

When a process is being *created*, a search is made for the first available entry in the table of process descriptions. This entry again becomes available when the process has been *removed*. The order in which processes are created and removed is unpredictable; so the order in which processes are arranged in this table does not reflect the structure of the process tree.

We therefore introduce another table which contains the indices of existing processes in *hierarchal* order. In this table, the index of a parent process always precedes the indices of its child processes. When a child process is created, its index is placed at the end of this table. When a child process and its descendants have been removed, their indices are removed from this table by compacting the remaining indices.

In the previous example (Fig. 8.8), the processes could have been arranged in the two tables in the order shown in Fig. 8.9.

Process
descriptions

| S |
|---|
| F |
| A |
| C |
| G |
| D |
| B |
| H |
| E |

Process
hierarchy

| B |
|---|
| A |
| E |
| F |
| G |
| C |
| D |
| H |

Fig. 8.9. An example of the ordering of processes within the table of process descriptions and the table defining the process hierarchy corresponding to Fig. 8.8.

Algorithm 8.7 defines the *data structures* needed to control process communication and scheduling. Each *process description* has been extended with the identity of the *parent process* and a boolean indicating whether the given process is a *candidate* for starting, stopping, or removal. (Initially, this boolean is *false*.)

The basic operating system $S$ is assumed to have process index 1. Since $S$ is never a candidate for starting, stopping, or removal, it is excluded from the hierarchy table.

*ALGORITHM 8.7   The Extended Monitor Data Structure*

```
type P = 1. .max number of processes;
     H = 2. .max number of processes;
     B = 1. .max number of buffers;
     C = array 1. .8 of integer;

var v: shared
     record
        process: array P of
                 record
                    state: (removed, started,
                       stopped directly, stopped indirectly);
                    parent: 0. .max number of processes;
                    candidate: boolean;
                    claim: 0. .max number of buffers;
                    queue: sequence of B;
                    arrival: event v;
                 end
        hierarchy: array H of P;
        buffer: array B of
                 record
                    state: (empty, sent, received, returned);
                    content: C;
                    to, from: 0. .max number of processes;
                 end
        pool: sequence of B;
     end

     function running: P;
     begin . . . end
```

Algorithm 8.8 defines the monitor procedure *create process*. It checks whether the calling process has the resources it wants to assign to its child (including a process description). To omit trivial details, the only resource mentioned explicitly here is the buffer claim. Following this, an empty process description is assigned to the child, and initialized with the parent index and the resources mentioned while the state is set to *stopped directly*. Finally, the hierarchy table is extended with the child index. (This trivial operation is considered a primitive here.)

Algorithm 8.9 defines the monitor procedure *start process*. It checks whether the calling process is the parent of the given child and whether the child is in the state *stopped directly*; if it is, all existing processes are scanned in hierarchal order to identify the candidates for starting: They are the child process itself and all processes in the state *stopped indirectly*

*ALGORITHM 8.8   The Monitor Procedure Create Process*

```
procedure create process
(var child: P; const resources: B);

region v do
begin
  with process(running) do
  if claim ⩾ resources then
  label done
  begin
    claim := claim − resources;
    for every child do
    with process(child) do
    if state = removed then
    begin
      state := stopped directly;
      parent := running;
      claim := resources;
      extend hierarchy(child);
      exit done;
    end
  end
end
```

*ALGORITHM 8.9   The Monitor Procedure Start Process*

```
procedure start process
(child: P);

var h: H; p: P;

region v do
begin
  with process(child) do
  if parent = running & state = stopped directly then
  for every h do
  begin
    p := hierarchy(h);
    with process(p) do
    if p = child
    or  state = stopped indirectly &
        process(parent). candidate then
    begin
      state := started;
      candidate := true;
```

```
        resume(p, arrival);
      end
      else candidate := false;
    end
  end
```

whose parents are themselves candidates. When a candidate has been recognized, it is resumed in the state *started*. Since we have already discussed details of processor multiplexing in Chapter 4, the operation *resume* is considered a primitive here. If the process is waiting for an arrival, *resume* will cause one; otherwise, it will return the process to the ready queue.

Algorithm 8.10 defines the monitor procedure *stop process*. It checks

**ALGORITHM 8.10** *The Monitor Procedure Stop Process*

```
      procedure stop process
      (child: P);

      var h: H; p: P;

      region v do
      begin
        with process(child) do
        if parent = running & state ≠ stopped directly then
        for every h do
        begin
          p := hierarchy(h);
          with process(p) do
          if p = child then
          begin
            state := stopped directly;
            candidate := true;
            preempt(p);
          end else
          if state ≠ stopped directly &
            process(parent). candidate then
          begin
            state := stopped indirectly;
            candidate := true;
            preempt(p);
          end
          else candidate := false;
        end
      end
```

whether the calling process is the parent of the given child and whether the child has *not* already been *stopped directly*; if it is not, all existing processes are scanned in hierarchal order to identify the candidates for stopping: They are the child process itself and all processes that are *not* in the state *stopped directly* and whose parents are themselves candidates. When a candidate has been recognized, it is preempted from the ready queue (if it is in that queue). The short-term scheduling primitive *preempt* is considered a primitive here.

*ALGORITHM 8.11   The Monitor Procedure Remove Process*

```
procedure remove process
(child: P);

var h: H; p: P;
    index: B; resources: 0. .max number of buffers;

region v do
begin
  with process(child) do
  if parent = running & state = stopped directly then
  begin
    resources:= 0;
    for every h do
    begin
      p:= hierarchy(h);
      with process(p) do
      if p = child
      or process(parent). candidate then
      begin
        state:= removed;
        candidate:= true;
        scan buffers;
        resources:= resources + claim;
        parent:= 0;
        claim:= 0;
        reset(arrival);
      end
      else candidate:= false;
    end
    with process(running) do
    claim:= claim + resources;
    compact hierarchy;
  end
end
```

Algorithm 8.11 defines the monitor procedure *remove process*. It checks whether the calling process is the parent of the given child and whether the child is in the state *stopped directly*; if it is, all existing processes are scanned in hierarchal order to identify the candidates for removal: They are the child process itself and all processes whose parents are themselves candidates. When a candidate has been recognized the following is done: All message buffers are scanned as shown in Algorithm 8.12. If a buffer was sent by the candidate, it is removed from the queue of

**ALGORITHM 8.12**  *The Monitor Procedure Remove Process (cont.)*

*"scan buffers"*

```
for every index do
with buffer(index) do
if state ≠ empty then
begin
  if from = p then
  begin
    claim:= claim + 1;
    if state ≠ returned then
    with process(to) do remove(index, queue);
    state:= empty;
    from:= 0; to:= 0;
    put(index, pool);
  end else
  if to = p then
  begin
    remove buffer(index, queue);
    state:= returned;
    content:= dummy answer;
    to:= 0;
    with process(from) do
    if state = started then cause(arrival);
  end
end
```

the receiver and returned to the pool. If a buffer was sent to the candidate, it is removed from the queue of the latter and returned to the sender with a dummy answer. Following this, the process description of the candidate is made available for future creation. Finally, all resources assigned to the child and its descendants are returned to the calling process and the hierarchy table is compacted (the latter operation is considered a primitive here).

### 8.10.3. Preemption and Input/Output

So far, we have only considered internal processes. In the actual system, preemption is complicated by input/output from external processes. This is handled as follows:

When a parent wants to stop a child, the state of the child is changed to *awaiting direct stop*, and all started descendants of the child are described as *awaiting indirect stop*. At the same time, these processes are removed from the ready queue.

What remains to be done is to ensure that all input/output started by these processes is terminated. To control this, each internal process description contains an integer called the *stop count*. The stop count is initialized to zero and increased by one each time the internal process starts input/output. On arrival of an answer from an external process, the monitor decreases the stop count by one and examines the state of the internal process. If the stop count becomes zero and the process is awaiting stop (directly or indirectly), its state is changed to stopped (directly or indirectly).

The call of *stop process* is completed only when all involved processes have been stopped. This can last for some time and it may not be acceptable to the parent (being an operating system with many other duties) to be inactive for so long. For this reason, the stop operation is split in two parts. The stop procedure

$$stop\ process(name, buffer, result)$$

only initializes the stopping of a child and selects a *message buffer* for the parent. When the child and its descendants have been completely stopped, the monitor delivers an answer to the parent in this buffer. So the parent can use the procedures *wait answer* or *wait event* to wait for the completion of the stop.

In principle, an internal process cannot be stopped until all input/output requested by it has been completed. This requirement is inevitable for high-speed devices such as a drum or a magnetic tape station, which are beyond program control during input/output. But it is not strictly necessary to enforce this for low-speed devices controlled by the monitor on a character-by-character basis. In practice, the monitor handles the stop situation as follows:

Before an external process starts *high-speed input/output*, it examines the state of the sending process. If the sender is stopped (or waiting to be stopped), the input/output is not started; instead, the external process returns an answer indicating a block length of zero. The sender must then repeat the input/output after being restarted. If the sender has not been stopped, its stop count is increased and the input/output is started. Note that if the stop count were increased immediately after the sending of a message, the sending process could only be stopped after the completion of all previous operations pending in external queues. By delaying the increase of the stop count as much as possible, we ensure that high-speed peripherals at most prevent the stopping of internal processes during a single block transfer.

*Low-speed devices* never increase the stop count. During output, an external process fetches one word at a time from the sending process and outputs it character-by-character regardless of whether the sender is stopped meanwhile. Before fetching a word, the external process examines the state of the sender. If it is stopped (or waiting to be stopped), the output is terminated by an answer defining the actual number of characters output; otherwise, the output continues. During input, an external process examines the state of the sender after each character. If the sender is stopped (or waiting to be stopped), the input is terminated by an answer; otherwise, the character is stored and the input continues. Low-speed devices therefore never delay the stopping of a process.

### 8.10.4.  Interruptable Monitor Procedures

Some monitor procedures are too long to be executed entirely in the uninterruptable state; in particular, those which update the catalog on the backing store and create, start, stop, and remove processes. They are called as other monitor procedures, but behind the scenes they are executed by an anonymous internal process that only operates in the uninterruptable state for short intervals while updating monitor tables; otherwise, the anonymous process shares processor time with other internal processes.

When an internal process calls an interruptable monitor procedure, the following takes place: The state of the calling process is changed to *awaiting monitor response*. At the same time, its process description is linked to the event queue of the anonymous process. The anonymous process serves the calling processes one by one and returns them to the ready queue after completion of their calls.

So monitor calls of long duration (3 to 30 msec) are interruptable as other internal processes. From the point of view of a calling process however, these monitor procedures are still indivisible primitives since: (1) they are executed only by the anonymous process one at a time in their order of request; and (2) the calling processes are delayed until their requests are honored.

## 8.11.  A CRITICAL REVIEW

I conclude the case study of the *RC 4000* multiprogramming system with a critical review of its advantages and disadvantages.

### 8.11.1. System Advantages

Among the more attractive attributes of the system are the following:

(1) *Well-defined objectives.* It implements a nucleus which can be extended with a variety of operating systems. It has been successfully used to design a spooling system and a number of real-time systems which supervise industrial plants.

(2) *Simple structure.* The monitor implements about 30 operations. The concepts involved and their relationships are fully explained in a manual of 160 pages. Compared to the actual machine language implementation, the manual omits only trivial programming details.

(3) *Moderate size.* A monitor of 4800 words and a basic operating system of 1400 words is reasonably small by most standards.

(4) *Reliability.* Although the monitor was written in machine language, its simplicity and moderate size made it possible to develop a set of programs which were executed as internal processes and tested the monitor systematically, starting with processor multiplexing, followed by process communication, and ending with process scheduling. The monitor was extended with a procedure of about 20 instructions which would stop the system temporarily and output one or two monitor variables (addresses of process descriptions or message buffers) in the uninterruptable state each time a significant event occurred (such as a preemption or resumption of a process, or a change of a message buffer state). This simple test mechanism ensured that the response to and recording of an event was executed as a critical region. By careful design of the test programs, it was ensured that they would be executed as reproducible, concurrent processes. As a result, the monitor was practically error-free after a test period of one month (Brinch Hansen, 1973).

(5) *Readable documentation.* A report entitled "An Undergraduate Course on Operating Systems Principles," published by the National Academy of Engineering (Cosine report, 1971) recommends that the study of operating system concepts be accompanied by a detailed study of a particular system embodying these concepts. The report emphasizes that "the system should be documented adequately, so that recourse to the operating system code is not necessary for a detailed understanding of its implementation" and further states that "the committee is aware of only a few systems that meet these requirements." One of the three systems mentioned in the report is the *RC 4000* multiprogramming system.

## 8.11.2.  System  Disadvantages

Although our attitude toward program design was guided by reasonably sound principles, our particular solution to the problem at hand was far from ideal. The system nucleus is unsatisfactory in the following respects:

(1) *Error detection*. Today I question the most basic assumption of the system: That it tries to make multiprogramming safe at the machine level of programming. The monitor defines a set of language primitives for multiprogramming that may be called by correct or incorrect programs written in machine language. We had to make this assumption when the system was built because no high-level language available at that time was both sufficiently well-structured and efficient for general programming. The resulting lack of structure in user programs makes it impossible to detect multiprogramming errors at compile time; the monitor therefore spends a considerable amount of processor time verifying the validity of calls at run time. Unfortunately, this checking only catches simple errors of parameter values or violations of protection rules, but gives no assistance whatsoever in the detection of time-dependent errors.

(2) *Concurrent processes*. In retrospect, I realize that the event primitives were introduced as an *ad hoc* means of simulating concurrent activities within a common store area. This enables the basic operating system to be engaged in conversations with several terminals at the same time. It was also used in the implementation of a spooling system. It would have been conceptually more clear to have designed these operating systems as a set of cooperating, internal processes. But the designers of these operating systems felt that it would have been too expensive (in terms of system resources) to establish several internal processes and too cumbersome to share large data structures among them (for reasons explained in the following paragraphs).

(3) *Mutual exclusion*. The data structure controlled by the monitor (consisting of process descriptions and scheduling queues) is a global shared variable. The monitor ensures mutual exclusion of operations on it by the crude method of interrupt inhibition. This means that all process interactions (including the synchronization of input/output) exclude one another in time. Since some of them last several milliseconds, this makes the monitor a bottleneck. To alleviate this problem, we resorted to an *ad hoc* solution by introducing an anonymous internal process which permits processor multiplexing to continue during the most extensive monitor calls. But the real problem was that we did not realize the need to establish critical regions for an arbitrary number of shared variables and, therefore, we did not solve that problem. This is also evident at higher levels of

programming: The only way a set of cooperating, internal processes can achieve mutual exclusion of their access to a shared data structure is by placing the data structure within one of the processes and accessing it by sending messages to that process—a safe, but very expensive method since each communication requires 2 msec of monitor time.

(4) *Process communication.* Our desire to solve protection problems at the machine language level made it necessary to implement a fairly restrictive mechanism for process communication within the monitor. This created an artificial resource restriction (a finite number of message buffers shared by all processes), an artificial data structure restriction (a fixed message length of eight words for all processes), and an inefficient implementation (physical copying of messages). The problem was simply that we had no clear understanding of the need for establishing arbitrary rules of process synchronization.

So the language features for multiprogramming implemented by the nucleus—*create, start, stop,* and *remove process,* as well as *send* and *wait message*—are unstructured and somewhat impractical. It would have been far more natural to program operating systems in terms of concurrent statements, shared variables, and critical regions (simple and conditional) as proposed in this book. But this was by no means obvious when the system was built.

(5) *Medium-term scheduling.* We saw the advantages of being able to use an internal process to simulate an external process, but we did not make it practical to do so. To avoid transmitting large data blocks as a sequence of small messages, input/output is handled by communicating addresses to peripheral devices, which then transfer blocks directly to or from the store through a high-speed data channel. The problem of preventing process preemption and reassignment of the store while input/output is in progress is solved correctly by means of the stop count for external processes. But, when an internal process $A$ sends an address to another internal process $B$ to enable the latter to access a large data block directly within the former, there is no guarantee that the operating system of process $A$ will not preempt it from the store while this is being done (unless the operating system is process $B$). Again, this shows that the mutual exclusion problem is unsatisfactorily solved in general. Furthermore, medium-term scheduling is complicated considerably by our use of unstructured multiprogramming features: This forces the monitor to examine all process descriptions and sometimes also all message buffers before an internal process can be started, stopped, or removed.

(6) *Short-term scheduling.* At an early stage in the design, a distinction was made between processes that control input/output and those that perform computations. This distinction between external and internal processes was based on differences in process scheduling and store

addressing. It had a drastic influence on the real-time characteristics of the system. On the one hand, input/output processes could be activated immediately by interrupts and run without preemption for several milliseconds. On the other hand, due to the use of fixed round-robin scheduling, computational processes could only respond to urgent, external events within 10 to 100 msec. The maintenance of the system was also strongly affected by this decision. The input/output processes enjoyed privileges of addressing which enabled them to enter global critical regions and execute shared procedures within the nucleus. But the smallest modification of any of them required reassembly and testing of the entire nucleus. In contrast, computational processes were unable to share procedures, but were easy to implement and test separately. The system nucleus was indeed built to create and execute computational processes dynamically. We should have treated all processes uniformly at the short-term level of scheduling and made it possible to assign priorities to them when they were started.

(7) *File system.* The difficulty of establishing arbitrary critical regions within processes and exchanging arbitrary data structures between them led to the inclusion of too many functions in the system nucleus—among others, the file system. The file system itself has several limitations: It requires that file names be unique throughout the installation (which is impractical); it uses contiguous allocation of backing storage, (which makes it almost impossible to prevent a deadlock of unrelated computations); and it does not prevent the loss of data in the case of hardware malfunction. Since the file system is a part of the system nucleus, its replacement requires reassembly and testing of the nucleus.*)

It is, however, to the credit of the system that all these deficiencies are apparent to a keen reader of the system manual and not hidden as undocumented implementation details.

## 8.12. LITERATURE

The following is a list of literature describing a number of excellent operating systems in some detail.

The *Scope* operating system for the *CDC 6600* computer is a remarkably simple operating system for one of the fastest machines in the world. It permits concurrent execution of up to seven non-interactive jobs at a time. It is described by Thornton (1964) and Wilson (1971a).

The *Master control program* for the *B5500* computer is also a system

---

*A later version of the system has removed some of the limitations of the file system (Andersen, 1972).

for concurrent execution of non-interactive jobs. An unusual aspect of this system is that it was written in extended Algol 60. It is described by Lonergan (1961) and McKeag (1971a).

The *Titan supervisor*, designed at Cambridge University in England and described by Fraser (1971) and Wilson (1971b), permits conversational access from 26 terminals simultaneously. It is also noteworthy for its simple file system.

Most multiprogramming concepts discussed in this book evolved during the design of *THE multiprogramming system* at the Technological University of Eindhoven, The Netherlands; that is, critical regions, semaphores, deadlock prevention, and hierarchal program design. Various aspects of this system are described by Bron (1971), Dijkstra (1965 and 1968), and McKeag (1971b).

The *Multics* system is a large interactive system which can serve about 50 users simultaneously. Its development has required 200 man-years. It is described in great detail by Organick (1972).

BRON, C., "Allocation of virtual store in THE multiprogramming system," *International Seminar on Operating System Techniques*, Belfast, Northern Ireland, Aug.-Sept. *1971*.

DIJKSTRA, E. W., "Cooperating sequential processes," Technological University, Eindhoven, The Netherlands, *1965*. (Reprinted in *Programming Languages*, F. Genuys, ed., Academic Press, New York, New York, 1968).

DIJKSTRA, E. W., "The structure of THE multiprogramming system," *Comm. ACM 11*, 5, pp. 341-46, May *1968*.

FRASER, A. G., "The integrity of a disc based file system." *International Seminar on Operating System Techniques*, Belfast, Northern Ireland, Aug.-Sept. *1971*.

LONERGAN, W. and KING, P., "Design of the B5000 system," *Datamation 7*, 5, pp. 28-32, May *1961*.

McKEAG, R. M., "Burroughs B5500 Master control program," The Queen's University of Belfast, Northern Ireland, *1971a*.

McKEAG, R. M., "THE Multiprogramming system," The Queen's University of Belfast, Northern Ireland, *1971b*.

ORGANICK, E. I., *The Multics System: An Examination of its Structure*. MIT Press, Cambridge, Massachusetts, *1972*.

THORNTON, J. E., "Parallel operation in the Control Data 6600," *Proc. AFIPS Fall Joint Computer Conf.*, pp. 33-40, *1964*.

WILSON, R., "CDC Scope 3.2," The Queen's University of Belfast, Northern Ireland, *1971a*.

WILSON, R., "The Titan supervisor," The Queen's University of Belfast, Northern Ireland, *1971b*.

# EXERCISES

The purpose of these exercises is to:

(1) bring to your attention *practical problems* encountered in most operating systems;

(2) give you some *experience* in using the techniques presented in the text;

(3) give you the pleasure of deriving additional *theoretical results*; and

(4) suggest *research projects* which will increase our understanding of operating system concepts.

## CHAPTER 1

1.1.  Study the *manual of an operating system* for a computer to which you have access and ask yourself the following questions:
Is the manual *easy to read*?
*How many pages* must I read to understand the system well enough to use it efficiently?
Does the manual clearly explain: the *purpose* of the system; the *effect* of its operations; the *cost* of these operations (in terms of storage and execution time); the overall internal *structure*; and the system's main *limitations*?
Find out from the operators how frequently the system crashes and for what reasons. Start to think about how you would design and document a better system.

1.2.  The classical *batch-processing* system completely ignores the cost of increased waiting time for users. Consider a single batch characterized by the following parameters:

|  |  |
|---|---|
| $M$ | average mounting time |
| $T$ | average service time per job |
| $N$ | number of jobs |
| $S$ | unit price of service time |
| $W$ | unit price of waiting time per user |

(a) Show that the optimal batch size which minimizes the cost of service time and waiting time per user (within a single batch) is

$$N_{opt} = \sqrt{\frac{MS}{TW}}$$

(b) In an installation in which $M = 5$ min, $T = 1$ min, and $S = \$300/\text{hour}$, the operators choose $N = 50$. Assuming that this is an optimal choice, find the unit cost of user waiting time $W$?

1.3. The operating systems of some computers in the 1960's were protected against destruction by their jobs by being placed in store locations which all programs (including the operating system itself) could *read* from, but *none* could *write* into. What was the defect of this early *protection system*?

1.4. A university uses a spooling system to execute student programs written in a single high-level language. Measurements show that the execution phase of an average job uses the processor as follows:

| | |
|---|---|
| job scheduling | 3 sec |
| compiler loading from drum | 2 — |
| compilation | 5 — |
| execution | 15 — |
| | 25 sec |

Suggest a method for increasing the *throughput* of this system.

1.5. In the *Exec II* system, users would submit a large number of jobs in the morning. These jobs took hours to complete and thereby prevented fast response. Suggest a modification of the scheduling policy which would discourage users from doing this.

1.6. "*Warm start.*" The backing store of a spooling system may hold the input and output of as many as 10 to 50 jobs at any time. What methods would you propose to ensure that the operating system will be able to continue scheduling these jobs and printing their output after a breakdown and repair of the central processor or the internal store?

1.7. In the *Scope* system for the *CDC 6600* computer, system resources (processor time, storage, and so on) can remain idle while running jobs wait for operators to mount magnetic tapes. Suggest a solution to this problem.

1.8. (Research project) Define protection and scheduling rules for an installation that maintains a library of 30,000 magnetic tapes of which 1000 are mounted on 30 stations each day. (*Hint*: Take the installation environment into consideration—the manual handling of tapes, their organization on shelves, and the ways in which one can collect and utilize data about their expected frequency of usage.)

1.9. In the *CTSS* system, a single processor and an internal store are multiplexed among user computations by swapping. The amount of internal store required by each job during execution is known. How would you use this information about the expected workload to make swapping more efficient?

1.10. In the original version of the *SDC Q-32* system, swapping reduced processor utilization by 50 per cent. Suggest a modification of swapping that will increase processor utilization without degrading user response.

1.11. How does the solution to Exercise 1.10 complicate store management?

1.12. The *CTSS* system uses swapping to ensure immediate response to user requests from terminals. Measurements showed that about one-half of all user requests could be classified as file manipulation, program input, and editing. How would you use this information about the expected workload to improve processor utilization at a reasonable cost without degrading user response?

1.13. In the *SDC Q-32* system, a significant number of jobs required long processing time with little or no interaction. To require that a user remain at a terminal during these periods would clearly be undesirable. Suggest a system feature which would enable users to be absent during their computations and at the same time permit the terminals to be used by others.

1.14. In the *RC 4000* multiprogramming system, all *files* on the backing store must have unique *names*. In a large installation one cannot expect users to solve name conflicts among themselves. Suggest a structure of the file system that enables each user to be unaware of the names used by other users unless one of them needs access to a file created by another.

1.15. Consider a simple file system that enables users to create, use, and delete files on a disk which is not backed up by magnetic tapes. Suggest a reasonable *classification of files* that can be used to select some of them for automatic deletion when the disk is full and more space is needed. Also consider how you would implement this algorithm.

1.16. A file system automatically copies files from disk to magnetic tape at regular intervals as an insurance against *disk malfunction*. However, it is possible that parts of these tapes cannot be read when they are needed to reestablish the file system after a disk failure. What measures would you propose to ensure that tape errors do not bring a system restart to a complete halt?

1.17. Suggest a simple method of limiting the periodic copying of files from disk to magnetic tape in Exercise 1.16 as much as possible. (It is not an acceptable solution to increase the interval between successive copy operations since this interval is determined mainly by the reliability of the disk.)

1.18. Propose a system in which the problem of protecting files stored on disk against hardware malfunction is viewed consistently as an *insurance problem*; that is, each user must decide whether to pay a premium for having some of his files automatically copied to magnetic tape at a certain frequency or else run the risk of losing them completely.

1.19. (S. Lauesen) Outline the implementation details of a simple *job control language* for a non-interactive system in which named files can be stored either on a backing store or on other peripherals. A command has the following format:

$$O := P(I, A, B, \ldots, Z)$$

It will cause the execution of a program $P$ with input from a file $I$ and output on a file $O$. $A, B, \ldots, Z$ are optional parameters (booleans, numbers, or textstrings) that are meaningful to $P$ only. The user can specify a sequence of such commands, pass parameters between programs, and specify conditional execution, for example:

> **var** *correct: boolean;*
> *source:= edit(source);*
> *object:= create file(10);*
> *object:= algol(source, correct);*
> **if** *correct* **then** *object;*
> *delete file(object);*

where *edit*, *create file*, *algol*, and *delete file* are programs, while *source* and *object* are data files (after compilation, *object* becomes a program file).

1.20. In a shared computer system, users are identified by *passwords*. Since the list of passwords is stored within the operating system, management is worried about the possibility that a malicious user may write a program which examines the entire store and finds this list. Assuming that this is possible, choose an internal representation of passwords that is useless for external identification.

1.21. A *password* which identifies a user and on which accounting of resource usage is based may become known to other users. Suggest a simple method of detecting possible misuse of passwords and propose a countermeasure.

1.22. An operating system uses an alphanumeric *display* to keep the main operator informed about the current *status* of the system. Consider what data would be meaningful to him in a spooling system and in a conversational system. Decide which of them would be useful to display continuously and which of them should be available only on request. Make suggestions about how the operator might use the data displayed to interact with the system and improve its performance on a time scale comparable to human reaction time (of the order of minutes).

## CHAPTER 3

3.1. (C. A. R. Hoare) *"Triple buffering."* Write an algorithm which can input, process, and output a sequence of data elements of type $T$ using three buffers—$A$, $B$, and $C$—cyclically as follows:

> *phase* 1: *input(A);*
> *phase* 2: *process(A); input(B);*
> *phase* 3: *output(A); process(B); input(C);*
>  . . .        . . . . .

Overlapping of input, processing, and output in time should be achieved by means of concurrent statements without the use of critical regions. *Input, process,* and *output* can be considered primitive operations; a boolean function *more* is *true* if the input sequence contains one or more data elements; otherwise, it is *false*. The solution should also work when the input sequence contains 0, 1, or 2 data elements.

3.2. What is the maximum factor *f* by which the execution time can be reduced by the triple-buffering scheme of Exercise 3.1 compared to a strictly sequential execution of input, processing, and output (ignoring the overhead of concurrent statements)?

3.3. The algorithm below is Dekker's solution to the *mutual exclusion* problem for two processes, *P1* and *P2*. Outline an informal argument which shows that:

```
var outside1, outside2: boolean; turn: 1. .2;
begin
  outside1:= true; outside2:= true; turn:= 1;
  cobegin
  "P1" repeat
          label enter
          begin
            repeat
              outside1:= false;
              repeat
                if outside2 then exit enter;
              until turn = 2;
              outside1:= true;
              repeat until turn = 1;
            forever
          end
          P1 inside;
          turn:= 2; outside1:= true;
          P1 outside;
        forever

  "P2" repeat
          label enter
          begin
            repeat
              outside2:= false;
              repeat
                if outside1 then exit enter;
              until turn = 1;
              outside2:= true;
              repeat until turn = 2;
            forever
          end
          P2 inside;
          turn:= 1; outside2:= true;
          P2 outside;
        forever
  coend
end
```

(1)  one process at most is inside its critical region at a time;

(2)  if both processes are trying to enter their critical regions simultaneously, a decision will be made within a finite time as to which one should be permitted to do so; and

(3)  if a process is stopped outside its critical region, this cannot influence the progress of the other process.

3.4.   A computer has an instruction which exchanges the contents of two store locations. *Exchange operations* on a given store location exclude one another in time. Comment on the following solution to the *mutual exclusion* problem with *n* processes:

> **var** *free*: *boolean*; *turn*: array 1. .*n* of *boolean*;
> "*Initially free is true, and all turns are false*"
>
> "*Process i*"
> **repeat**
>   **repeat** *exchange(free, turn(i))* **until** *turn(i)*;
>   *critical region*;
>   *exchange(free, turn(i))*;
>   *outside region*;
> **forever**

3.5.   Propose a language feature which enables concurrent processes to exchange *large messages* by *reference* instead of by *value*. This language feature must enable a compiler and its run-time system to ensure that:

(1)  a reference either points to a message element or is undefined;

(2)  one process at a time at most can access a given message element; and

(3)  a process cannot reference a message element while it is within a buffer.

3.6.   Comment on the following version of Algorithm 3.7:

> **type** *B* = **shared record**
>                  *buffer*: **array** 0. .*max*-1 **of** *T*;
>                  *p*, *c*: 0. .*max*-1;
>                  *full*, *empty*: *semaphore*;
>             **end**
>
> "*Initially p = c = full = 0 & empty = max*"
>
> **procedure** *send*(*m*: *T*; **var** *b*: *B*);
> **region** *b* **do**

```
begin
  wait(empty);
  buffer(p):= m;
  p:= (p + 1) mod max;
  signal(full);
end


procedure receive(var m: T; b: B);
region b do
begin
  wait(full);
  m:= buffer(c);
  c:= (c + 1) mod max;
  signal(empty);
end
```

3.7. *"Pipeline system."* A stream of data elements of type $T$ produced by a process $P0$ passes through a sequence of processes, $P1$, $P2$, ... , $Pn-1$, which operate on the elements in that order:

$$P0 \to P1 \to P2 ---- \to Pn-1$$

Define a generalized message buffer which contains all the partially consumed data elements and write an algorithm for process $Pi$ $(0 \leqslant i \leqslant n - 1)$

```
              "Process Pi"
              repeat
                receive from predecessor;
                consume element;
                send to successor;
              forever
```

(Process $P0$ receives empty elements sent by process $Pn-1$.) The algorithm should enable the processes to operate directly on messages stored in the buffer so that copying is unnecessary.

3.8. Show that the processes, $P0$, $P1$, . ., $Pn-1$, in Exercise 3.7 cannot be *deadlocked* with respect to the common pipeline.

3.9. Show that Algorithms 3.8 and 3.9 maintain the *invariant*

$$D \equiv (rr = 0 \text{ implies } rw = aw) \ \& \ (aw = 0 \text{ implies } rr = ar)$$

which was used to show the absence of deadlocks.

**3.10.** (P. J. Courtois, F. Heymans, and D. L. Parnas) The following is a solution to a variant of the *readers and writers* problem in which *no priority* is given to waiting writers:

> **var** *ar*: **shared** *integer*; *s*: *semaphore*;
> "*Initially ar = 0 and s = 1*"
>
> "*reader*"                                "*writer*"
> **region** *ar* **do**                   *wait*(*s*);
> **begin**                                 *write*;
>   *ar*:= *ar* + 1;                        *signal*(*s*);
>   **if** *ar* = 1 **then** *wait*(*s*);
> **end**
> *read*;
> **region** *ar* **do**
> **begin**
>   *ar*:= *ar* − 1;
>   **if** *ar* = 0 **then** *signal*(*s*);
> **end**

Use the *semaphore invariant* to prove that readers and writers exclude each other in time and that writers also exclude one another.

**3.11.** Cars coming from the north and south must pass a bridge across a river. Unfortunately, there is only one lane on the bridge. So at any moment, it can be crossed only by *one or more* cars coming from the same direction (but not from opposite directions). Write an algorithm for a southern and a northern car as they arrive at the bridge, cross it, and depart on the other side. (See Fig. E3.11.)

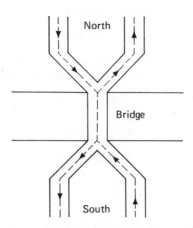

**Fig. E3.11.**

3.12. Refine the solution to Exercise 3.11 so that the direction of traffic across the bridge will change each time 10 cars have crossed from one direction while one or more cars were waiting to cross it from the opposite direction.

3.13. Processes $P1$, $P2$, $\ldots$, $Pn$ share a single resource $R$ but, one process at most can use it at a time. A process can start using it immediately if the resource is free; otherwise, the process must wait until the resource has been released by another process. If one or more processes are waiting when the resource is released, it is granted to the process with the highest priority. The priority rule is the following: Process $Pi$ has priority number $i$ $(1 \leqslant i \leqslant n)$, with low numbers indicating high priority. Program the procedures used to *reserve* and *release* the resource:

> *"process Pi"*
> *reserve(i)*;
> *use resource*;
> *release*;

3.14. In a system with non-preemptive resource allocation, resources can be requested and released one at a time. When resources are available and no processes are waiting for them, they can be granted to any process. But, when resources are being released and one or more processes are waiting for them, those resources are granted to waiting processes on the basis of *priorities* assigned to user computations by installation management. Is this policy feasible?

3.15. (R. C. Holt) 3 processes share 4 resource units which can be reserved and released only one at a time. Each process needs a maximum of 2 units. Show that a *deadlock* cannot occur in this system.

3.16. (R. C. Holt) $n$ processes share $m$ resource units, which can be reserved and released only one at a time. The maximum need of each process does not exceed the capital $m$, and the sum of all maximum needs is less than $m + n$. Show that a *deadlock* cannot occur in this system.

3.17. (R. C. Holt) (Research project) Develop *probabilistic models* of resource allocation which can predict the mean time between *deadlocks* and permit designers to determine whether the deadlocks occur so infrequently that prevention is unnecessary.

3.18. *"The banker's algorithm applied."* Write two procedures which enable a customer to ask the banker to *increase* and *decrease* his *loan* by a single coin of a given currency (see Algorithm 2.6). (Notice that the identity of coins is relevant to the customers.)

3.19. (E. W. Dijkstra) *"The dining philosophers."* Five philosophers sit around a table. Each philosopher alternates between thinking and eating:

**repeat** *think*; *eat* **forever**

In front of each philosopher there is a plate with spaghetti. When a philosopher wishes to eat, he picks up two forks next to his plate. There are, however, only five forks on the table. (See Fig. E3.19.)

Fig. E3.19.

So a philosopher can only eat when none of his neighbors are eating. Write the algorithm for philosopher $i$ ($0 \leqslant i \leqslant 4$). (*Hint*: Prevent *deadlock*.)

3.20. Comment on the following solution to the problem of the dining philosophers (see Exercise 3.19):

> **var** *fork*: **array** 0. .4 **of shared** *boolean*;
>
> "*Philosopher i*"
> **repeat**
>   *think*;
>   **region** *fork*(*i*) **do**
>   **region** *fork*((*i* + 1) **mod** 5) **do** *eat*;
> **forever**

3.21. Comment on the following solution to the problem of the dining philosophers (see Exercise 3.19):

> **var** *thinking*: **shared array** 0. .4 **of** *boolean*;
>             "*initially all true*"
>
> "*Philosopher i*"
> **repeat**
>   *think*;
>   **region** *thinking* **do**
>   **begin**
>     **await** *thinking*((*i* − 1) **mod** 5) &
>             *thinking*((*i* + 1) **mod** 5);
>     *thinking*(*i*):= *false*;
>   **end**
>   *eat*;
>   **region** *thinking* **do** *thinking*(*i*):= *true*;
> **forever**

**3.22.** Comment on the following solution to the problem of the dining philosophers (see Exercise 3.19): A hungry philosopher first picks up his left fork; if his right fork is also available, he starts eating; otherwise, he puts down his left fork again and repeats the cycle.

**3.23.** A *spooling system* consists of an input process $I$, a user process $P$, and an output process $O$ connected by two buffers. (See Fig. E3.24.)

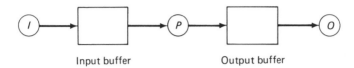

Input buffer             Output buffer

**Fig. E3.23.**

The processes exchange data in units of equal size called *pages*. These pages are buffered on a drum using a floating boundary between the input and the output, depending on the speed of the processes. The communication primitives used ensure that the following resource constraint is satisfied:

$$i + o \leqslant max$$

where

| | |
|---|---|
| $max$ | maximum number of pages on drum |
| $i$ | number of input pages on drum |
| $o$ | number of output pages on drum |

The following is known about the processes:

(1) As long as the environment supplies data, process $I$ will eventually input it to the drum (provided drum space becomes available).

(2) As long as input is available on the drum, process $P$ will eventually consume it and output a finite amount of data on the drum for each page input (provided drum space becomes available).

(3) As long as output is available on the drum, process $O$ will eventually consume it.

Show that this system can be *deadlocked.*

**3.24.** Suggest an additional *resource constraint* that will prevent the deadlock in Exercise 3.23, but still permit the boundary between input and output to vary in accordance with the present needs of the processes.

**3.25.** (C. Bron) In *THE* multiprogramming system, a drum is divided into *input buffers, processing areas,* and *output buffers* with floating boundaries, depending on the speed of the processes involved. The current state of the drum can be characterized by the following parameters:

> *max*      maximum number of pages on drum
> *i*        number of input pages on drum
> *p*        number of processing pages on drum
> *o*        number of output pages on drum
> *reso*     minimum number of pages reserved for output
> *resp*     minimum number of pages reserved for processing

Formulate the necessary *resource constraints* that guarantee that the drum capacity is not exceeded and that a minimum number of pages is reserved permanently for output and processing. Illustrate these constraints geometrically in an $(i, o, p)$ coordinate system.

**3.26.** In *THE* multiprogramming system (see Exercise 3.25), a page can make the following *state transitions*:

> (1)  empty → input buffer          (input production)
> (2)  input buffer → processing area   (input consumption)
> (3)  processing area → output buffer  (output production)
> (4)  output buffer → empty          (output consumption)
> (5)  empty ↛ processing area        (procedure call)
> (6)  processing area → empty        (procedure return)

Define the effect of these transitions in terms of the quantities $i$, $o$, and $p$. Can any of them lead to a *deadlock* if the assumptions made in Exercise 3.23 about input processes, user processes, and output processes hold?

**3.27.** Represent the drum in Exercise 3.23 by an array of pages:

> **var** *drum*: **array** 1..*max* **of** *page*

and implement the following communication procedures

> *send input(p)*
> *receive input(p)*
> *send output(p)*
> *receive output(p)*

(where $p$: *page*) such that the resource constraints of Exercises 3.23 and 3.24 are satisfied.

# CHAPTER 4

**4.1.** A process that is operating on a *shared variable* delays all other processes that are waiting to do the same. Suggest a method for alleviating this problem.

**4.2.** A multiprogramming system *measures* the *processor time* used by each computation. How does this influence the design of the short-term scheduling primitives (Algorithms 4.1-4.6)?

**4.3.** To which process would you *charge* the *processor time* used to honor an *interrupt*? Present the cases for and against alternatives.

**4.4.** In several computers, an *interrupt* causes the *machine state* (register values) to be stored in fixed locations associated with the given interrupt signal. Under what circumstances is this a practical technique? Explain why it is inconvenient in general.

**4.5.** Choose a representation of the *ready queue* and implement processor multiplexing according to a *round-robin* algorithm.

**4.6.** Choose a representation of the *ready queue* and implement processor multiplexing according to a *round-robin* algorithm with the following additional constraint: Processes outside *critical regions* are only executed when no processes are inside critical regions and *ready* to run.

**4.7.** Represent the *multi-level queue* defined in Section 4.2.5

$$\text{type } N = 1..n;$$
$$\text{var } q: \text{queue } N \text{ of } T; t; T; p:N;$$
$$enter(t,p,q);$$
$$remove(t,p,q);$$

in terms of records, arrays, and sequences.

**4.8.** How would you *test* the correctness of the *short-term scheduling primitives* (Algorithms 4.1-4.6) in a systematic, reproducible manner? (*Hint*: Modify the algorithms slightly to obtain a recording of significant events and design a series of processes that will force the basic monitor through all of its relevant states at least once.)

**4.9.** Write an algorithm which executes the statement

$$y:= (a + b)/(c - d) + e * f$$

by *concurrent evaluation* of subexpressions. The variables involved are distinct integer variables.

Evaluate whether this is practical to do on a multiprocessor system with the following *execution times*:

| | |
|---|---|
| + − | 2 μsec |
| * / := | 10 μsec |
| intermediate result | 5 μsec |
| cobegin coend | 500 μsec per process |

**4.10.** (Research project) Design a *multiprocessor system* consisting of a number of identical processors connected to a common store which is able to continue its operation after a *hardware malfunction* of a single processor. Consider hardware and software aspects of this reliability problem at the lowest level of programming. Try also to make the system tolerant of other kinds of failure. Do not expect to solve the problem with present machines and programming languages.

# CHAPTER 5

5.1. Choose a representation of segments and holes in a store with *contiguous segments* and write *reserve* and *release* operations (with *compacting*) using the *first fit* placement algorithm.

5.2. (D. E. Knuth) *"Fifty per cent rule."* Consider an internal store shared by contiguous segments and show that under equilibrium conditions it contains, on the average, half as many holes as segments.

5.3. What guidance does the fifty per cent rule of Exercise 5.2 give toward an efficient implementation of a placement algorithm for contiguous segments?

5.4. (P. J. Denning) *"Sequential placement with compacting."* Consider a store in which contiguous segments $S1, S2, \ldots, Sn$ are placed strictly in their order of creation from one end of the store to the other. (See Fig. E5.4.)

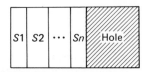

Fig. E5.4.

When segment $Sn+1$ is being created, it is placed immediately after segment $Sn$ even though some of the segments $S1, S2, \ldots, Sn$ may already have been deleted. When the boundary between segments (in use or deleted) and the hole reaches the other end of the store, the segments in use are compacted.

(a) Let $s$ and $t$ denote the average length and lifetime of a segment (measured in words and store references) and let $f$ denote the fraction of the store which is unused under equilibrium conditions. Show that the fraction of time $F$ spent on compacting is constrained as follows:

$$F \geqslant \frac{1 - f}{1 + kf} \text{ where } k = \frac{t}{2\,s} - 1$$

(*Hint*: Find the average speed at which the boundary crosses the store and assume that copying of a single word requires at least two store references.)

(b) Find $F$ for $f = 0.2$, $t = 1000$, and $s = 50$.

5.5. A computer is shared by computations that all use a modest number of variables (compared to the capacity of the internal store); the compiled programs may, however, be fairly large. Suggest a *simplified* and more efficient form of *demand paging* which takes advantage of this knowledge.

5.6. (P. Naur) Suggest a simple experiment which will demonstrate the *locality principle* for a given program in the demand paging system of Exercise 5.5.

**5.7.** How would you *measure thrashing* in a single processor system with a single backing store in such a way that the system does not register overcommitments of very short duration?

**5.8.** (L. A. Belady, R. A. Nelson, and G. S. Shedler) *"Demand paging anomaly."* A process refers to five pages, $A$, $B$, $C$, $D$, and $E$, in the following order:

$$A; B; C; D; A; B; E; A; B; C; D; E$$

Assume that the replacement algorithm is *first-in, first-out* and find the number of page transfers during this sequence of references starting with an empty internal store with 3 and 4 page frames.

**5.9.** (A. Alderson, W. C. Lynch, and B. Randell) *"Load control by external priorities."* Simulate the behavior of a *demand paging* system which executes a fixed number of identical processes indefinitely. The system is characterized by the parameters $t$, $T$, and $s$ and the function $p(s) = a\, e^{-bs}$ as defined in Section 5.4.2.

(a) Measure the processor utilization $\eta$ as a function of the number of processes $n$ for an internal store of fixed capacity. The simulation should only keep track of the number of page frames assigned to each process (but should not be concerned with individual page frames).

(b) Repeat the experiment with the following modification: Assign priorities $1, 2, \ldots, n$ to the $n$ processes and use the following scheduling rule (due to R. M. Wharton): Assign the processor to the process of the highest priority that is ready to run. When a page must be transferred to a full store on demand from a given process, select a page frame from the process of the lowest priority that has one (provided the priority of the latter process is less than that of the former). If no such process exists, delay the given process (leaving its page frames unchanged) until a process of higher priority releases page frames (this will never occur in this simple model in which processes continue forever).

**5.10.** In a *demand paging* system, it is discovered that a significant amount of processor time is lost while computations wait for *slow peripherals*. The scheduling algorithm is therefore modified as follows: When idle processor time has exceeded a certain limit, another computation is started. Comment on this proposal.

**5.11.** A *drum* consisting of 512 tracks of 1024 words each must be divided into *page frames* of 512 words each. Suggest an arrangement of page frames which ensures that there will always be a page frame which can be accessed with a negligible waiting time (equal to $\frac{1}{1024}$ of the revolution time at most).

**5.12.** In *THE* multiprogramming system, processes can be *deadlocked* with respect to the *backing store*. (See Exercises 3.25 and 3.26.) Suggest a scheduling policy which tries to avoid this as long as possible.

**5.13.** In the *SDS 940* computer, the internal store is divided into 16 page frames of 2 K words each. The virtual store of a process is a single segment consisting of up to 8 pages. Address mapping is done by 8 registers which define the base addresses of page frames available to the currently running process (some of these addresses may be undefined, indication that no frames have been assigned to the corresponding pages). Comment on the usefulness of this machine for (a) sequential computations; (b) concurrent computations; and (c) demand paging.

5.14. For a computer with *demand paging*, the *magnetic tapes* are built to transfer blocks of variable length to contiguous store locations. Outline the manner in which you would handle store allocation in such a system (assuming that it is unacceptable to management that blocks on tape can only be smaller than or equal to one page). Could the problem be simplified by a different machine structure at a reasonable cost?

5.15. (K. Fuchel and S. Heller) In a *CDC 6600* installation, a *single processor* is multiplexed among $n$ independent jobs placed in an internal store. When a running job awaits the completion of *input/output*, the processor is assigned to a *ready* job in the internal store. However, if all $n$ jobs wait for input/output at the same time, the processor is idle. Measurements show that with an internal store of 65 K words, the average number of scheduled jobs $n$ is 2, while the processor utilization $\eta$ is only 36 per cent. Assuming that idle processor time is caused only by input/output, find the average probability $p$ that a single job is waiting for input/output?

5.16. Use the result of Exercise 5.15 to evaluate the amount of internal store required to *increase processor utilization* to 90 per cent, assuming that the operating system and an average job need 10 K and 25 K words, respectively.

5.17. (a) If an internal store contains $n$ independent jobs, each characterized by an average input/output probability $p$ as derived in Exercise 5.15, what would the utilization $\eta$ of a processor then be in a *dual processor* system?
(b) Evaluate $\eta$ for $n = 2$ and $p = 0.8$.

5.18. (Design project) Implement concurrent statements, critical regions, and event queues efficiently on a computer. If you feel that the available computer is less than ideal for this purpose, then use this insight to suggest more appropriate machine features. If you cannot carry out such a project for economic reasons, take the time to outline the main problems and their solutions.

5.19. (Research project) Develop realistic *dynamic models* of the *store requirements* of computations and use them to define meaningful comparisons of various store management techniques under well-defined circumstances. (Part of the project is to find out what these "circumstances" are.)

# CHAPTER 6

6.1. Consider how you would *measure* the service time distribution $F(t)$; and the *service and arrival rates*, $\mu$ and $\lambda$, continuously during system operation by simple means (rather than by laborious analysis of measurements of individual jobs collected over an extensive period of time).

6.2. Interarrival times which follow an exponential distribution

$$F(x) = 1 - e^{-x} \qquad \text{where } x = \lambda t$$

can be simulated by the following statement:

> **var** $x$: *real*;
> $x := -ln(random)$;

where *random* is a real function which delivers a random number uniformly distributed between 0 and 1. How can the same method be used to *simulate service times* which follow a hyperexponential distribution?:

$$F(x) = 1 - a\, e^{-bx} - (1 - a)\, e^{-cx} \qquad \text{where } x = \mu t$$

6.3.  Refine the *demand paging* model of Exercise 5.9 to account for different, finite service times and working sets (for example, selected from exponential and uniform distributions). Also make suggestions for the modelling of input/output delays caused by slow peripherals and the distribution of page demands over drum sectors.

6.4.  "*Finite input queue.*" Consider a queuing system with a single processor, Poisson input, and exponential service times which can hold a maximum of $n$ jobs (including the one being served). (See Fig. E6.4.)

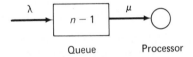

Queue       Processor

**Fig. E6.4.**

Jobs which arrive when the system is full leave without returning. The system can be in $n + 1$ states with either $0, 1, \ldots$ , or $n$ jobs waiting or in service. Let $p_0$, $p_1, \ldots$ , $p_n$ denote the steady state probabilities of these states. Find the relations between these probabilities and show that

$$p_n = \frac{\rho^n (1 - \rho)}{1 - \rho^{n+1}}$$

where $\rho = \lambda/\mu$ is the utilization factor. (*Hint*: The same technique was used to derive equation (6.31).)

6.5.  Use the result of Exercise 6.4 to determine the necessary *queue capacity* when $\rho = 0.93$ so that the probability that a job will find the queue full upon arrival does not exceed 1 per cent, assuming that an average job occupies 15 K words of store.

6.6.  "*Message buffer.*" Consider a system in which a sequence of jobs is executed by two processors in series. (See Fig. E6.6.)

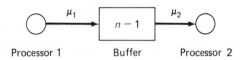

**Fig. E6.6.**

Service times are exponential with means of $1/\mu_1$ and $1/\mu_2$, respectively. The processors are connected by a buffer which can hold a maximum of $n - 1$ partially completed jobs. When the buffer is full, processor 1 is delayed until processor 2 removes another job from it. We define the performance measure $R$ as the ratio of the throughput of jobs with and without buffering. (If no buffer is used, processor 1 is always forced to wait while processor 2 completes a job, and vice versa.) Use the result of Exercise 6.4 to show that

$$
R = \begin{cases} (1 + \rho)\dfrac{1 - \rho^n}{1 - \rho^{n+1}} & \rho \neq 1 \\[3mm] 2\dfrac{n}{n + 1} & \rho = 1 \end{cases} \qquad \text{where } \rho = \dfrac{\mu_1}{\mu_2}
$$

**6.7.** Consider a *spooling system* in which a central processor is connected to a line printer by a buffer on a backing store. Use the result of Exercise 6.6 to determine the *buffer capacity* necessary to maintain a throughput that is 97 per cent of the maximum achievable, assuming that execution and printing times are exponential with means 1 and 0.5 min. What is the value of the performance measure $R$?

**6.8.** The *shortest job next* algorithm minimizes the average response time. Prove this for a batch of $n$ jobs which arrive at the same time with service times

$$
t_1 \leqslant t_2 \leqslant \ldots \leqslant t_n
$$

ignoring further arrivals.

**6.9.** Design and carry out a simulation experiment which measures the effect of *inaccurate user estimates* of service times on the average waiting times in a non-preemptive queuing system with a single processor using the *shortest job next* algorithm.

**6.10.** Use the result of Exercise 6.2 to *simulate* the *highest response ratio next* algorithm by a sequential program. Test the accuracy of the approximations, equations (6.27) and (6.28), for various values of $\rho$, using the constants $a = 0.11$, $b = 0.21$, and $c = 1.88$. (*Hint*: To achieve a steady state equilibrium, the program must simulate a reasonable number of jobs before measurements are collected.)

**6.11.** (S. Lauesen) "*Minimax response ratio scheduling.*" In a non-preemptive single processor system, the queue contains three jobs at time $t$ immediately after the completion of a job. These jobs arrived at times $t_1$, $t_2$, and $t_3$ with estimated run times $r_1$, $r_2$, and $r_3$. Fig. E6.11 shows the linear increase of their response ratios in time.

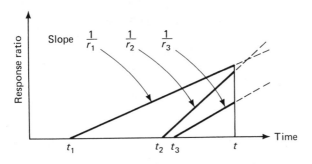

**Fig. E6.11.**

Use this example to find a variant of *response ratio scheduling* which minimizes the maximum response ratio for a given batch of jobs ignoring further arrivals. (*Hint*: Decide first which job to schedule as the last one.)

6.12. Compare the performance of the *minimax response ratio* algorithm of Exercise 6.11 to the *highest response ratio next* algorithm by a simulation similar to the one used to solve Exercise 6.10.

6.13. (P. Mondrup) Prove that the *minimax response ratio* algorithm of Exercise 6.11 minimizes the maximum response ratio for a given batch of jobs. (*Hint*: Focus attention on the job which will achieve the highest response ratio and all jobs executed before it. Consider the same subset of jobs scheduled in any other order and observe the response ratio of the job which is executed as the last one among them. Notice that this subset may now be mixed with other jobs from the total set.)

6.14. "*Guaranteed response ratio scheduling.*" How can the algorithm of Exercise 6.11 be used to implement a non-preemptive system that guarantees that response ratios never exceed a given limit? (*Hint*: Upon arrival of a job, the system must decide whether to accept the job or reject it.)

6.15 The algorithm in Exercise 6.14 tends to be *unfair* to *very short jobs*. Explain why and suggest a remedy.

6.16 "*Non-preemptive foreground-background scheduling.*" In a non-preemptive queuing system with a single processor, jobs with service times below a threshold $t$ enter a *foreground queue*, while longer jobs enter a *background queue*. Each queue is served in *first-come first-served* order, but a job in the background queue is only started when the foreground queue is empty. Arrivals in both queues are Poisson processes. The overall service time distribution $F(x)$ can be arbitrary. The arrival rate of all jobs is denoted $\lambda$. Show that the average waiting times, $W1$ and $W2$, for foreground and background jobs are

$$W1 = \frac{W_0}{1 - \rho_t} \quad \text{and} \quad W2 = \frac{W1}{1 - \rho}$$

where $\rho$, $W_0$, and $\rho_t$ are given by equations (6.14), (6.17), and (6.25), respectively. (*Hint*: Use the conservation law.)

**6.17.** In the *foreground-background* system of Exercise 6.16, the *threshold* $t$ must be chosen such that the average waiting time $W1$ in the foreground queue does not exceed a given limit $W_{max}$ for utilization factors $\rho \leqslant 1$.

(a) Show that for hyperexponential service times, $t$ is defined by the relation

$$G(t) \leqslant 1 - \frac{d}{\mu W_{max}}$$

where $\frac{1}{\mu}$ and $\rho$ are the mean service time and utilization factor for all jobs, while $G(t)$ and $d$ are defined by equations (6.13) and (6.21).

(b) Compute $t$, $W1$, and $W2$ for the case in which $\frac{1}{\mu} = 1$ min, $d = 2.75$, $\rho = 0.93$, and $W_{max} = 5$ min.

**6.18.** (L. Kleinrock) *"Process sharing."* A processor is multiplexed at infinite speed among all jobs present in a queuing system with no overhead. (This is an idealized model of round-robin scheduling among jobs kept in an internal store using time quanta that are very small compared to the mean service time.) Show that for Poisson input from an infinite source with exponential service times, the mean response time of a job with a service time $t$ is given by:

$$R_t = \frac{t}{1 - \rho}$$

(*Hint*: Consider the mean workload $U$ in the system upon arrival of the given job.)

**6.19.** (L. Kleinrock) *"Selfish round robin."* In a queuing system, new jobs must wait for a while before being served. While a job waits, its priority increases linearly with time from zero at a rate $\alpha$. A job waits until its priority reaches the priority of the jobs in service; then, it begins to share the processor equally with other jobs in service while its priority continues to increase at a slower rate $\beta$. The algorithm is called "selfish" because the jobs in service try (in vain) to monopolize the processor by increasing their priority continuously. Use Fig. E6.19 to show that the mean response time $R_t$ for a job of service time $t$ is given by:

$$R_t = \frac{\frac{1}{\mu}}{1 - \rho} + \frac{t - \frac{1}{\mu}}{1 - \rho'}$$

where

$$\rho = \frac{\lambda}{\mu} \qquad \rho' = \rho\left(1 - \frac{\beta}{\alpha}\right) \qquad 0 \leqslant \beta \leqslant \alpha$$

assuming that arrival and service times are exponentially distributed with means $1/\lambda$, and $1/\mu$, respectively. (*Hint*: Consider the total system and the two subsystems separately.)

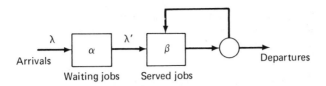

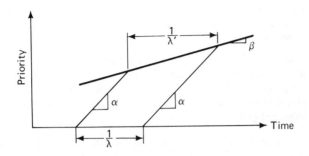

**Fig. E6.19.**

**6.20.** (E. G. Coffman and L. Kleinrock) *"Shortest elapsed time next."* A processor is multiplexed at infinite speed among all jobs in a queuing system according to the rule *shortest elapsed time next.* Arrival and service times are exponential with means $1/\lambda$ and $1/\mu$. Show that the mean response time $R_t$ for a job with service time $t$ is given by

$$R_t = \frac{W_0^t}{(1 - \rho_t)^2} + \frac{t}{1 - \rho_t}$$

where

$$\rho_t = \int_0^t \lambda x \, dF(x)$$

$$W_0^t = \tfrac{1}{2} \int_0^t \lambda \, x^2 \, dF(x)$$

$$F(x) = \begin{cases} 1 - e^{-\mu x} & 0 \leqslant x < t \\ 1 & t \leqslant x < \infty \end{cases}$$

(*Hint*: A job of service time $t$ will be delayed by all jobs present upon its arrival (including the one in service) and by all jobs arriving while it is in the system, until these jobs have either been completed or have been served for a maximum period $t$ each.)

**6.21.** A queuing system uses the scheduling algorithm *shortest elapsed time next* in a *foreground queue.* Jobs that have received service for a period $T$ enter a *background queue* in which they are served to completion in *first-come, first-served* order in periods when the foreground queue is empty. Use the method of solution from Exercise 6.20 to find the mean response time $R_t$ of long running jobs $(t > T)$.

**6.22.** A university computing center is shared by users from different departments. Suggest a scheduling algorithm that guarantees a certain fraction of the processor time to each department on a weekly basis. What priority rules would you suggest for competing users from one or more departments as long as none of them have exceeded their weekly quota?

**6.23.** An interactive system using *round-robin* scheduling and *swapping* tries to give guaranteed response to trivial requests as follows: After completing a round-robin cycle among all active jobs, the system determines the quantum for the next cycle by dividing a maximum response time by the number of jobs requiring service. Is this a practical policy?

**6.24.** Simulations showed that a multi-queue algorithm would reduce the swap time from 40 to 20 per cent in the *SDC Q-32* system. When it was implemented, this did indeed happen, but no corresponding increase of processor utilization was observed. Where would you expect to find the reason for this and how would you try to improve the processor utilization?

**6.25.** In a preemptive queuing system with a single processor using *foreground-background* scheduling, long jobs can experience indefinite waiting times when the system is heavily used for conversational access. Propose a scheduling algorithm which gives rapid response to a moderate number of conversational users and at the same time guarantees a certain fraction of the processor time to background jobs.

**6.26.** Suggest a scheduling algorithm which will share a single processor among three classes of jobs as proposed in Section 1.4.1:

   (1) Conversational editing and preparation of jobs

   (2) Non-interactive scheduling of small jobs with fast response

   (3) Non-interactive scheduling of large jobs

with response times of the order of seconds, minutes, and hours, respectively. The system may deny service to additional users when it is heavily loaded.

# ANSWERS

## CHAPTER 1

**1.2.** (a) The time required to execute a batch is $M + N * T$, and the cost of using the processor for this amount of time and letting $N$ users wait meanwhile is $(M + N * T) * (S + N * W)$. So the total cost of service time and waiting time per customer is

$$C = (M + N * T) * (S + N * W)/N$$

The result follows by setting $\frac{dC}{dN} = 0$.
(b) 60¢/hour(!)

**1.3.** Since no program (including the operating system) could write into a protected location, an operating system was forced to place its *variables* in *unprotected* locations.

**1.4.** Notice that *job scheduling* and *compiler loading* account for 20 per cent of the execution phase. This can virtually be eliminated by designing the compiler to compile and execute a sequence of programs (rather than one) each time the compiler is scheduled and loaded. Excellent examples are the Fortran compilers developed at Purdue University (PUFFT) and the University of Waterloo (WATFOR).

**1.5.** The countermeasure taken was to cancel any job request which had been waiting for more than one hour without being honored.

**1.7.** The problem was solved in the *Atlas* system by postponing the execution of a job until all its tapes were mounted.

**1.9.** The solution used in *CTSS* is to use the same base address for all jobs in the internal store; but, instead of removing a job completely from the internal store at the end of its time slice, the system only transfers as much of it to the backing store as is required to make room for the next job.

**1.10.** Divide the internal store into two areas and execute a job in one area while another job is being swapped into the other area. This is called *overlapped swapping and execution*.

**1.11.** It requires *program relocation* by means of base and limit registers. This is easily seen if you consider overlapped swapping and execution of an odd number of jobs in two store areas.

**1.12.** An effective solution is to keep a single copy of the most frequently used procedures for file manipulation, program input, and editing permanently (or semi-permanently) in the internal store and thus enable user programs to call them directly. If the system does not distinguish between utility programs and user programs, it will spend a considerable amount of time swapping multiple copies of the former for different users.

**1.13.** Permit user computations to take input from and deliver output to the file system and permit users to input and output these data at terminals at their own convenience before and after execution.

**1.14.** In the *Titan supervisor*, each user has his own catalog describing the names and locations of files owned by him. The locations of *user catalogs* are defined in a *master catalog* (Fraser, 1971). In the *Multics* system, this idea is generalized to a *tree* of catalogs with files as leaves. This enables user groups to establish local nomenclature within project components in a hierarchal manner (Daley, 1965).

**1.17.** Copy only those files which have been changed since the previous copy operation.

**1.20.** In the *Titan supervisor*, passwords quoted by users are scrambled by an algorithm and compared with a list of scrambled passwords. The scrambling algorithm is not kept secret since there is no economical way of performing the reverse operation.

**1.21.** When a user successfully quotes a password to the *Titan supervisor*, he is told the date and time at which it was last quoted. If he suspects an infringement, he can immediately choose another password.

# CHAPTER 3

**3.1.**

```
var last, this, next: T;
if more then
begin
  input(next);
  if more then
  begin
    this:= next;
    cobegin
      process(this); input(next);
    coend
    while more do
```

```
            begin
              last:= this; this:= next;
              cobegin
                output(last); process(this); input(next);
              coend
            end
            output(this);
          end
          process(next);
          output(next);
        end
```

3.2.    Let $I$, $P$, and $O$ denote the execution times of the input, processing, and output operations. Then we have

$$f = \frac{I + P + O}{max(I, P, O)} \leqslant 3$$

3.3.

(1)  Notice that each process only changes its own variable *outside* and that

*outside1* implies $P1$ *outside* &
*outside2* implies $P2$ *outside*

Since process $P1$ only enters its critical region when *outside2* holds (and vice versa for $P2$), mutual exclusion is guaranteed.

(2)  The variable *turn* is only changed at the end of a critical region; it can therefore be regarded as a constant when both processes are trying to enter their critical regions at the same time.

If *turn* = 1, then process $P1$ can only cycle in the statement

```
        repeat
          if outside2 then exit enter;
        until turn = 2;
```

and process $P2$ can only cycle in the statement

```
        repeat until turn = 2;
```

But the latter implies that *outside2* holds, so $P1$ will enter its region. A similar argument can be made when *turn* = 2.

(3)  If $P1$ is stopped outside its critical region, we have

*outside1*

This will immediately permit process *P2* to enter its critical region independent of the value of *turn*.

3.4.    Before process *i* enters its critical region, we have

$$\text{not } turn(i)$$

If *free* = *true*, we have after an exchange operation:

$$\text{not } free \text{ \& } turn(i)$$

and process *i* will enter its critical region. However, if *free* = *false*, we have after an exchange operation:

$$\text{not } free \text{ \& not } turn(i)$$

and process *i* will not enter its critical region. So at most one process at a time can be inside its critical region. And, since exchange operations are executed one at a time, the decision as to which process should enter its critical region first cannot be delayed indefinitely. Whether or not the scheduling of critical regions will be fair depends entirely on the hardware implementation of exchange operations and on the scheduling policy used to execute concurrent processes. The disadvantage of the solution is that it uses the *busy form of waiting*.

3.5.    The notation

$$\textbf{var } v\text{: } \textbf{pool } max \textbf{ of } T;$$
$$b\text{: } \textbf{sequence of } v;$$
$$s, t\text{: } \textbf{ref } v;$$

declares (1) a *pool v* consisting of a maximum number of message elements of type *T*; (2) a *sequence b* of such elements sent by one process to another; and (3) two *references, s* and *t*, to message elements.

An element is reserved, produced, and sent by a process *P* as follows:

> *reserve(s)*;
> **with** *s* **do** *produce element*;
> *send(s, b)*;

An element is received, consumed, and released by a process *Q* as follows:

> *receive(t, b)*;
> **with** *t* **do** *consume element*;
> *release(t)*;

As soon as an element is sent or released, the reference to it is made undefined.

The compiler will check that concurrent processes use disjoint sets of reference variables; and the compiler's run-time system will check that references are defined when they are used.

3.6.  If a receiver is waiting for a full buffer element inside a critical region, a sender cannot enter its critical region and signal the availability of a full buffer element. So the solution can lead to a *deadlock*.

3.7.  The *buffer* is declared to be an array of shared elements of type $T$. Another array defines the number of input elements *available* to each process. Each process keeps track of the index $j$ of the buffer element it is referring to at the moment.

```
var buffer: array 0. .max-1 of shared T;
    available: shared array 0. .n-1 of 0. .max;

"Initialization"
var k: 1. .n-1;
region available do
begin
  available(0):= max;
  for every k do available(k):= 0;
end

"Process i"
var j: 0. .max-1; succ: 0. .n-1;
begin
  j:= 0; succ:= (i + 1) mod n;
  repeat
    region available do
    await available(i) > 0;
    region buffer(j) do consume element;
    region available do
    begin
      available(i):= available(i) - 1;
      available(succ):= available(succ) + 1;
    end
    j:= (j + 1) mod max;
  forever
end
```

3.8.  A deadlock is a situation in which

$$P0 \text{ waits for } Pn-1 \ \&$$
$$P1 \text{ waits for } P0 \ \&$$
$$\cdots$$
$$Pn-1 \text{ waits for } Pn-2$$

because

$$available(0) = 0 \ \&$$
$$available(1) = 0 \ \&$$
$$. . . . .$$
$$available(n-1) = 0$$

But if $max > 0$, this condition cannot hold since the critical regions satisfy the following invariant:

$$\sum_{i=0}^{n-1} available(i) = max$$

**3.10.** Let $rr$ and $rw$ denote the number of *running readers* and *running writers*. Evidently, we have

(1) $\qquad\qquad\qquad 0 \leqslant rr \ \& \ 0 \leqslant rw$

(2) $\qquad\qquad\qquad 0 \leqslant waits(s) \leqslant signals(s) + 1$

Now suppose $rr$ readers and $rw$ writers are using the resource simultaneously. Then we also have

(3) $\qquad waits(s) - signals(s) = $ **if** $rr > 0$ **then** $rw + 1$ **else** $rw$

since one *wait* and one *signal* operation at most are executed for each group of running readers which use the resource for a continuous period of time. From this we find the following *invariant*:

$$0 \leqslant rr \ \& \ 0 \leqslant rw \ \& \ (\text{if } rr > 0 \text{ then } rw + 1 \text{ else } rw) \leqslant 1$$

*case 1:*
    If $rr > 0$ then $rw = 0$.
*case 2:*
    If $rr = 0$ then $0 \leqslant rw \leqslant 1$.
Q. E. D.

**3.11.** This is a variant of the readers and writers problem (Algorithm 3.10). No priority is specified for southern and northern cars, but they must exclude each other in time on the bridge:

        **var** *bridge*: **shared record** *southern, northern*: *integer* **end**
                "*Initially both zero*"

      "*southern car*"
      **begin**
        **region** *bridge* **do**

```
begin
  await northern = 0;
  southern:= southern + 1;
end
cross bridge;
region bridge do
  southern:= southern - 1;
end
```

The algorithm for a northern car is symmetrical.

3.12. The data structure represents the following for cars coming from both directions: The number of cars *waiting* to cross the bridge; the number of cars *crossing* the bridge; and the number of cars which have entered the bridge *ahead* of waiting cars coming from the opposite direction.

```
type direction = record
                   waiting, crossing, ahead: integer;
                 end
                 "Initially all zero"

var bridge: shared record
                   southern, northern: direction;
                 end

"southern car"
begin
  region bridge do
  with southern do
  begin
    waiting:= waiting + 1;
    await northern.crossing = 0 & ahead < 10;
    waiting:= waiting - 1;
    crossing:= crossing + 1;
    if northern.waiting > 0 then
    ahead:= ahead + 1;
  end
  cross bridge;
  region bridge do
  with southern do
  begin
    crossing:= crossing - 1;
    if crossing = 0 then
    northern.ahead = 0;
  end
end
```

**3.13.** A straightforward (but not too efficient) implementation is the following:

```
type I = 1. .n;
var v: shared record
                free:boolean;
                waiting: array I of boolean;
                grant: array I of event v;
            end

procedure reserve(i: I);
region v do
begin
  if free then
  free:= false else
  begin
    waiting(i):= true;
    await(grant(i));
  end
end

procedure release;
var i: I;
region v do
label done
begin
  for every i do
  if waiting(i) then
  begin
    waiting(i):= false;
    cause(grant(i));
    exit done
  end
  free:= true;
end
```

**3.14.** No, it is not. External priorities that only reflect the attitude of management toward users cannot prevent *deadlocks*. They can be used to determine when computations should be started, but during execution, additional rules must be used, as is explained in Sections 2.6 and 3.5.

**3.15.** A deadlock is a state in which all resource units are reserved while one or more processes are waiting indefinitely for more units. But, if all 4 units are reserved, at least one process has acquired 2 units. Consequently, that process will be able to complete its work and release both units, thus enabling another process to continue.

**3.16.** Using the terminology of Section 2.6.1 we have

$$(1) \ \sum_{1}^{n} need(i) = \sum_{1}^{n} claim(i) + \sum_{1}^{n} loan(i) < m + n$$

In a deadlock situation, all resource units are reserved:

$$(2) \ \sum_{1}^{n} loan(i) = m$$

and some processes are waiting for more units indefinitely. But from (1) and (2), we find

$$(3) \ \sum_{1}^{n} claim(i) < n$$

This means that at least one process $j$ has acquired all its resources ($claim(j) = 0$) and will be able to complete its task and release all its resources again, thus ensuring further progress in the system. So a deadlock cannot occur.

3.19. Deadlock is avoided by ensuring that a hungry philosopher picks up *both* forks at the same time (instead of one at a time). A shared array defines the number of unused forks next to each plate; each array element is initially equal to 2 and can assume the values 0, 1, or 2.

```
var forks: shared array 0. .4 of 0. .2;

procedure philosopher(i: 0. .4);
var left, right: 0. .4;
begin
  left:= (i - 1) mod 5;
  right:= (i + 1) mod 5;
  repeat
    think;
    region forks do
    begin
      await forks(i) = 2;
      forks(left):= forks(left) - 1;
      forks(right):= forks(right) - 1;
    end
    eat;
    region forks do
    begin
      forks(left):= forks(left) + 1;
      forks(right):= forks(right) + 1;
    end
  forever
end
```

**3.20.** This program leads to a *deadlock* when all philosophers pick up their left forks at the same time and wait for their right forks to become available. They will then starve to death.

**3.21.** It is possible for two non-adjacent philosophers to alternate in such a manner that at any moment at least one of them is eating. Thus, they manage to prevent the philosopher between them from ever eating.

**3.22.** The philosophers can starve while repeatedly picking up and putting down their left forks in perfect unison.

**3.23.** A *deadlock* occurs when process $I$ has filled the drum with input ($i = max$) and process $I$ is waiting to transfer more input to the drum, while process $P$ is waiting to transfer more output to the drum and process $O$ is waiting to transfer more output from the drum.

**3.24.** Reserve a minimum number of pages (called *reso*) permanently for output buffering, but permit the number of output pages to exceed this limit when drum space is available. The resource constraints now become:

$$i + o \leqslant max$$

$$i \leqslant max - reso$$

where

$$0 < reso < max$$

This is illustrated by Fig. A3.24.

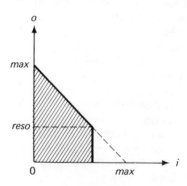

Fig. A3.24.

If process $P$ is waiting to deliver output on the drum, process $O$ will eventually consume all previous output and make at least *reso* pages available for further output, thus enabling $P$ to continue. So $P$ cannot be delayed indefinitely by $O$. Process $I$ can be delayed if the drum is full of input/output; but sooner or later, all previous input will be consumed by $P$ and the corresponding output will be consumed by $O$, thus enabling $I$ to continue.

**3.25.** Resource constraints:

(a) $\qquad\qquad i + o + p \leqslant max$

(b) $\qquad\qquad i + o \quad\ \leqslant max - resp$

(c) $\qquad\qquad i + p \quad\ \leqslant max - reso$

(d) $\qquad\qquad i \qquad\ \leqslant max - (reso + resp)$

See also Fig. A3.25.

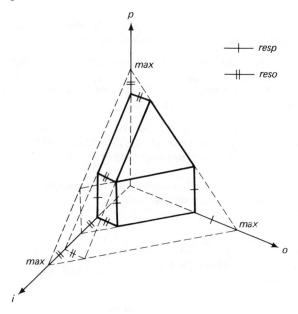

**Fig. A3.25.**

Typical values used in *THE* multiprogramming system are $max = 1000$, $resp = 744$, and $reso = 64$.

**3.26.** The effects of the state transitions are the following:

(1) $\qquad\qquad i := i + 1$

(2) $\qquad\qquad i := i - 1; \quad p := p + 1$

(3) $\qquad\qquad p := p - 1; o := o + 1$

(4) $\qquad\qquad o := o - 1$

(5) $\qquad\qquad p := p + 1$

(6) $\qquad\qquad p := p - 1$

By examining the resource constraints illustrated in the solution to Exercise 3.25, we see the following:

(6) *Procedure returns* can take place immediately since they only release resources.

(5) *Procedure calls* may exhaust the drum ($p = max - reso$) and lead to deadlock.

(4) *Output consumption* can take place immediately after output becomes available.

(3) *Output production* can be delayed temporarily until all previous output has been consumed and made at least *reso* pages available for further output.

(2) *Input consumption* can take place immediately after input becomes available.
So input/output consumption will continue as long as the user processes do not deadlock themselves by procedure calls.

(1) *Input production* can be delayed until all previous input and the corresponding output has been consumed. At this point, when $i = o = 0$, input can be produced provided the user processes have not exhausted the drum ($p < max - reso$).
*Conclusion*: The uncontrolled amount of storage assigned to the user processes is the only possible source of a storage deadlock.

3.27.

```
const reso = desired value;
type N = 1..max;
var v: shared record
            drum: array N of page;
            input, output, empty: sequence of N;
            i, o: 0..max;
            current: N;
        end
"Initially all pages are empty and i = o = 0"

procedure send input(p: page);
region v do
begin
  await i + o < max & i < max - reso;
  get(current, empty);
  drum(current):= p;
  put(current, input);
  i:= i + 1;
end

procedure receive input(var p: page);
region v do
```

```
begin
  await i > 0;
  get(current, input);
  p:= drum(current);
  put(current, empty);
  i:= i - 1;
end
```

The procedures *send output* and *receive output* await the holding of $i + o < max$ and $o > 0$, respectively. Apart from that, they are quite similar to *send input* and *receive input*.

# CHAPTER 4

4.1. In *THE* multiprogramming system, a process is given a higher priority of execution while it is within a critical region.

4.2. The system must include a *clock* that measures time in units comparable to the access time of the internal store. The procedure *initiate process* must set the elapsed processor time for a new child process to zero; the procedure *terminate process* must add the amount used by the calling process to that used by its parent process. When a running process is *entered* in a queue, the interval that has elapsed since it was last *continued* must be added to its elapsed processor time.

4.3. Processor time spent on an interrupt that terminates an action (for example, input/output) started by a particular process ought to be charged to that process. But this fairness may be expensive since it increases the overhead at the lowest level of scheduling. A simpler method is to let the currently running process pay for all interrupts which occur while it is running and hope that in the long run the cost will be evenly distributed among all processes.

4.4. This technique is based on the assumption that an interrupted process $A$ will continue to run after the response to an interrupt. But, in general, an interrupt may cause the basic monitor to preempt a process $A$ in favor of another process, $B$. It is now necessary to copy the execution state of process $A$ from the locations associated with the interrupt to the process description associated with $A$. The machine might as well have stored them there in the first place.

4.5.

```
var ready: sequence of P;

procedure preempt process;
var candidate: P;
region v do
begin
  put(process, ready);
  get(candidate, ready);
  continue(candidate);
end
```

**4.6.**

```
type process description = record
                    . . . . .
                  urgent: boolean;
               end
   "Initially, urgent is false; it is true within critical regions"


var ready: record
            foreground, background: sequence of P;
          end
      "Urgent processes enter the foreground queue;
      other processes enter the background queue"


procedure preempt process;
var candidate: P;
region v do
begin
  with ready do
  begin
    if process table(process).urgent then
    put(process, foreground) else
    put(process, background);
    if not empty(foreground) then
    get(candidate, foreground) else
    get(candidate, background);
  end
  continue(candidate);
end
```

**4.7.**

```
type Q = record
          level: array N of sequence of T;
          top: N;
          waiting: integer;
        end
      "Initially all levels are empty and waiting = 0"


procedure enter(t: T; p: N; var q: Q);
begin
  with q do
  begin
    put(t, level(p));
    if waiting = 0 then top:= p else
    if p < top then top:= p;
```

```
        waiting:= waiting + 1;
    end
end

procedure remove(var t: T; p: N; q: Q);
begin
    with q do
    begin
        get(t, level(top)); p:= top;
        waiting:= waiting - 1;
        if waiting > 0 then
        while empty(top) do top:= top + 1;
    end
end
```

4.8.  The following technique was used to test the *RC 4000* multiprogramming system:
The procedures

$$enter(process, queue) \quad continue(process)$$

will stop processor multiplexing temporarily and print one or two integers identify-
ing the process and the queue involved.
To test processor multiplexing, the system is initialized with two processes, *A* and
*B*:

> **cobegin**
> "*A*" **repeat forever**
> "*B*" **repeat forever**
> **coend**

and the timer is replaced with an interrupt key. Assuming that the short-term
scheduling algorithm is round-robin, the test output will have the following
format (shown here in symbolic form to make it more readable):

>      continue *A*
> \*  enter *A*, *ready queue*
>      continue *B*
> \*  enter *B*, *ready queue*
>      continue *A*
>      . . . . .

The lines marked \* are the responses to timer interrupts simulated by pushing the
interrupt key.
To test the *wait* and *signal* operations, the system is started with two processes, *C*
and *D*, in the *ready queue* (in that order):

```
var v: shared boolean; i: integer;
cobegin
  "C" begin
        region v do
        for i:= 1 to some limit do;
          . . . . .
      end
  "D" begin
        region v do . . . ;
          . . . . .
      end
coend
```

The test output will appear as follows:

|   | | |
|---|---|---|
| | continue C | "C enters its region" |
| * | enter C, ready queue | "C preempted within its region" |
| | continue D | |
| | enter D, semaphore queue | "D waiting to enter its region" |
| | continue C | |
| | enter D, ready queue | "C leaves its region" |
| * | enter C, ready queue | "C preempted outside its region" |
| | continue D | "D enters its region" |

. . . . .

and so on. (See also Brinch Hansen, 1973.)

4.9.

```
var y, a, b, c, d, e, f, g, h, i: integer;
begin
  cobegin
    g:= a + b;
    h:= c - d;
    i:= e * f;
  coend
  y:= g/h + i;
end
```

The execution times of the sequential and concurrent versions of the statement are 51 and 1542 μsec, respectively (!).

# CHAPTER 5

5.2.  Let s and h denote the average number of segments and holes, respectively. The probability that a given segment is followed by a hole in the store (and not by another segment) is $\frac{1}{2}$ because deletions and creations are equally probable in equilibrium. So with s segments in store, the average number of holes h must be

$s/2$. It is intuitively reasonable that the number of holes must be less than the number of segments because neighboring segments can be combined into a single hole upon deletion.

5.3.  It is advantageous to represent the state of the store by a list of holes because, on the average, it will only be half as long as a list of segments.

5.4.  (a) Consider a store of $c$ words immediately after compacting when the hole consists of $f c$ words. In equilibrium, an average segment of $s$ words is deleted and another one is created every $t$ references. So the boundary moves at the speed of $s/t$ words per reference. Consequently, it crosses the hole after $f c t/s$ references. At this point, $(1 - f)c$ words must be compacted; this requires at least $2(1 - f)c$ references. So the fraction of time spent on compacting is

$$F \geqslant \frac{2(1 - f)c}{2(1 - f)c + f c t/s}$$

which reduces to the equation given.

(b) $F = 0.29$.

5.5.  In the *GIER Algol* system, stack pages remain fixed in the internal store, whereas program pages are transferred to and from a drum on demand.

5.6.  Extend the given program $P$ with the following data structure

var $A$: **array** 1. .*max* **of**
        **array** 1. .*page length* **of** *integer*:

and execute it as the only process on the machine. The amount of store available to program $P$ itself can be changed by means of the constant *max*.

5.8.  9 and 10 page transfers, respectively.

5.10. Idle processor time can also be caused by processes waiting for page transfers. In that case, the modified algorithm will soon cause *thrashing* by increasing the computational workload.

5.11. In *THE* multiprogramming system, all frames pass the access heads once, in order of (cyclically) increasing frame number during each revolution. (See Fig. A5.11.)

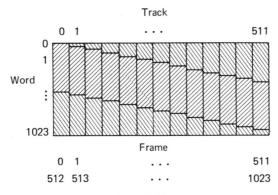

Fig. A5.11.

The track number $t$ and the word number $w$ of the beginning of frame number $f$ are defined as follows:

$$t := f \bmod 512 \qquad w := f$$

where

$$0 \leqslant f \leqslant 1023$$

**5.12.** From the solution to Exercise 3.25, we find that the dangerous boundaries are $i = max - (reso + resp)$ and $i + p = max - reso$. Here, further *input production* ($i := i + 1$) depends on *input consumption* ($i := i - 1$; $p := p + 1$) and *procedure returns* ($p := p - 1$); in short, it depends on activities within user processes, whereas *output consumption* ($o := o - 1$) is of no help. Unfortunately, it is also possible that user processes will do exactly the opposite and lead the system right into a deadlock by an excessive number of *procedure calls* ($p := p + 1$). A possible solution is to use *load control*, that is, to try to stay away from these boundaries and prevent the scheduling of further computations if the system comes close to them. In *THE* multiprogramming system, the operator is notified of a tight store situation and is expected to act accordingly.

**5.13.** (a) *sequential computations*: The machine can be used to implement a *stack* not exceeding 16 K words efficiently. This is satisfactory for a large class of sequential programs.
(b) *concurrent computations*: If the machine is used to implement *nested segments*, it would seem to be a serious limitation that a parent process can only assign a segment to a child process that is at least 2 K words (= 1 page) smaller than its own segment. It is possible, however, to implement a general *tree-structured stack* of non-nested segments by using the page registers to define that (linear) part of the stack which is accessible to the currently running process. But the requirement that each process be assigned at least 2 K words of internal store will certainly limit the usefulness of concurrent statements. One can therefore conclude that this machine is not very practical for concurrent computations. Nevertheless, it has been used for that purpose (Lampson, 1966).
(c) *demand paging*: It is also doubtful that the machine is adequate for this purpose considering that working sets are restricted to eight pages. Most programs would need all eight pages in the internal store to run efficiently.

**5.15.** The probability that $n$ independent jobs are waiting for input/output at the same time is $p^n$, so we have

$$\eta = 1 - p^n$$

or

$$p = (1 - \eta)^{1/n}$$

For $n = 2$ and $\eta = 0.36$, we find $p = 0.8$. In other words, the average job waits for input/output 80 per cent of the time.

**5.16.** Since $\eta = 1 - p^n$ we have

$$n = \frac{ln(1 - \eta)}{ln\ p}$$

Using $\eta = 0.9$ and $p = 0.8$, we find $n = 10$. So we need $10 * 1 + 25 * 10 = 260$ K words.

**5.17.** If all jobs wait, both processors are idle; the probability of this is $p^n$. And, if all jobs except one wait, one processor is idle; the probability of this is $n\ p^{n-1}(1 - p)$. So the utilization of each processor is

$$\eta = 1 - (p^n + n\ p^{n-1}(1 - p)/2)$$

For $n = 2$ and $p = 0.8$, we find $\eta = 0.2$.

## CHAPTER 6

**6.2.** The trick is to look upon $F(x)$ as a mixture of two exponential distributions

$$F(x) = a(1 - e^{-b\ x}) + (1 - a)(1 - e^{-c\ x})$$

from which jobs are chosen with probabilities $a$ and $1 - a$. This leads to the following statement:

> **var** $x$: *real*;
> **if** *random* $< a$ **then** $x := -ln(random)/b$
> **else** $x := -ln(random)/c$;

**6.4.** The relations between the steady state probabilities are:

$$p_0 = p_0(1 - \lambda dt) + p_1 \mu dt$$

$$p_j = p_{j-1}\lambda dt + p_j(1 - (\lambda + \mu)dt) + p_{j+1}\mu dt \qquad (0 < j < n)$$

$$p_n = p_{n-1}\lambda dt + p_n(1 - \mu dt)$$

The middle equation shows that, during a time interval $dt$, the state $j$ can be entered either: (1) from the state $j - 1$, after an arrival; (2) from the state $j$, if no arrival or departure occurs; or (3) from the state $j + 1$, after a departure. By solving these equations, we find

$$p_j = \rho^j p_0 \qquad (0 \leqslant j \leqslant n)$$

and, since the sum of the probabilities is one, we have

$$p_0 = \frac{1-\rho}{1-\rho^{n+1}}$$

From this, the result for $p_n$ follows immediately.

**6.5.** For $\rho = 0.93$ and $n = 28$, we have $p_n = 0.01$. The store capacity needed is $28 * 15 = 420$ K words.

**6.6.** The input rate to the buffer is $\mu_1$ when it is not full so the average input rate is

$$\mu_1(1-p_n)$$

In a steady state, this is equal to the average output rate.
Without a buffer, the service rate is

$$\frac{1}{\frac{1}{\mu_1}+\frac{1}{\mu_2}} = \frac{\mu_1}{1+\rho}$$

So we find

$$R = (1+\rho)(1-p_n) \quad \text{for } \rho \neq 1$$

The result for $\rho = 1$ follows by using L'Hospital's rule.

**6.7.** Let $\frac{1}{\mu_1}$ and $\frac{1}{\mu_2}$ denote the means of execution and printing times, respectively. The maximum throughput is $\mu_1$ (for an infinite buffer). If the buffer capacity is $n - 1$, the throughput is $\mu_1(1-p_n)$. For $\rho = 0.5$ and $n = 4$, we find $p_n = 0.03$ and $R = 1.45$.

**6.8.** $n$ users must wait for the execution of job 1; $n - 1$ users must wait for the execution of job 2; and so on. Therefore, the average response time is

$$(n * t_1 + (n-1) * t_2 + \ldots + t_n)/n$$

If we make any changes in this schedule, for example by exchanging jobs $j$ and $k$ (where $j < k$), the average response time is increased by the amount

$$(k-j) * (t_k - t_j)/n \geqslant 0$$

In other words, the average response time can only increase if the *shortest job next* algorithm is not used.

**6.9.** One method described by Conway, Maxwell, and Miller (1967) is to generate actual processing times $t$ (for example, as proposed in Exercise 6.2) and multiply them by a scaled random number to obtain estimated processing times that are uniformly distributed between $(1-p)t$ and $(1+p)t$ where $p$ is the maximum error of estimates.

**6.11.** First, the scheduler computes the response ratios at time $t + r_1 + r_2 + r_3$, when all

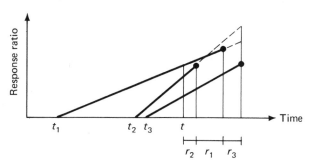

**Fig. A6.11.**

three jobs will have been finished (see Fig. A6.11). At that time, job 3 will have the smallest response ratio of the three; so the scheduler decides to execute this job last and proceeds to examine jobs 1 and 2 at time $t + r_1 + r_2$, when they will both be finished. Here the response ratio of job 1 is the smaller, and consequently, job 2 is selected for service at time $t$. This algorithm is repeated each time a job is completed to take new arrivals into account. Note that this algorithm is not quite the same as *highest response ratio next*: The latter would schedule job 1 at time $t$. Intuitively, it is clear that the present algorithm attempts to minimize the maximum response ratio by consistently postponing those jobs that will suffer the least increase of their response ratios.

6.13. Consider the queue at time $t$ immediately after a departure and ignore further arrivals. The waiting jobs are numbered 1 to $n$ in the order in which they will be scheduled:

| job: | 1 | 2 | ... | $i$ | ... | $n$ |
|------|------|------|------|------|------|------|
| arrival time: | $t_1$ | $t_2$ | ..... | $t_i$ | ... | $t_n$ |
| service time: | $r_1$ | $r_2$ | ... | $r_i$ | ... | $r_n$ |

Among these we assume that job $i$ will reach the highest response ratio before its departure. When the jobs 1 to $i$ have been executed, time becomes

$$T_i = t + r_1 + r_2 + \ldots + r_i$$

and job $i$ has the response ratio

$$R_i(T_i) = (T_i - t_i)/r_i$$

The reason for executing job $i$ last in the sequence 1 to $i$ is that its response ratio will be the lowest one among these jobs at time $T_i$:

$$R_i(T_i) = min[R_1(T_i), R_2(T_i), \ldots, R_i(T_i)]$$

Consider now the consequences of scheduling the same $n$ jobs in any other sequence:

job:                     $a$  $b$  ... $j$  ... $z$
arrival time:            $t_a$ $t_b$ ... $t_j$ ... $t_z$
service time:            $r_a$ $r_b$ ... $r_j$ ... $r_z$

In the new sequence, we select the smallest subsequence of jobs, $a$ to $j$, that contains all the jobs, 1 to $i$, of the original subsequence. (This implies that job $j$ is itself one of the jobs 1 to $i$.) When the jobs $a$ to $j$ have been served, time becomes

$$T_j = t + r_a + r_b + \ldots + r_j$$

and job $j$ reaches the response ratio

$$R_j(T_j) = (T_j - t_j)/r_j$$

Since the jobs 1 to $i$ are a subset of the jobs $a$ to $j$, the sum of their service times $T_i - t$ must be less than or equal to the sum of service times $T_j - t$. And since response ratios increase with time, $T_i \leqslant T_j$ implies

$$R_j(T_j) \geqslant R_j(T_i)$$

It is also known that job $j$ is one of the jobs 1 to $i$, of which job $i$ has the smallest response ratio at time $T_i$. The above inequality can therefore be extended as follows:

$$R_j(T_j) \geqslant R_j(T_i) \geqslant R_i(T_i)$$

In other words, when the scheduling algorithm is changed, there will always be a job $j$ that reaches a response ratio $R_j(T_j)$, which is greater than or equal to the highest response ratio $R_i(T_i)$ obtained with the original algorithm.

Notice that this proof is valid in general for priorities which are non-decreasing functions of time. For example, in a *first-come, first-served* system, priorities increase linearly with waiting time at the same rate for all jobs. Therefore, the present proof shows that the *first-come, first-served* algorithm minimizes the maximum waiting time for a given batch of jobs.

6.14. When a customer arrives with a request for service of a certain length, the scheduler computes the sequence in which jobs would be executed if the request were accepted. If this simulation shows a response ratio exceeding the given limit, the request is rejected; otherwise, it is accepted.

6.15. When a very short job is requested, there is a high probability that its response ratio will exceed the given limit while the job in service is being completed. You can easily see this if you consider *average* response ratios: If the very short job requires a service time $t$, then its average response ratio will be $W_0/t$ after the completion of the job in service. This will exceed a limit $R$ if $t < W_0/R$. For $\rho = 0.93$, $d = 2.75$, and $R = 10$ we find $\mu t < 0.26$. According to Fig. 6.3, this means that about 30 per cent of all jobs will be denied service. A reasonable cure would be to require that either the response time be less than a certain limit (say 5 min) or the response ratio be less than another limit (say 10).

**6.16.** When a foreground job arrives, a job from either queue may be in service; its expected completion time is $W_0$. Apart from that, a foreground job can only be delayed by other foreground jobs already present. So the equation for $W1$ follows directly from equation (6.22) by replacing $\rho$ with $\rho_t$.
From the conservation law (6.19), we find:

$$W1 \int_0^t \lambda x \, dF(x) + W2 \int_t^\infty \lambda x \, dF(x) = \frac{\rho W_0}{1 - \rho}$$

or

$$\rho_t W1 + (\rho - \rho_t) W2 = \frac{\rho W_0}{1 - \rho}$$

From this result, the equation for $W2$ follows directly by substitution of the equation for $W1$.

**6.17.** (a) From Exercise 6.16, we have

$$\frac{W_0}{1 - \rho_t} \leqslant W_{max}$$

By using $\rho_t = \rho \, G(t)$, we find

$$G(t) \leqslant \left(1 - \frac{W_0}{W_{max}}\right) \frac{1}{\rho}$$

Furthermore, we have

$$W_0 = \frac{\rho d}{\mu}$$

Using these results for $\rho \leqslant 1$, we find the given relation.
(b) We require $G(t) \leqslant 0.45$. According to Fig. 6.4, this is satisfied for $\mu t = 2.5$ or $t = 2.5$ min. Furthermore, $W1 = 4.4$ min and $W2 = 63$ min.

**6.18.** Let $N$ denote the total number of jobs present (waiting or in service) when the given job arrives and let $U$ denote their mean completion time. Since the service times are exponential, the mean completion time per job remains $1/\mu$ independent of the scheduling algorithm used. This combined with equation (6.18) gives

$$U = \frac{N}{\mu} = \frac{1}{\mu} \frac{\rho}{1 - \rho}$$

or

$$N = \frac{\rho}{1 - \rho}$$

And, since all jobs share the processor equally, we have for the newly arrived job

$$R_t = (N + 1) t$$

which can be reduced to the given result.

**6.19.** The total number of jobs $N$ waiting or in service when the given job arrives is given by

$$N = \frac{\rho}{1 - \rho}$$

independent of the scheduling algorithm (see Exercise 6.18). From this we derive the mean overall response time $R$ by using Little's law (6.15):

$$R = \frac{N}{\lambda} = \frac{\frac{1}{\mu}}{1 - \rho}$$

Now let $W$ and $S_t$ denote the mean times spent waiting and in service by a job of service time $t$. Since priorities are initially based only on elapsed waiting time, $W$ is clearly independent of the service time $t$. Evidently, we have

$$R_t = W + S_t$$

Since service is based on *processor sharing*, we have from Exercise 6.18:

$$S_t = \frac{t}{1 - \rho'} \quad \text{where} \quad \rho' = \frac{\lambda'}{\mu}$$

By taking the averages of $R_t$ and $S_t$, we find

$$R = W + S$$

or

$$W = \frac{1}{\mu} \left( \frac{1}{1 - \rho} - \frac{1}{1 - \rho'} \right)$$

And from the priority diagram, we find the relation

$$\frac{\beta}{\lambda'} = \left( \frac{1}{\lambda'} - \frac{1}{\lambda} \right) \alpha$$

which defines $\lambda'$ (and thereby $\rho'$).

**6.20.** Let $T_1$ denote the delay of a newly arrived job with service time $t$ caused by *earlier arrivals* (waiting or in service). The mean time required for the job in service to either complete or reach a service time $t$ is $W_0^t$ (see Section 6.1.4). In a steady state, the mean number of earlier arrivals waiting which have been served less than $t$ is $\lambda T_1$, and the mean time required to serve them for a maximum period $t$ is

$$\int_0^t \lambda T_1 x \, dF(x) = \rho_t T_1$$

So we have

$$T_1 = W_0^t + \rho_t T_1$$

or

$$T_1 = \frac{W_0^t}{1 - \rho_t}$$

Now, let $T_2$ denote the delay caused by *later arrivals*. During the mean response time $R_t$ of the given job, the mean number of arrivals is $\lambda R_t$, and the mean time required to serve them for a maximum period $t$ is

$$T_2 = \int_0^t \lambda R_t x \, dF(x) = \rho_t R_t$$

By setting

$$R_t = T_1 + T_2 + t$$

the given result follows.

**6.21.** A long-running job must wait for the completion of all earlier arrivals. So we have

$$T_1 = \frac{W_0}{1 - \rho} = \frac{1}{\mu} \frac{\rho}{1 - \rho}$$

The delays caused by later arrivals is

$$T_2 = \rho_T R_t$$

And, since

$$R_t = T_1 + T_2 + t$$

we find

$$R_t = \frac{1}{\mu} \frac{\rho}{(1 - \rho)(1 - \rho_T)} + \frac{t}{1 - \rho_T} \qquad t > T$$

**6.23.** Only as long as there are comparatively few users in the system. When the quantum is decreased to satisfy more users rapidly two things happen: (1) processor utilization decreases; and (2) at a certain point, the quantum becomes too small to satisfy most trivial requests. Users will then experience a sudden *increase* of response times because their requests must pass through the round-robin queue several times.

**6.24.** The 20 per cent savings went to idle time caused by slow peripherals (Schwartz, 1967). The solution used was to increase the number of background jobs (in queue 3) by adding 350,000 words of drum storage to the installation.

**6.25.** The *batch/time-sharing system* for the *SDS Sigma 5 and 7* computers uses a particularly simple algorithm (Shemer, 1969): The system always keeps a background job in the internal store ready to run. While foreground jobs are being swapped, the processor serves the background job. When a swap has been completed, the corresponding foreground user is given one quantum (provided the background job has already used its quantum).

# *VOCABULARY*

The following is a glossary of the most basic terms used in the text. The entries are arranged according to the logic of the subject, with an alphabetic index at the end. New terms are printed in **bold face** type. References to previously defined terms are printed in *italics*. My main purpose is to be consistent in the use of terminology within the framework of this book. I am not seeking general acceptance of the present vocabulary and have made no attempt to list alternative terms for the concepts or distinguish between preferred and deprecated terms.

## COMPUTERS AND OPERATING SYSTEMS

**Data.** Physical phenomena chosen by convention to represent certain aspects of our conceptual and real world. The meanings we assign to data are called their **Information**. Data are used to transmit information between human beings, to store information for future use, and to derive new information by manipulating the data according to formal rules.

**Operation.** A rule for deriving a finite set of *data*, called the **Output**, from another finite set of data, called the **Input**. Once initiated, an operation is completed within a finite time. An operation always delivers the same output when it is applied to a given input, regardless of the time required to carry it out.

**Computation.** A finite set of *operations* applied to a finite set of *data* in an attempt to solve a problem. If a computation solves the given problem, it is also called an **Algorithm**; but a computation can be meaningless.

**Process.** A *computation* in which the *operations* are carried out strictly one at a time.

**Program.** A description of a *computation* in a formal language called a **Programming Language**.

**Computer.** A physical system capable of carrying out *computations* by interpreting *programs*. A computer consists of a **Store**, a physical component in which *data* and programs can be retained for future use, and one or more **Processors**, physical components which can carry out *processes* defined by stored programs.

**Virtual Machine.**  A *computer* simulated partly by *program*.

**Operating System.**  A set of manual and automatic procedures that enable a group of people to share a *computer* efficiently. An operating system receives requests from users and determines the order in which their *computations* are carried out. It provides users with long-term storage of *programs* and *data*, and protects them against unauthorized usage. Finally, it performs accounting of the cost of computation and assists management in measuring performance.

**Non-interactive System.**  An *operating system* that does not permit *computations* to interact with the environment of a *computer*.

**Interactive System.**  An *operating system* that permits *computations* to interact with the environment of a *computer*.

## CONCURRENT PROCESSES

**Concurrent Processes.**  *Processes* that overlap in time. Concurrent processes are called **Disjoint** if each of them only refers to **Private Data**; they are called **Interacting** if they refer to **Common Data**.

**Multiprogramming.**  Programming techniques used to control *concurrent processes*.

**Synchronization.**  A general term for any constraint on the order in which *operations* are carried out. A synchronizing rule can, for example, specify the precedence, priority, or mutual exclusion in time of operations.

**Critical Regions.**  A set of *operations* on a *common data* structure which exclude one another in time.

**Semaphore.**  A *common data* structure used to exchange timing signals between *concurrent processes*.

**Message Buffer.**  A *common data* structure used to exchange *data* between *concurrent processes*.

**Monitor.**  A *common data* structure and a set of meaningful *operations* on it that exclude one another in time and control the *synchronization* of *concurrent processes*.

**Running.**  The state of a *process* that is being executed by a *processor*.

**Waiting.**  The state of a *process* that is suspended temporarily until a *synchronizing* condition, called an **Event**, holds.

**Deadlock.**  A situation in which two or more *processes* are *waiting* indefinitely for *events* that will never occur.

## SCHEDULING

**Job.**  A general term for a *computation* requested by a user.

**Resource.**  A general term for any object (*processor, store, program, data*, and so on) shared by *computations*.

**Scheduling Algorithm.** An *algorithm* that determines the order in which competing *jobs* are allowed to use *resources*.

**Arrival Rate.** The average number of *jobs* requested per time unit.

**Service Rate.** The average number of *jobs* completed per time unit when the system is being used.

**Utilization Factor.** The ratio of the *arrival rate* to the *service rate*. In the steady state, the utilization factor represents the average fraction of time that the system is being used.

**Service Time.** The amount of time required to execute a *job*.

**Waiting Time.** The amount of time during which a *job* waits to be executed.

**Response Time.** The time interval between the request for execution of a *job* and the return of its results to a user. The response time is the sum of the *waiting time* and the *service time*.

**Response Ratio.** The ratio of the *response time* to the *service time* of a *job*. The response ratio represents the degradation in execution speed experienced by a given job as a result of the presence of other jobs and the *scheduling algorithm* used.

**Equitable Sharing.** A form of *scheduling* under which the *response ratio* is proportional to the number of *jobs* present in the system.

**Non-preemptive Scheduling.** A form of *scheduling* in which *jobs* can use *resources* exclusively until they release them again.

**Preemptive Scheduling.** A form of *scheduling* in which *jobs* can be interrupted and their *resources* transferred to more urgent jobs. An interrupted job can be either **Terminated** completely or **Resumed** later.

**Multiplexing.** The sharing of a single *resource* among several *jobs*—one at a time—by frequent *preemption* and *resumption*.

**Priority.** A number used to establish an order of precedence among *jobs* competing for *resources*. Priorities can be either fixed or dynamic.

**Queue.** A set of *jobs* waiting for a given type of *resource* and ordered according to *priorities*.

**Time Slice.** An interval of time during which a *job* can use a *resource* without being *preempted*.

**Round Robin.** Cyclical *multiplexing* of a *resource* among *jobs* with fixed *time slices*.

## PROCESSOR AND STORE MANAGEMENT

**Short-term Scheduling.** That part of a *scheduling algorithm* that assigns *processors* and *storage* to *processes* as soon as they become available to maintain efficient utilization of a *computer*. This level of programming also implements *synchronizing operations*, which enable processes to *interact*.

**Medium-term Scheduling.** That part of a *scheduling algorithm* that initiates and terminates *processes* in accordance with the policy of computer management towards users. This level of programming establishes the identity and authority of users; inputs and analyzes their requests; initiates and terminates *jobs*; performs accounting of *resource* usage; and maintains system integrity in spite of hardware malfunction.

**Interrupt.** A timing signal that causes a *processor* to suspend the execution of its current *process* and start another process.

**Store Location.** A *store* component that can represent any one of a finite set of *data* values.

**Store Capacity.** The number of *locations* in a *store*.

**Access Time.** The average time required to record or obtain the value of a *store location*. For *stores* with moving physical media (magnetic tapes, drums, and disks), the access time consists of a **Waiting Time**, required to position the media, and a **Transfer time**, required to transfer *data to* or from the store.

**Internal Store.** A *store* with a moderate *capacity* and fast *access* used to hold *data* and *programs* during execution.

**Backing Store.** A *store* with a large *capacity* and slow *access* used to hold *data* and *programs* until they are needed in an *internal store*.

**Address.** A number used to identify a *store location*. A **Real Address** is unique within the entire *store*; a **Virtual Address** is only unique within a part of the store. The conversion of a virtual address into a real address is called **Address Mapping**.

**Store Allocation.** The assignment of *store locations* to *data* and *programs* prior to their use. Store allocation can be done: (1) at compile time (**Fixed Allocation**); (2) prior to execution (**Dynamic Allocation**); or (3) during execution (**Dynamic Relocation**).

**Segment.** A set of *data* that can be placed anywhere in a *store* and *addressed* relative to a common origin. The origin and number of *locations* of a segment are called its **Base Address** and its **Length**, respectively.

**Placement Algorithm.** An *algorithm* that determines where in an *internal store segments* should be placed prior to their use.

**Contiguous Segmentation.** A form of *placement* in which each *segment* is placed in *store locations* with contiguous *real addresses*.

**Paged Segmentation.** A form of *placement* in which the *store* is divided into units of equal length, called **Page Frames**, while *segments* are divided into units of the same length, called **Pages**. During execution, a page can be placed in any available page frame.

**Compacting.** A form of *dynamic relocation* in which *contiguous segments* are moved to one end of the *store* to combine all unused storage at the other end.

**Store Fragmentation.** Unused storage wasted between *contiguous segments* (**External Fragmentation**) or within *paged segments* (**Internal Fragmentation**).

**Demand Fetching.** A form of *store multiplexing* in which *segments* are kept on a *backing store* and only *placed* in an *internal store* when *computations* refer to them.

**Locality.** The tendency of *processes* to refer heavily to a subset of their *segments* over a period of time.

**Working Set.** The minimum amount of *internal storage* needed by a *process* to utilize a *processor* efficiently.

**Thrashing.** A state in a *demand fetching* system in which *processors* spend most of their time waiting for *segments* to be transferred from the *backing store* to the *internal store*.

**Load Control.** A method that prevents *thrashing* by measuring the utilization of *processors* and *backing storage*, and (if necessary) *preempting processes* to reduce the computational load.

**Replacement Algorithm.** An *algorithm* used in a *demand fetching* system to determine which *segment* (or which part of it) to remove when another segment must be *placed* in a full *internal store*.

**Transfer Algorithm.** An *algorithm* used in a *demand fetching* system to determine the order in which *segments demanded* by *concurrent processes* are transferred from a *backing store* to an *internal store*.

**Swapping.** A form of *store multiplexing* in which *jobs* are kept on a *backing store* and periodically transferred entirely to an *internal store* to be executed for a fixed *time slice*.

**Resource Protection.** The use of automatic procedures to ensure that *resources* are accessed by well-defined *operations* within *computations* authorized to use these resources.

# *INDEX TO VOCABULARY*

# REFERENCES

The following is a complete list of the literature referenced in the text.

ALDERSON, A., LYNCH, W. C., and RANDELL, B., "Thrashing in a multiprogrammed paging system," *International Seminar on Operating System Techniques*, Belfast, Northern Ireland, Aug.-Sept. *1971*.

ALEXANDER, S. L. and KONIGSFORD, W. L., "TSS/360: a time-shared operating system," *Proc. AFIPS Fall Joint Computer Conf.*, pp. 15-28, *1968*.

ANDERSEN, P. L., "RC 4000 datamatics: monitor 3," Regnecentralen, Copenhagen, Denmark, Feb. *1972*.

ARDEN, B. and BOETTNER, D., "Measurement and performance of a multiprogramming system," *The 2d ACM Symposium on Operating System Principles*, Princeton, New Jersey, Oct. *1969*.

BATSON, A., JU, S., and WOOD, D., "Measurements of segment size," *Comm. ACM 13*, 3, pp. 155-59, March *1970*.

BELADY, L. A., "A study of replacement algorithms for a virtual-store computer," *IBM Systems Journal 5*, 2, pp. 78-101, *1966*.

BELADY, L. A., NELSON, R. A., and SHEDLER, G. S., "An anomaly in space-time characteristics of certain programs running in a paging machine," *Comm. ACM 12*, 6, pp. 349-53, June *1969*.

BELL, G. and NEWELL, A., *Computer Structures: Readings and Examples.* McGraw-Hill Book Company, New York, New York, *1971*.

BRATMAN, H., and BOLDT, I. V., "The SHARE 709 system: supervisory control," *Journal ACM 6*, 2, pp. 152-55, April *1959*.

BREDT, T. H., "A survey of models for parallel computing," Stanford University, Palo Alto, California, Aug. *1970*.

BRIGHT, H. S., CHEYDLEUR, B. F., and GROWE, W., "On the reduction of turnaround time," *Proc. AFIPS Fall Joint Computer Conf.*, pp. 161-69, Dec. *1962*.

BRINCH HANSEN, P. (ed.), "RC 4000 software: multiprogramming system," Regnecentralen, Copenhagen, Denmark, April *1969*.

BRINCH HANSEN, P., "The nucleus of a multiprogramming system," *Comm. ACM 13*, 4, pp. 238-50, April *1970*.

BRINCH HANSEN, P., "An analysis of response ratio scheduling," *IFIP Congress 71*, Ljubljana, Yugoslavia, Aug. *1971a*.

BRINCH HANSEN, P., "An outline of a course on operating system principles," *International Seminar on Operating System Techniques*, Belfast, Northern Ireland, Aug.-Sept. *1971b*.

BRINCH HANSEN, P., "A comparison of two synchronizing concepts," *Acta Informatica 1*, 3, pp. 190-99, *1972a*.

BRINCH HANSEN, P., "Structured multiprogramming," *Comm. ACM 15*, 7, pp. 574-78, July *1972b*.

BRINCH HANSEN, P., "Testing a multiprogramming system," *Software—Practice & Experience 3*, 2, pp. 145-50, April-June *1973*.

BRON, C., "Allocation of virtual store in THE multiprogramming system," *International Seminar on Operating System Techniques*, Belfast, Northern Ireland, Aug.-Sept. *1971*.

COFFMAN, E. G. and WOOD, R. C., "Interarrival statistics for time-sharing systems," *Comm. ACM 9*, 7, pp. 500-03, July *1966*.

COFFMAN, E. G. and KLEINROCK, L., "Computer scheduling methods and their countermeasures," *Proc. AFIPS Spring Joint Computer Conf.*, pp. 11-21, April *1968a*.

COFFMAN, E. G. and VARIAN, L. C., "Further experimental data on the behavior of programs in a paging environment," *Comm. ACM 11*, 7, pp. 471-74, July *1968b*.

COFFMAN, E. G. and KLEINROCK, L., "Feedback queuing models for time-shared systems," *Journal of ACM 15*, 4, pp. 549-76, Oct. *1968c*.

COFFMAN, E. G., ELPHICK, M. J., and SHOSHANI, A., "System deadlocks," *Computing Surveys 3*, 2, pp. 67-78, June *1971*.

COMEAU, L. W., "A study of the effect of user program optimization in a paging system," *ACM Symposium on Operating System Principles*, Gatlinburg, Tennessee, Oct. *1967*.

COMFORT, W. T., "A computing system design for user service," *Proc. AFIPS Fall Joint Computer Conf.*, pp. 619-28, *1965*.

CONWAY, M. E., "Design of a separable transition-diagram compiler," *Comm. ACM 6*, 7, pp. 396-408, July *1963*.

CONWAY, R. W., MAXWELL, W. L., and MILLER, L. W., *Theory of Scheduling*, Addison-Wesley, Reading, Massachusetts, *1967*.

CORBATO, F. J., MERWIN-DAGGETT, M., and DALEY, R. C., "An experimental time-sharing system," *Proc. AFIPS Fall Joint Computer Conf.*, pp. 335-44, May *1962*.

CORBATO, F. J. and VYSSOTSKY, V. A., "Introduction and overview of the MULTICS system," *Proc. AFIPS Fall Joint Computer Conf.*, pp. 185-96, Nov. *1965*.

COSINE REPORT on "An undergraduate course on operating systems principles," Commission on Education, National Academy of Engineering, Washington, D.C., June *1971*.

COURTOIS, P. J., HEYMANS, F., and PARNAS, D. L., "Concurrent control with 'readers' and 'writers.'" *Comm. ACM 14*, 10, pp. 667-68, Oct. *1971*.

COX, D. R. and SMITH, W. L., *Queues*, John Wiley and Sons, New York, New York, *1961*.

DAHL, O.-J., MYHRHAUG, B., and NYGAARD, K., "Simula 67—Common base Language," Norsk Regnesentral, Oslo, Norway, May *1968*.

DAHL, O.-J. and HOARE, C. A. R., "Hierarchal program structures," Unpublished draft, *1971*.

DALEY, R. C. and NEUMAN, P. G., "A general purpose file system for secondary storage," *Proc. AFIPS Fall Joint Computer Conf.*, pp. 213-29, *1965*.

DALEY, R. C. and DENNIS, J. B., "Virtual memory, processes, and sharing in Multics," *Comm. ACM 11*, 5, pp. 306-12, May *1968*.

DeMEIS, W. M. and WEIZER, N., "Measurements and analysis of a demand paging time sharing system," *Proc. ACM National Meeting*, pp. 201-16, *1969*.

DENNING, P. J., "The working set model for program behavior," *Comm. ACM 11*, 5, pp. 323-33, May *1968*.

DENNING, P. J., "Virtual memory," *Computing Surveys 2*, 3, pp. 153-89, Sept. *1970*.

DENNIS, J. B., "Segmentation and the design of multiprogrammed computer systems," *Journal of ACM 12*, 4, pp. 589-602, Oct. *1965*.

DENNIS, J. B. and VAN HORN, E. C., "Programming semantics for multiprogrammed computations," *Comm. ACM 9*, 3, pp. 143-55, March *1966*.

DIJKSTRA, E. W., "Cooperating sequential processes," Technological University, Eindhoven, The Netherlands, *1965*. (Reprinted in *Programming Languages*, F. Genuys, ed., Academic Press, New York, New York, 1968).

DIJKSTRA, E. W., "The structure of THE multiprogramming system," *Comm. ACM 11*, 5, pp. 341-46, May *1968*.

DIJKSTRA, E. W., "A short introduction to the art of programming," Technological University, Eindhoven, The Netherlands, Aug. *1971a*.

DIJKSTRA, E. W., "Hierarchal ordering of sequential processes," *Acta Informatica 1*, 2, pp. 115-38, *1971b*.

DIJKSTRA, E. W., "A class of allocation strategies inducing bounded delays only," *Proc. AFIPS Spring Joint Computer Conf.*, pp. 933-36, May *1972*.

ESTRIN, G. and KLEINROCK, L., "Measures, models, and measurements for time-shared computer utilities," *Proc. ACM National Meeting*, pp. 85-96, Aug. *1967*.

FELLER, W., *"An Introduction to Probability Theory and its Applications,"* Vol. I, 2 ed., John Wiley and Sons, New York, New York, *1957*.

FIFE, D. W., "An optimization model for time-sharing," *Proc. AFIPS Spring Joint Computer Conf.*, pp. 97-104, April *1966*.

FINE, G. H., JACKSON, C. W., and McISAAC, P. V., "Dynamic program behavior under paging," *Proc. ACM National Meeting*, pp. 223-28, *1966*.

FRASER, A. G., "The integrity of a disc based file system," *International Seminar on Operating System Techniques*, Belfast, Northern Ireland, Aug.-Sept. *1971*.

FREEMAN, D. N. and PEARSON, R. R., "Efficiency vs responsiveness in a multiple-services computer facility," *Proc. ACM National Meeting*, pp. 25-34B, *1968*.

FUCHEL, K. and HELLER, S., "Consideration in the design of a multiple computer system with extended core storage," *The ACM Symposium on Operating System Principles*, Gatlinburg, Tennessee, Oct. *1967*.

GLASER, E. L., COULEUR, J. F., and OLIVER, G. A., "System design of a computer for time sharing applications," *Proc. AFIPS Fall Joint Computer Conf.*, pp. 197-202, *1965*.

GRAHAM, R. M., "Protection in an information processing utility," *Comm. ACM 11*, 5, pp. 365-69, May *1968*.

HABERMANN, A. N., "On the harmonious cooperation of abstract machines," Technological University, Eindhoven, The Netherlands, *1967*.

HABERMANN, A. N., "Prevention of system deadlocks," *Comm. ACM 12*, 7, pp. 373-85, July *1969*.

HABERMANN, A. N., "Synchronization of communicating processes," *Comm. ACM 15*, 3, pp. 171-76, March *1972*.

HAVENDER, J. M., "Avoiding deadlock in multitasking systems," *IBM Systems Journal 7*, 2, pp. 74-84, *1968*.

HOARE, C. A. R., "An axiomatic basis for computer programming," *Comm. ACM 12*, 10, pp. 576-83, Oct. *1969*.

HOARE, C. A. R., "Proof of a program: Find," *Comm. ACM 14*, 1, pp. 39-45, Jan. *1971a*.

HOARE, C. A. R., "Towards a theory of parallel programming," *International Seminar on Operating System Techniques*, Belfast, Northern Ireland, Aug.-Sept. *1971b*.

HOARE, C. A. R. and McKEAG, R. M., "A survey of store management techniques," *International Seminar on Operating System Techniques*, Belfast, Northern Ireland, Aug.-Sept. *1971c*.

HOLT, R. C., "On deadlock in computer systems," Cornell University, Ithaca, New York, *1971*.

HOOVER, E. S. and ECKHART, B. J., "Performance of a monitor for a real-time control system," *Proc. AFIPS Fall Joint Computer Conf.*, pp. 23-25, Nov. *1966*.

HORNING, J. J. and RANDELL, B., "Process structuring," University of Newcastle upon Tyne, England, *1972*.

HUME, J. N. P. and ROLFSON, C. B., "Scheduling for fast turnaround in job-at-a-time processing," *IFIP Congress 68*, Edinburgh, Great Britain, Aug. *1968*.

IRONS, E. T., "A rapid turnaround multiprogramming system," *Comm. ACM 8*, pp. 152-57, March *1965*.

KILBURN, T., HOWARTH, D. J., PAYNE, R. B., and SUMNER, F. H., "The Manchester University Atlas operating system. Part I: Internal organization," *Computer Journal 4*, 3, pp. 222-25, Oct. *1961*.

KILBURN, T., EDWARDS, D. B. G., LANIGAN, M. J., and SUMNER, F. H., "One-level storage system," *IRE Transactions on Electronic Computers 11*, 2, pp. 233-35, April *1962*.

KLEINROCK, L., "A conservation law for a wide class of queuing disciplines," *Naval Research Logistics Quarterly 12*, pp. 181-92, June *1965*.

KLEINROCK, L., "Certain analytic results for time-shared processors," *IFIP Congress 68*, Edinburgh, Great Britain, Aug. *1968*.

KLEINROCK, L., "A continuum of time-sharing scheduling algorithms," *Proc. AFIPS Spring Joint Computer Conf.*, pp. 453-58, *1970*.

KNUTH, D. E., *The Art of Computer Programming*, Volume 1. Addison-Wesley, Reading, Massachusetts, *1969*.

LAMPSON, B. W., LICHTENBERGER, W. W., and PIRTLE, M. W., "A user machine in a time-sharing system," *Proc. IEEE 54*, 12, pp. 1766-74, Dec. *1966*.

LAMPSON, B. W., "A scheduling philosophy for multiprocessing systems," *Comm. ACM 11*, 5, pp. 347-60, May *1968*.

LAMPSON, B. W., "Dynamic protection structures," *Proc. AFIPS Fall Joint Computer Conf.*, pp. 27-38, *1969*.

LAMPSON, B. W., "On reliable and extensible operating systems," *Infotech State of the Art Proceedings*, *1970*.

LICKLIDER, J. C. R. and CLARK, W. E., "On-line man-computer communication," *Proc. AFIPS Spring Joint Computer Conf.*, pp. 113-28, May *1962*.

LISKOW, B. H., "The design of the Venus operating system," *Comm. ACM 15*, 3, pp. 144-49, March *1972*.

LITTLE, J. D. C., "A proof of the queuing formula $L = \lambda W$," *Operations Research 9*, pp. 383-87, *1961*.

LONERGAN, W. and KING, P., "Design of the B5000 system," *Datamation 7*, 5, pp. 28-32, May *1961*.

LYNCH, W. C., "Description of a high capacity fast turnaround university computing center," *Proc. ACM National Meeting*, pp. 273-88, Aug. *1967*.

LYNCH, W. C., "An operating system design for the computer utility environment," *International Seminar on Operating System Techniques*, Belfast, Northern Ireland, Aug.-Sept. *1971*.

McCULLOUGH, J. D., SPEIERMAN, K. H. and ZURCHER, F. W., "A design for a multiple user multiprocessing system," *Proc. AFIPS Fall Joint Computer Conf.*, pp. 611-17, *1965*.

McKEAG, R. M., "Burroughs B5500 Master control program," The Queen's University of Belfast, Northern Ireland, *1971a*.

McKEAG, R. M., "THE Multiprogramming system," The Queen's University of Belfast, Northern Ireland, *1971b*.

McKINNEY, J. M., "A survey of analytical time-sharing models," *Computing Surveys 1*, 2, pp. 105-16, June *1969*.

MEALY, G. H., "The functional structure of OS/360. Part I—Introductory survey," *IBM Systems Journal 5*, 1, *1966*.

MINSKY, M. L., *Computation: Finite and Infinite Machines*. Prentice-Hall, Inc., Englewood Cliffs, New Jersey, *1967*.

MORENOFF, E. and McLEAN, J. B., "Inter-program communications, program string structures and buffer files," *Proc. AFIPS Spring Joint Computer Conf.*, pp. 175-83, *1967*.

MORRIS, D., SUMNER, F. H., and WYLD, M. T., "An appraisal of the Atlas supervisor," *Proc. ACM National Meeting*, pp. 67-75, Aug. *1967*.

MOTOBAYASHI, S., MASUDA, T. and TAKAHASHI, N., "The HITAC 5020 time sharing system," *Proc. ACM National Meeting*, pp. 419-29, *1969*.

NATO REPORT on "Software Engineering,," Garmisch, Germany, Oct. *1968*.

NATO REPORT on "Software Engineering," Rome, Italy, Oct. *1969*.

NAUR, P., "The design of the GIER Algol compiler," *BIT 3*, 2-3, pp. 124-40 and 145-66, *1963*.

NAUR, P., "The performance of a system for automatic segmentation of programs within an Algol compiler (GIER Algol)," *Comm. ACM 8*, 11, pp. 671-77, Nov. *1965*.

NAUR, P., "Program translation viewed as a general data processing problem," *Comm. ACM 9*, 3, pp. 176-79, March *1966*.

OPPENHEIMER, G. and WEIZER, N., "Resource management for a medium-scale time-sharing operating system," *Comm. ACM 11*, 5, pp. 313-22, May *1968*.

ORGANICK, E. I. and CLEARY, J. G., "A data structure model of the B6700 computer system," *Proc. Symposium on Data Structures in Programming Languages*, Gainsville, Florida, pp. 83-145, Feb. *1971*.

ORGANICK, E. I., *The Multics System: An Examination of its Structure*. MIT Press, Cambridge, Massachusetts, *1972*.

PATIL, S. S., "Closure properties of interconnections of determinate systems," *Record of the Project MAC Conference on Concurrent Systems* and *Parallel Computations*, ACM, New York, New York, pp. 107-16, June *1970*.

PHIPPS, T. E., "Machine repair as a priority waiting-line problem," *Operations Research 4*, pp. 76-85, *1956*.

RANDELL, B. and RUSSELL, L. J., *Algol 60 Implementation*. Academic Press, New York, New York, *1964*.

RANDELL, B., "A note on storage fragmentation and program segmentation," *Comm. ACM 12*, 7, pp. 365-72, July *1969*.

ROSIN, R. F., "Determining a computing center environment," *Comm. ACM 8*, 7, pp. 463-68, July *1965*.

ROSIN, R. F., "Supervisory and monitor systems," *Computing Surveys 1*, 1, pp. 15-32, March *1969*.

ROSS, D. T., "Introduction to software engineering with the AED-0 language," Massachusetts Institute of Technology, Cambridge, Massachusetts, Oct. *1969*.

SALTZER, J. H., "Traffic control in a multiplexed computer system," *MAC-TR-30*, Massachusetts Institute of Technology, Cambridge, Massachusetts, July *1966*.

SCHERR, A. L., "An analysis of time-shared computer systems," *MAC-TR-18*, Massachusetts Institute of Technology, Cambridge, Massachusetts, June *1965*.

SCHROEDER, M. D. and SALTZER, J. H., "A hardware architecture for implementing protection rings," *Comm. ACM 15*, 3, pp. 157-70, March *1972*.

SCHWARTZ, J. I., COFFMAN, E. G., and WEISSMAN, C., "A general purpose time-sharing system," *Proc. AFIPS Spring Joint Computer Conf.*, pp. 397-411, April *1964*.

SCHWARTZ, J. I. and WEISSMAN, C., "The SDC time-sharing system revisited," *Proc. ACM National Meeting*, pp. 263-71, Aug. *1967*.

SHEMER, J. E. and HEYING, D. W., "Performance modeling and empirical measurements in a system designed for batch and time-sharing users," *Proc. AFIPS Fall Joint Computer Conf.*, pp. 17-26, *1969*.

SIMON, H. A., "The architecture of complexity," *Proc. American Philosophical Society 106*, 6, pp. 468-82, *1962*.

SIMON, H. A., "Reflections on time sharing from a user's point of view," *Computer Science Research Review*, Carnegie-Mellon University, Pittsburgh, Pennsylvania, *1966*.

STRACHEY, C., "Time sharing in large fast computers," *Proc. International Conference on Information Processing, UNESCO*, Paris, France, pp. 336-41, June *1959*.

THORNTON, J. E., "Parallel operation in the Control Data 6600," *Proc. AFIPS Fall Joint Computer Conf.*, pp. 33-40, *1964*.

VANDERBILT, D. H., "Controlled information sharing in a computer utility," *MAC-TR-67*, Massachusetts Institute of Technology, Cambridge, Massachusetts, Oct. *1969*.

VAREHA, A. L., RUTLEDGE, R. M., and GOLD, M. M., "Strategies for structuring two-level memories in a paging environment," *The 2d ACM Symposium on Operating System Principles*, Princeton, New Jersey, Oct. *1969*.

WALTER, E. S. and WALLACE, V. L., "Further analysis of a computing center environment," *Comm. ACM 10*, 5, 266-72, May *1967*.

WILSON, R., "CDC Scope 3.2," The Queen's University of Belfast, Northern Ireland, *1971a*.

WILSON, R., "The Titan supervisor," The Queen's University of Belfast, Northern Ireland, *1971b*.

WIRTH, N., "On multiprogramming, machine coding, and computer organization," *Comm. ACM 12*, 9, pp. 489-98, Sept. *1969*.

WIRTH, N., "The programming language Pascal," *Acta Informatica 1*, 1, pp. 35-63, *1971a*.

WIRTH, N., "The design of a Pascal compiler," *Software—Practice and Experience 1*, pp. 309-33, *1971b*.

WULF, W. A., "Performance monitors for multiprogramming systems," *The 2d ACM Symposium on Operating System Principles*, Princeton, New Jersey, Oct. *1969*.

The following papers: ALDERSON, *1971*; BRINCH HANSEN, *1971b*; BRON, *1971*; DIJKSTRA, *1971b*; FRASER, *1971*; HOARE, *1971b* and *1971c*; and LYNCH, *1971* have been reprinted in:

*Operating Systems Techniques—Proceedings of a Seminar held at Queen's University, Belfast, 1971*. Edited by C. A. R. Hoare and R. H. Perrott. Academic Press, New York, *1972*.

DAHL, *1971 is included in:*

DAHL, O.-J., DIJKSTRA, E. W. and HOARE, C. A. R. *Structured Programming*, Academic Press, New York, *1972*.

HORNING, 1972 has been reprinted in:

*ACM Computing Surveys 5*, 1, pp. 5-30, Mar. *1973*.

McKEAG, *1971a* and *1971b*; and WILSON, *1971a* and *1971b* have been reprinted in:

*Studies in Operating Systems*, Academic Press, New York, *1974*.

# INDEX TO ALGORITHMS

# INDEX